Praise for *Innovation for Social Change*

"Chock-full of real-world examples, Kral goes way beyond the theoretical by drawing on her more than two decades of practical experience helping organizations achieve meaningful results. *Innovation for Social Change* shares sophisticated yet easy to follow lessons to help empower social entrepreneurs and the organizations they lead."

—Brian Hooks,
Chairman & CEO, Stand Together and coauthor,
Believe in People: Bottom-Up Solutions for a Top-Down World

"A must-read for every nonprofit organization wanting to thrive in the modern era. *Innovation for Social Change* highlights the benefits to humankind when nonprofits leverage innovation, and the consequences when they do not. Throughout, Kral helps nonprofits overcome innovation deficits by offering thoughtful principles and actionable practices to build an ecosystem that fosters a perpetual culture of innovation."

—Nathan Chappell,
Inventor for Social Good and author of *The Generosity Crisis*

"If your nonprofit needs a boost of innovation and inspiration. Leah Kral's *Innovation for Social Change* is just what the doctor ordered. Through practical examples and modern research, this book encourages nonprofit leaders to trust creativity, take risks, and, perhaps most importantly, learn from failure."

—Arthur C. Brooks,
Professor, Harvard Kennedy School and Harvard Business School,
and #1 *New York Times* best-selling author

"A brilliant combination of useful frameworks, practical advice, and real-world stories that bring everything to life. *Innovation for Social Change* reflects many of the experiences we've had while building Recidiviz and shares new lessons that will continue to guide our growth. It's a must-read for leaders, founders, and anybody who cares about high-impact, creative solutions to pressing challenges."

—Clementine Jacoby,
Cofounder and CEO, Recidiviz

"This is an enormously helpful book, charting ways for us all toward real transformational change. Leah Kral helps us see nonprofit innovation as a way to imagine a circle of compassion, and then imagine no one standing outside that circle."

—Fr. Greg Boyle,
Founder of Homeboy Industries and best-selling author,
Tattoos on the Heart: The Power of Boundless Compassion

"Leah Kral has crafted an invaluable resource for philanthropic professionals of all levels to discover and apply best practices of innovation in their work. She draws together vivid examples from the nonprofit and for-profit worlds to help practitioners find creative and innovative solutions to the problems their organizations face."

—Heather Templeton Dill,
President, John Templeton Foundation

"Radical impact to longstanding, deeply rooted social issues requires grit, ingenuity, and courage. We have to funnel the compassion often found in the nonprofit sector into true action for systemic change. *Innovation for Social Change* provides a roadmap to doing just that, transforming bold baby steps into sustainable, innovative practices that can change our work for the better."

—Tina Postel, CEO,
Loaves & Fishes/Friendship Trays

"Innovation is not just for commercial businesses. This fascinating book tells stories from innovative nonprofits, deriving vital lessons for how social entrepreneurs can and do turn new ideas into affordable, reliable, and available improvements in people's lives."

—Matt Ridley,
author of *How Innovation Works*

INNOVATION
for
SOCIAL CHANGE

INNOVATION
for
SOCIAL CHANGE

How wildly successful nonprofits inspire and deliver results

LEAH KRAL

WILEY

Published by John Wiley & Sons, Inc., Hoboken, New Jersey.
Published simultaneously in Canada.

For general information on our other products and services or for technical support, please contact our Customer Care Department within the United States at (800) 762-2974, outside the United States at (317) 572-3993 or fax (317) 572-4002.

Wiley also publishes its books in a variety of electronic formats. Some content that appears in print may not be available in electronic formats. For more information about Wiley products, visit our web site at www.wiley.com.

Library of Congress Cataloging-in-Publication Data

Names: Kral, Leah, author.
Title: Innovation for social change : how wildly successful nonprofits
  inspire and deliver results / Leah Kral.
Description: Hoboken, New Jersey : John Wiley & Sons, Inc., [2023] |
  Includes bibliographical references and index.
Identifiers: LCCN 2022029472 (print) | LCCN 2022029473 (ebook) | ISBN
  9781119987468 (hardback) | ISBN 9781119987482 (adobe pdf) | ISBN
  9781119987475 (epub)
Subjects: LCSH: Nonprofit organizations--Management | Social change.
Classification: LCC HD62.6 .K7275 2023 (print) | LCC HD62.6 (ebook)
 | DDC
   658/.048—dc23/eng/20220624
LC record available at https://lccn.loc.gov/2022029472
LC ebook record available at https://lccn.loc.gov/2022029473

Cover Design: Wiley
Cover Image: © natrot/Getty Images

SKY10036524_101822

This book is dedicated to all of the innovators with big hearts who make life better for others, through small acts of kindness or courageous deeds of justice.

I am especially thankful for Richard and Ethel, whose generosity and love have made all the difference in my life.

Contents

Acknowledgments

*Find a group of people who challenge and inspire you, spend a lot
of time with them, and it will change your life.*

—Amy Poehler

I am grateful to the many practitioners who made time to talk with me,
among them an executive at Justice Ventures International, whose
team works to rescue victims of human trafficking, an evaluation expert
at Maya Angelou Public Charter School, who works with teams that are
pioneering new education best practices in the juvenile justice system,
and many others. Many experts graciously took the time to share their
stories and provide feedback as chapter reviewers. I would like to thank
Adriana Rodriguez, Leigh McAfee, Annie Sweeney, Jerry Burden, Adam
Millsap, Emily Chamlee-Wright, Katie Keilman, Christy Horpedahl, Sam
Staley, Dirk Brown, and many others, for their time and insights.

I consider myself extremely fortunate to work alongside smart,
generous people at the Mercatus Center at George Mason University
who challenge and inspire me. This nonprofit is the home of heterodox
thinkers and brainy economists who work to discover what aspects of
institutions and culture help societies prosper. These are people for
whom economics is not just an abstraction, but a way of thinking that
is applied in our daily work. They take to heart the maxim from Nobel
Laureate F. A. Hayek that "nobody can be a great economist who is only
an economist—and I am even tempted to add that the economist who
is only an economist is likely to become a nuisance if not a positive
danger."[1]

Thanks to the lived experiences of my colleagues, many of the stories throughout this book demonstrate economic principles applied
in the nonprofit workplace. These are concepts such as public goods,

externalities, incentives, trade-offs, unintended consequences, and opportunity costs—which, in plain English, is about surfacing information so we can make better decisions.

I would especially like to thank my Mercatus colleagues Virgil Storr, Dan Butler, Ashley Schiller, Chris Myers, Dan Barrett, Robin Currie, Christina Behe, Matt Mitchell, Eileen Norcross, Ben Klutsey, Sarah Wright, Devin Scanlon, Gary Leff, Kim Hemsley, Sarah Jones, Jackie Cooper-Fulton, Roman Hardgrave, and Adam Thierer for taking the time to talk with me and share their expertise.

I am grateful to Wanchen Zhao for her gorgeous and clever illustrations.

I want to express my gratitude to Dan Rothschild, executive director of the Mercatus Center, who saw the potential of this project even before I did. Both he and Chief Operating Officer Jennifer Zambone suggested that I should write a book based on my workshops and consulting on nonprofit innovation. I am grateful to them for their time, excellent advice, and for granting me the time to focus on it.

I am thankful to have had the good fortune to learn from risk takers and entrepreneurial problem solvers, such as Denny Solomon, Betty Jo Jennings, Shamus Janko, Tiffany Smith, Brian Hooks, and many others.

I have been beyond fortunate to benefit from the wise counsel of Garrett Brown, senior director of Publications at Mercatus. Thanks to his shepherding, high-quality editing, and thoughtful advice, this book sailed through the publication process. Every first-time author should be so lucky to have confidence-boosting guidance like this.

I would like to thank Brian Neill, Debbie Schindlar, and the wonderful folks at Wiley for their enthusiasm for the project and for helping to bring the idea of the book into concrete form.

I am deeply grateful to John Paine, whose skilled eye took a first draft and made it sing. I am grateful for his sound judgment about what belonged on the cutting room floor and what needed to be elaborated.

Most of all, my endless gratitude to Richard, for his willingness to listen to me obsess about things like theory of change and design thinking, and for his patience on evenings and weekends where I was hunched over my laptop. His sharp eye and judgment strengthened the book. I am thankful for his love, generosity, and zest for life which brings brightness to each day.

Introduction

Innovation and Nonprofits

Why does innovation matter—to a nonprofit's staff and volunteers, to the beneficiaries of a nonprofit's work, to its donors and supporters?

Nonprofits provide some of the greatest gifts to the world and take on some of its hardest problems. Nonprofits are building civil society. Our work eases hunger, conserves nature and wildlife, and fights injustice. Nonprofits advancing education help break the chains of ignorance and poverty. Recovery programs, mental health counseling, medical care, and research provide healing. Arts programs lift the human spirit.

Think about your day-to-day nonprofit operations: what does it look like when your nonprofit is operating at its innovative and effective best?

- Ideating: regularly turning "aha" moments into game changers; thinking through where you want to go and how to know you are getting there
- Clarifying what's working and what's not, to accelerate your impact
- Designing small experiments that lead to discoveries
- Confidently saying no to things—preventing mission creep
- Getting green lights for projects
- Inspiring others who want to be a part of your efforts (talented superstars, partners, donors)
- Creating a work environment where team members are empowered, creative, and fulfilled
- Improving services and lowering costs

1

- Making a meaningful difference that improves people's lives
- Offering solutions to society's most pressing problems

Wow, right? Though as we know, not every nonprofit team would describe itself this way. Why not? Even with the best of intentions and the worthiest of missions, nonprofits struggle. We may feel unfocused or spread too thin. Teams aren't always inspired or rowing in the same direction. We often have blind spots. Sometimes teams are siloed. We may be underfunded and overworked. Perhaps our results are luke-warm. Aspects of how a nonprofit is structured or managed might be an obstacle to innovation.

How do we break out of ruts? How do we challenge the status quo? How do we make better decisions when we don't have a complete map of all of our options and possibilities?

These are common challenges that most organizations struggle with, but for a nonprofit it probably means not delivering the best outcomes to those it serves. Imagine the life-altering ramifications when a mediocre program fails to meet the needs of an at-risk young person. For the causes and people we lovingly serve, we need organizations that empower us to ask courageous questions, and experiment to discover what works best.

Nonprofit innovation matters because the stakes are high, the needs are many, and the world's needs keep changing. We can always do better.

The good news is that human ingenuity and creativity are limitless. There are many ways to innovate, big or small. In these pages, we will read about inspiring examples of innovative nonprofits. Some closely resemble the earlier description. They find creative ways to bring about meaningful improvements in the lives of stakeholders. Team members know that their efforts and collective brainpower make a difference. Donors feel energized and confident when they invest in an innovative nonprofit, and they remain committed because they know their money fuels good work. These are nonprofits that *endure*, that are built to ad-just and continue to be impactful as the world changes around us.

These are nonprofits that are innovating in a variety of ways, includ-ing internal process improvements (small or large), fundraising models, organizational or program strategy, technology, or inventions. This book will dive into *how* they do it.

These stories are lighthearted and accessible, and they can inspire us and help us think in new ways. We will draw on stories representing a diversity of nonprofits with a variety of missions, some whose names you will recognize, as well as some that will be unfamiliar. We will explore how real nonprofits innovate, like the Mayo Clinic, Fred Rogers's nonprofit production company, Aravind Eye Hospital, Greyston Foundation and Bakery, the LeBron James Foundation IPromise School, and many others. This book also includes examples of nonprofits that have struggled, like Chicago's Hull House, The Newseum, the One Laptop Per Child Initiative, and others. It is important for us to consider both scenarios, from the innovation success stories to the lukewarm or failed efforts, which teach us what *not* to do.

Based on lessons from these nonprofits and from interviews with people working on the front lines of social change, this book surfaces six basic, mutually reinforcing principles that can help you be more innovative:

1. Like a detective, be a fearless and relentless problem solver. Identify hidden needs.

2. Ideate. Start small but dream big: whether designing modest experiments or identifying partners and building ecosystems for social change, boldly think through where you want to go and how you might get there.

3. Unlock potential. Create a collaborative workplace culture that leaves room for experiment and play, for spontaneity and discovery.

4. Unlock even more potential. Empower bottom-up decision making, encourage savvy risk taking, and reward tough-minded trade-off thinking.

5. Clarify what's working and what's not through continuous learning and stress testing to accelerate your impact. Build a common-sense evaluation approach that supports agility, experimentation, and team learning.

6. Persuade. You must be really good at this. Stand out from the crowd, secure resources, and win buy-in for your idea.

For each of the six principles, this book provides practical how-to steps accompanied with real world stories that bring the lessons to life. Consider treating this book as your innovation boot camp.

When you think of innovation, in your role or at your nonprofit, what comes to mind?

learn **risk**
BOLD ADAPT probability
SOCIAL CHANGE discipline
resourceful **DARING** **PASSION**
CHALLENGE THE STATUS QUO BETS
AUDACITY gamble **continuous improvement**
TRIAL AND ERROR **TEAM IQ** play
ORIGINAL DREAM **EXPLORATION** ingenuity

INNOVATION

CREATIVITY TENACITY **entrepreneur**
MISSION ADVANCING **breakthrough** contrarian
PERMISSIONLESS INNOVATION TINKER **fearless** ITERATE
CURIOSITY possibility DISCOVERY **vision**
inspire **INVENT** focus outcomes
EXPERIMENT ingenuity **venture**
questioning **freedom**
IMAGINATION

Figure 0.1 Wanchen Zhao

While leaders and experts describe innovation in different ways, all are woven together by threads of common agreement:

- "Innovation is turning an idea into a solution that adds value from a customer's perspective."
- "Creativity is thinking of something new; innovation is the implementation of something new."[1]
- "It's about taking real needs and creating a bridge to a solution."[2]
- "Innovation is a process to bring new ideas, new methods or new products to an organization."[3]

Innovation involves creativity, originality, and some risk taking. An innovative leader asks, "What could be better?" and then tinkers and experiments. Innovation is the opposite of business as usual. A social entrepreneur can be anyone who has concern for an issue and dreams about possibilities for solving it.

While for-profits by their nature are structured to maximize profit, nonprofits are structured to advance a mission and provide value to the beneficiaries we serve. We are deeply committed to being a force for good, whether building a civil society, advancing human flourishing, or solving social problems.

One common misconception is that we in nonprofits don't have enough resources (time, staff, money) to pursue innovative ideas. The truth is, inefficiencies and lost opportunities are by far the greater loss.

A nonprofit's limited size and budget is not a constraint to achieving widespread social change and setting the world ablaze. The smallest nonprofit may start with nothing more than a spark of an idea and a few passionate volunteers. For example, international powerhouse Habitat for Humanity began at an impoverished communal farm in rural Georgia with a handful of volunteers and unwanted donated materials.

Sure, innovation can be big, like creating a civil rights movement, but more often than not it happens on the margins. According to a retired executive who coaches young entrepreneurs, "Innovation doesn't have to be about creating the next iPad. It can be the way you treat a customer."[4] A humble process improvement such as replacing paper-based client intake forms with an electronic form on a handheld tablet can save time and steps. Seemingly small innovations open the way for our time, energy, and resources to be put to better use elsewhere.

What inspired the creation of this book? I felt compelled to share these innovation stories so that they could be useful for other nonprofits. These stories surfaced from decades of stress-testing these insights with nonprofit teams and through the lens of my own management experience, from interviews with nonprofit professionals in a variety of settings, as well as from my own freewheeling adventures as a US Peace Corps volunteer. Increasingly often in my work, teams would reach out to me for help when they found themselves spread too thin or dissatisfied with lukewarm results. With a little help, teams can get unstuck. That's what this book is meant to be, a wellspring of inspiration and practical low-cost ideas that you can actually use in the nonprofit workplace.

You will find insights from the discipline of economics in these stories. I have the good fortune to work alongside economists in nonprofits, people for whom economics is not just an abstraction, but a way of thinking and working. Throughout this book, you will find stories of how nonprofits apply economic principles, such as incentives, trade-offs, unintended consequences, public goods, externalities, and opportunity costs, which in plain English is about surfacing information so we can make better decisions. Economic thinking is great for sparking innovative thinking.

Excitingly, the nonprofit sector is growing. The federal government recognizes the nonprofit sector's built-in advantages for innovation and agile responses to social problems. In the last 60 years, government agencies at all levels have shifted a significant portion of taxpayer resources toward a grant-making model that relies on nonprofits to deliver such crucial social services as local job-training programs and homeless shelters. This shift may be partially because policymakers have realized that nonprofits have far greater freedom to innovate compared to government, which can be rigidly limited by strictly defined mandates or by accountability to oversight committees. As an example, local communities and the nonprofit and for-profit sectors far surpassed FEMA's response in disaster relief efforts in the wake of Hurricane Katrina in New Orleans.[5]

According to a 2013 study by the Urban Institute, US nonprofits account for over 5% of GDP, and contribute $900 billion to the US economy. Americans clearly believe in the nonprofit sector: a quarter of all adults volunteered with a nonprofit in 2014, contributing 8.7 billion hours.[6] In 2004, "nonprofits were the third-largest industry in the United States, behind retail and wholesale trade, but ahead of construction, banking, and telecommunications."[7] As of 2013, it is estimated that nonprofits employ over 14 million people.[8]

Though the needs in our society are vast, there is good reason to be optimistic. We work in a growing sector with significant resources. This book challenges us to ask, are we making the best use of those resources?

Whether you are running an NGO with a $50 million budget or a homeless shelter operating on a shoestring, this book will help you. It shares best practices that can be applied at any nonprofit, no matter what its annual revenue or staff size. These practices are not cost-prohibitive. They will improve nonprofits by helping a variety of actors, including:

- Social entrepreneurs of all stripes who want to advance a social good
- Social entrepreneurs working at the international, national, or local levels
- Leaders or managers of nonprofit programs
- Frontline staff or volunteers
- Board members
- Grants officers at foundations
- Donors
- Consultants
- Students planning careers in the nonprofit sector

While *Innovation for Social Change* was primarily written for those working in nonprofits, it also can help those working in philanthropy. The book can help develop a common language between donors and people working on the front lines of nonprofits. It can help foundation grants officers and donors to better understand the management challenges that nonprofits are grappling with as they strive to be more innovative and effective.

Let's also identify what this book is not. I did not write this book to tell you what to think; rather, the stories can help us with *how* to think. The principles, practices, and examples can help you find new ways to think about a problem or opportunity and give you a range of tools that you can apply to your nonprofit's situation and context.

Acknowledging that we live in an era of disagreement and polarization, the examples I share here reflect a variety of viewpoints. We will read examples of advocacy organizations with political orientations we may or may not agree with. There are both religious or secular missions and perspectives that we may or may not subscribe to. Nonetheless, the lessons of innovation can still be relevant to your nonprofit's particular situation and context.

This is not an academic or theoretical book. While practical, the book does not get bogged down in the weeds. It will not, for instance, cover the ins and outs of nonprofit tax law or go into the details of the best tactics for a social media campaign. This book focuses on systems that work together to enable nonprofits to become more effective and innovative.

The Plan of the Book

Chapter 1 begins with the story of a nonprofit that found new ways to punch above its weight. When faced with extinction, St. Benedict's Prep School turned difficulties into opportunity, and transformed itself through small experiments, attentiveness to the needs of its stakeholders, and in the process, created a novel approach to teaching at-risk young men.

How do we help great ideas bubble up? In **Part 1** we learn insights from the field of design thinking, a process lauded by industrial designers, engineers, and teams at movie companies like Pixar. Nonprofit teams can use these techniques as a disciplined process for exploring what's possible and thinking creatively and strategically. Are we good at identifying hidden needs? What if that seemingly small idea of yours has giant ramifications? And, when we have many possible opportunities, how do we narrow our focus? These ideation exercises are useful whether you are doing back-of-the-envelope thinking or surfacing ideas in team facilitations.

Part 2 helps us transform those ideas into action. Because we are often building the plane while flying, we can design small experiments, learn, and adjust before scaling. Based on what we learn, a vision begins to come into focus. We'll hear the origin stories of Habitat for Humanity and the Southern Christian Leadership Association. How did the founders go about identifying the social problem they wanted to solve? How did they develop a vision and a theory of change? Then, how do we know if what we are doing is working? We won't shy away from pointing out evaluation pitfalls. In contrast, we can design commonsense approaches to evaluation that support learning, innovation, and action.

In **Part 3**, we learn how successful nonprofits build an ecosystem for everyday innovation. First we ask, does workplace culture matter? Does it affect innovation? Nonprofit powerhouse Mayo Clinic built an innovation culture that any size nonprofit can learn from. We will explore how they encourage creative collaborations and build trust among colleagues, and how they ensure that team members and supervisors walk the talk. Further, what is the organization's role in supporting innovators? To get an idea across the finish line, the idea will need resources and perhaps approvals from decision makers. The idea may need support from downstream teams. It is important that our work is high quality and on time. We may find ourselves navigating organizational structures and processes that we like, or dislike.

Heavy-handed or bad organizational design can stifle creativity, decrease efficiency, create bottlenecks, and increase mistakes. And on the other hand, good organizational design helps teams to be their entrepreneurial best, constructively solve problems together, and achieve the best possible outcomes. Who gets to make decisions? Should it be bottom-up or top-down? Can we leave room for play and discovery? What's more, when is the best organizational design in fact no design at all?

As we think about building an ecosystem for innovation, what specific role do donors play related to a nonprofit's ability to innovate? Can they help or hinder innovation? How do nonprofits navigate donor partnerships—both opportunities and pitfalls—so that teams are empowered to innovate?

Last, **Part 4** asks, are there traits of social entrepreneurs that we can learn from? Through stories, we learn how social entrepreneurs are deeply passionate and genuinely love what they do. They are fearless and relentless problem solvers. They boldly challenge the status quo. They are persuasive—important because there are far more innovative ideas than there are resources. They find ways to stand out from the crowd of *good* ideas and make a compelling case that this is a *great* idea. Best of all, we can sharpen these skills with awareness and practice.

The stakeholders we care deeply about are counting on us to be our innovative and effective best selves. We need well-run nonprofits and an infrastructure that equips us to meet rapidly evolving challenges.

Through these stories we can see that nonprofit innovation is at the center of making our world a better place. What kind of human endeavors and social good will come about 50 years from now that we can't even imagine now? My hope is that the case studies and practices in this book will inspire social entrepreneurs and those with generous spirits to continue to dream big, experiment, and innovate boldly.

Are you ready to make transformational change happen through your nonprofit? Let's get started.

A Story of Transformative Innovation

The investigative television show *60 Minutes* began with its trademark rapid ticking of a stopwatch.[1] That evening's segment opened with a camera panning over the industrial skyline of Newark, New Jersey. A narrator described the city in 1967 as a time "when all hell broke loose"—high unemployment, police brutality, race riots, and white flight utterly changed the city. As the camera panned over city blocks, it paused on a high school campus, a 100-year-old prep school for boys. The narrator said that like so many others who abandoned the troubled city, even the Benedictine monks who taught here had lost faith in Newark, and they closed the school.

But a handful of dedicated monks decided to stay. Fast-forward from 1967 to 2018. The show views a morning convocation in a school gymnasium filled with teenage boys dressed in school uniforms. Nearly all the diverse student body comes from low-income neighborhoods. The gymnasium reverberates with energy as the students begin their day, shouting chants of positive affirmation and songs about facing daily challenges and conquering, their arms around each other, swaying to the music. When a senior student stands up with a raised hand, a hush falls over them. Five hundred high-energy boys become respectfully quiet and stand at attention. That's the signal for the elected student team leaders to begin their orderly roll calls. As it turns out, students are required to run much of the school. Students running the school?

That *60 Minutes* show isn't the only time the media has focused on St. Benedict's. The school has also been featured in the documentary *The Rule*, which aired on PBS, and in the book *Miracle on High Street*. Students are accustomed to a steady flow of curious visitors, including grant-making foundations and journalists.

Make no mistake, the program at St. Benedict's is rigorous, with an 11-month school year, a boot camp for new students, and a capstone student-led hike required for all first-year students. St. Benedict's will proudly tell anyone who asks that 98% of their students go to college, and 82% have completed college or are enrolled and on track to graduate. Compare this to 50% of Newark's families living in poverty and only 12% of the adult population having a college degree. Those are impressive results. What are those monks doing, and how did the school become such a shining example?

Back in the 1960s after Newark's riots, the school, with mostly white students, closed indefinitely. Many of the monks moved away. The school's prospects looked grim. Only a handful of monks felt a strong desire to serve Newark's diverse community. They stayed. A year later, they reopened the school.[2]

This would not be the old St. Benedict's, and not everyone was happy about the decision to create diversity in the new student body. The school faced an immediate backlash from angry alumni. "Why didn't you move out to the (white) suburbs? You could have saved the school," and "I won't give you a dime because of what you did."[3] Whereas tuition paid by the middle-class white families had previously covered all operating expenses, the new low-income families could not afford private school tuition. The monks had to learn how to raise money in a hostile environment.

To lead the reopening of the school, the council of monks made an unlikely choice of a youthful but intense 26-year-old monk, Fr. Edwin Leahy, to lead the school. "The no-nonsense leader intended to run a student-centered school based on self-respect and responsibility."[4] According to the 1,500-year-old Rule of Benedict that the monks live by, listening is one of the key precepts. Leahy laid out the approach: "We must be willing to constantly evaluate the community we serve and ask how we might better serve them."[5] "He believed that listening was the key to the early shaping of the school . . . keep our mouths shut as much as we could and keep our ears open."[6]

They became aware of the overwhelming challenges facing Newark students. Being a teenager is hard enough, but in the city's depressed economy, "St Benedict's relentless adversary was the street, where drugs and lethargy were ubiquitous, and where debased values compete with the school's good works."[7]

Based on what the monks learned, they began to experiment and transform the school. They offered group counseling sessions for those in emotional distress. They worked to ensure that a resident would be on site after hours for students who had an emergency or needed help. They added a small residence with six beds for students dealing with trauma who needed a safe place to stay.

Related to their goal to understand the needs of the students and build credibility and trust, sometimes the monks and faculty experimented with making surprise calls at the children's homes, which they called homework raids. As one of the monks noted, "I really think this was worthwhile, just to see where and how these kids live, while letting parents (often single mothers) know we're helping, and making the kid wonder a bit, too."[8]

St. Benedict's continued to transform itself. In 1976, a graduate and experienced Boy Scout leader led a rigorous 15-mile hike for small groups of first-year students on the Appalachian Trail. The rule was that no man would be left behind. The monks and faculty noticed that the hike had a positive effect on everyone involved, and they made the hike a capstone requirement for all first-year students.

The faculty noticed an improvement in self-esteem and performance.[9] In time, they decided to model the entire school on Boy Scout leadership principles that emphasize boys leading themselves. In addition, they added key practices from the house system of British private schools. They broke the student body into groups of 15, and the groups competed against each other academically. This began to create a new culture of norms among the students. The boys expanded the policy of no man left behind to academics. The students called each other brothers, and they worried about losing their brothers to the streets. One of their morning convocation chants is "Whatever hurts my brother hurts me!"

Out of this experience came another of the school's mottos: "Never do for students what they can do for themselves." The boys elect leaders from the student body. The student leaders coordinate events, set schedules, and lead the capstone hikes. The journalist on *60 Minutes* asked

A Story of Transformative Innovation

Fr. Leahy why the student-led model didn't lead to chaos. What do other educators think of this model of student empowerment and freedom? Without blinking, Fr. Leahy replied that the students also learn through failures, and that's OK.

One of the goals of the school is to build a community of peers. From those early days the vision has been to create "a tight-knit family atmosphere where everyone knew one another and each individual played an integral part in shaping something meaningful."[10] They have a daily convocation, which is "the most important thing we do and it's critical to have them together at least once a day."[11] "We were creating an alternative to the street," admitted Fr. Leahy, "especially since many kids coming here in the 1970s and 1980s did not have experiences of community. We were creating it for them."[12]

By all evidence, the St. Benedict's model is working extremely well. After those bleak years when most had lost faith, the parents, despite tough odds, have regained faith and hope in their children's school. "Many mothers over the years [have] arrived on the school's door step and said the same thing: 'I'm afraid I'm losing my boy and they told me to bring him to you, Father Ed.'"[13]

What St. Benedict's Can Teach Us About Innovation

In the best-selling classic *The Fifth Discipline: The Art and Practice of the Learning Organization*, management expert Peter Senge describes the importance of "building an organization where it is safe for people to create visions, where inquiry and commitment to the truth are the norm, and where challenging the status quo is expected—especially when the status quo includes obscuring aspects of current reality that people seek to avoid."[14]

The team members of St. Benedict's Prep School embody that ideal. During their start-up phase, they didn't get distracted by how a traditional school is supposed to operate. Instead, their practice of listening and learning led to radical innovation of the school's operational model. They paid close attention to the needs of the students and attempted experiments like implementing the first-year hike. They learned from their successes and failures, and then they scaled what worked.

If we were to diagram the approach they came to discover through trial and error, it might look like this:

IF ► the school staff deeply engage in radical listening to the needs of their students and immerse themselves in the lives of the students to better understand the students' obstacles, ►THEN they can design a school model that addresses those needs and diminishes those obstacles.

IF ► the students gain the opportunity to demonstrate leadership and form bonds of community, ► THEN they will experience personal transformation, and they will gain self-respect, confidence, and the inner strength to overcome the challenges of their community (poverty, drugs, gangs, lethargy, and ignorance).

▲ Social Change vision: Students and alumni have skills to be active members of their community, raise their own families, lead fulfilled lives, and break the cycle of poverty.

Similar to the idea behind the TV series *Undercover Boss*, the practice of radical listening, paying attention, and walking in another's shoes changes how an organization operates. "Humility allows leaders to benefit from other perspectives, because they realize they don't have a monopoly on insight. In fact, the people who are closer to the action often have the most practical, real-world knowledge. They help to solve problems or point out issues that would be hidden otherwise."[15]

As you read on, there will be more examples of innovative nonprofits surfacing needs, creating small experiments, taking risks, engaging in active listening, and other practices that we can learn from and emulate.

Part 1

Tools for Sparking Innovative Ideas

How do we in nonprofits go about drawing great ideas out into the open, pushing through hurdles, getting buy-in, exploring the ideas and then testing and improving them?

New insights are hovering around us at all times, and yet do we give voice to them, coax them out into the open, or follow through on them? Does our workplace empower us to explore them?

Industrial designers, engineers, movie companies like Pixar, and product development teams have long sung the praises of design thinking. Design thinking is a process for solving problems, discovery, and encouraging ideation. And when translated to the nonprofit setting, it works wonders for drawing out people's best thinking.

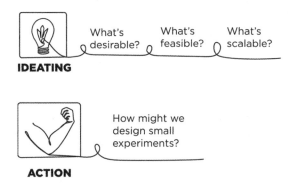

Figure 1.1 Wanchen Zhao

The first three practices help with ideation, while the fourth is meant to spur action. These steps are a feedback loop for generating ideas, concepts, asking "what if," learning, and adjusting.

Whether you are simply jotting down back-of-the-envelope ideas, or facilitating team discussion exercises at your nonprofit, design thinking can serve as an empowering guide.

Chapter 2

Surfacing Unmet Needs

Entrepreneurs see what no one else sees—because they make a systematic effort to ask questions and pay attention. Likewise, nonprofits can too, by assessing what's really in front of them. As surprising as this may sound to us today, tech entrepreneur and philanthropist Jean Case says that when AOL was founded, she often heard, "Why would I ever need email?" or "My business doesn't need a connection to the internet."[1] How often do we mindlessly accept little annoyances in our lives as a given? Perhaps some creative detective work on our part can help surface hidden opportunities.

The beneficiaries our nonprofits are serving may not know what specific improvements to ask for. But their unrealized needs exist, nonetheless. It is our responsibility to do the detective work to identify hidden needs and produce a better outcome.

At a nonprofit hospital in St. Louis, administrators hoped to renovate a wing of the hospital with a more patient-centric design. SSM DePaul Health Center hired a team of consultants for guidance. Thinking out of the box, one of the consultants faked an injury. He wore a hidden camera and captured the hospital experience from the perspective of a patient. When the consulting team showed the film footage to the hospital's leadership team, they were shocked. They saw poor communication, long wait times, and stark interiors. They had no idea. The footage provoked robust discussions and ideas for improving the patient experience.[2]

Opportunity doesn't just fall into our laps; we must proactively seek it out. We have to build a systematic search for unmet needs into our everyday practices. We start by looking at a problem from different vantage points. We walk around in someone else's shoes. What are latent needs or problems that people accept as the status quo but perhaps shouldn't?

For decades the eye care needs of India's rural poor went unmet. Health care institutions and practitioners either did not notice or did not believe anything could be done about it. That is, until the 1970s, when Indian eye specialist Dr. Govindappa Venkataswamy noticed that basics like cataract surgery and imported lenses from Western countries were impossibly expensive for this rural population. He put himself in their shoes. He asked himself, how might we make lenses affordable?

He considered how McDonald's revolutionized dining out, and with a team at Aravind Eye Hospital, began to relentlessly search for ways to adapt the efficiency, low cost, and high volume of the McDonald's fast-food model to the eye care system, without sacrificing quality. They experimented until they found approaches that worked. As word got around, they started performing in their local area 5 times the number of cataract surgeries than were performed in the entire country, and 16 times more than in the United States. Aravind Eye Hospital became a for-profit/nonprofit hybrid, using the funds from paying patients to subsidize surgeries for the poor. As of 2012, it had grown to a network of eye hospitals that has treated 32 million patients in 36 years, and performed more than 4 million eye surgeries, almost half of which are free,[3] without reducing quality—because someone didn't accept the status quo and instead, surfaced hidden needs.[4]

Identifying those unmet needs requires proactive and direct observation. As Henry Ford once put it, "If I'd asked my customers what they wanted, they'd have said 'a faster horse.'" If we rely only on what clients ask for, they may not be able to articulate needs for things that may not yet exist.

There is the famous story of how it took five years for 3M to find an application and market for one 3M scientist's discovery of a sticky adhesive, unlike scotch tape, that wouldn't permanently stick to surfaces. They didn't think the new technology mattered much; the adhesive didn't solve any obvious or known needs. But they kept searching. One day another 3M scientist who sang in his church choir noticed how choir members' bookmarks were always falling out of their songbooks—and the sticky note was born.[5]

In design thinking, asking what's desirable involves sleuthing, observing, and questioning. We leave no stone unturned and proactively look for the opportunity that no one else sees.

Bernie Glassman, an aeronautical engineer and Zen Buddhist, had a desire to help the unemployed of Yonkers, New York, who were most at risk, including felons, addicts, and the homeless. First, he wanted to understand their obstacles. This led Glassman to a bold immersion experiment. For a few weeks he chose to live on the street as a homeless person, sharing in their experiences and struggles.

He found the experience so profound that he began organizing similar homeless immersion experiences for others. After receiving safety training, immersion participants would then sleep under bridges and beg for food. Describing the experience, Glassman states, "When you're homeless and begging, people completely ignore you; you simply don't exist. Once you have been ignored like that, you can no longer do the same to other people; it becomes impossible to look away."[6]

Glassman founded Greyston Foundation in Yonkers, New York, which launched Greyston Bakery, a successful workforce development program. Glassman and his team set to work incorporating lessons from those direct observations to inform every detail of Greyston's highly unusual business model. They created an apprenticeship program open to anyone. The bakery has a first-come, first-served waiting list for positions, and no background checks or interviews are conducted. An on-site social worker helps employees solve obstacles such as stress management, transportation, child care, subsidized housing, and referrals for drug rehabilitation. Sometimes fights break out. Four out of five are gone within a week or two, but they can always sign up again. Everyone gets a chance, and some succeed. Greyston's model is a success in its field, providing the dignity of work to those highest-risk hires who were previously thought unemployable.[7]

Likewise, a UK charity that helps adults with autism and Asperger's syndrome live independently, Kingswood Trust, sought out immersion experiences with their clients so team members could get to know them better in the client's home environment. One Kingswood team member made an initial observation of an adult with autism and how he seemed to damage objects in the home, such as picking the stuffing of a leather sofa and rubbing indentations into the wall. Her first assumption was that this is problematic behavior and Kingswood should design programming or training to prevent this. But on further observation, as the team member tried to do the same actions herself, she noticed how pleasing the experience felt, and realized that he was identifying self-therapeutic effects and seeking a relaxing audio-tactile experience.[8]

As they made similar observations of their clients in their home environments, instead of treating those behaviors as a problem, they regarded them as helpful information and opportunities. Then they began to ask, how might Kingwood design methods for independent living, knowing the importance of tactile experiences for their clients? If a client is hypersensitive to sound, perhaps they could take on quieter chores like dusting or hanging up clothes on a clothesline, rather than vacuuming. They began asking, how could audio-tactile experiences be built into making a sandwich or washing clothes?

Unfortunately, however, sometimes we neglect to listen to our stakeholders, and we learn things the hard way. Take it from me. Some years ago, as a Peace Corps volunteer newly arrived in Jamaica, I joined with a team of other volunteers. One of our earliest training assignments was to find service opportunities in our community. One of the volunteers noticed an unsightly ravine full of trash and suggested a cleanup day. Soon we kicked into high gear, energetically planning the event, putting up posters, organizing how we would carry out the work. Then the day came. We American volunteers spent a very sweaty, dirty Saturday gathering many bags of trash. We noticed that none of the locals were out helping us, which was somewhat demoralizing. But by the end of the day the ravine looked much better.

Then the stunner. Two weeks later, the ravine was again full of trash. The culprit? None of us had spoken with people in the community about the trash cleanup day, whether they wanted it or had better ideas. We failed to ask questions and identify their true needs. It turns out that the ravine was their only option for disposing of trash. How arrogant and foolish they must have thought us. The lessons learned from that training assignment stick with me to this day.

Innovators make a systematic effort to ask questions and pay attention. What are the unspoken needs of your nonprofit's beneficiaries? How are teams at your nonprofit going about surfacing and discovering their hidden needs? How are team members asking questions, or immersing themselves in their circumstances to better understand the nuances?

A Thought Exercise: Exploring a Social Problem

For the sake of example, let's imagine you are creating educational programming for at-risk youth in an economically depressed suburb of Pittsburgh. Think about how you might go about describing the societal need or problem, approaching it from as many different angles as you can. Give yourself permission to explore and think big. Imagine the possible. At this stage of brainstorming, don't worry about budget constraints. Following are some imagined questions and answers:

Q. What is the societal problem that your nonprofit, program, or project intends to solve?

A. We aim to remove the barriers and obstacles in the way of the education of at-risk children in Pittsburgh.

Q. What is at stake? What is the urgency? What if you didn't act?

A. If no one acts, generations of Pittsburgh children's quality of life, including health and life expectancy, will be significantly affected. They will continue to be trapped in a cycle of poverty. We believe this can be prevented.

Q. Describe it at a personal level. How does this problem affect individuals, families, or workers?

A. These barriers prevent young people from being their best selves and contributing to their future families, community, and professional life. The cycle of poverty measurably impacts their health risks, lifetime earning potential, and upward mobility. As an at-risk youth grows into a young adult, we tend to see these risk factors impacting high school truancy, lower graduation rates, poverty, early pregnancy, addiction, violence, and recidivism. We estimate the dollar value to the community in terms of social services and lost taxable wages is $20 million per year.

Notice how the series of questions helps to make the thinking explicit. This is a good start; now let's ask deeper questions.

OK, but what's really the problem? What are those barriers? Let's borrow some wisdom from Six Sigma, which is a set of techniques and tools for process improvement pioneered by Motorola and General Motors in the 1980s and widely used today.[9] Though this is a playful example, it has a serious point.

Problem Statement: Leah becomes short-tempered with a work colleague.

WHY #1. DARREN:	Why were you short with me this morning? Was it because you didn't like the report I sent you yesterday?
LEAH:	I'm sorry for snapping at you Darren. I'm a bit hangry [hungry and angry] this morning.
WHY #2. DARREN:	Why are you hangry?
LEAH:	I set out to have a nice breakfast on my patio, and my cinnamon roll was stolen.
WHY #3. DARREN:	Why was your cinnamon roll stolen?
LEAH:	While I was watching the birds and sipping my coffee, a squirrel snuck up and stole the cinnamon roll from my plate.
WHY #4. DARREN:	What? Why did a squirrel steal your cinnamon roll?
LEAH:	I guess he was hungry.
WHY #5. DARREN:	Why was the squirrel bold enough to steal your breakfast?
LEAH:	My husband had been teaching this squirrel to eat peanuts out of his hand at the patio table. The squirrel probably thought my cinnamon roll was for him too.

This is a silly example, but what if the interviewer had stopped probing after the first question? Then our assessment of the situation would have been faulty. We may form an entirely different perspective as we dig deeper and prod with follow-on questions. This seemingly simple line of questioning challenges superficial thinking. This exercise is known as the "Five Whys" analysis from Six Sigma.

So, let's apply the Five Whys analysis to our imaginary nonprofit in Pittsburgh.

To start, give yourself permission to complain, vent, and get things off your chest and onto paper. You want to identify obstacles and problems. What are the problems that get in the way? Like the earlier story of the stolen breakfast, try asking why five times. Keep peeling back the layers of the problem and posing deeper questions. Include insights from direct, personal interactions and conversations with clients and their networks of relationships. Include insights about overt or hidden motivations and incentives, emotions, or anxieties they are experiencing.

As an example, following is how a team might answer these questions about the imaginary Pittsburgh nonprofit:

Q. The at-risk young person we serve can't focus on school. Why?

A. Based on our interviews with 30 families and from direct observation, we have learned that problems and adversity are different for each individual child. Problems range from poverty, discrimination, violence, parent's socioeconomic circumstances, unsafe neighborhoods, and unstable, disruptive conditions.

Q. Why?

A. We observe frequent relocation, uncertain housing, transportation issues, personal safety, homelessness, hunger, drugs, psychological stress, abuse, lack of support systems or community, and language barriers. We've learned from interviews that the family feels it has no choice but to prioritize other needs ahead of the child's educational needs, because those are more urgent. Survival is more urgent than education.

Q. Are schools part of the problem? If so, why?

A. Based on our interviews with 10 local teachers, we learned that they are overworked. Lack of funding and resources in the school system means that the needs of the most at-risk children aren't met. The teachers stated that the school bureaucracy leads to rigidity or prevents experimentation and innovation. Students may hide their circumstances from teachers or school staff out of fear, shame, or peer pressure.

Q. How are young people making good or bad decisions? Why?

A. Many of the at-risk youth we speak with and observe are living in high-stress circumstances, and thus are not trained in coping or stress-management techniques and have very little freedom or autonomy for decision making in their own lives. For escape, they may make bad decisions and turn to truancy, recreational drugs, or petty crime.

Notice how this exercise goes deeper into nuances. It requires walking in someone else's shoes. You might think about how asking layered questions as in the example might inform new programs or approaches at your nonprofit.

Visioning

As we explore the social problem we want to solve, this is a good time to pause and ask, what if the opposite of the problems were true? What would the world look like in a future where this problem no longer existed? And if someone sent a postcard from the future describing what the world looks like, say, 20 or 50 years from now, what would the postcard say? Imagine anything is possible.

What would good look like for the imaginary Pittsburgh nonprofit serving at-risk youth? For example:

Those formerly considered at-risk children in Pittsburgh have developed personal coping mechanisms and have family and community support systems that empower them to overcome barriers to education and social mobility. Later in life, as adults, they have a sense of purpose and fulfillment and are contributing members of families, communities, and workplaces.

To gain further clarity, another tool from design thinking is identifying specific "How might we?" questions.

The incidence of premature infant deaths was very high for families in rural villages in Nepal who did not live near hospitals. Students at Stanford studying design thinking were challenged with, *how might a nonprofit develop a low-cost solution to keep premature infants warm?* Using the principles of design thinking, the team came up with an idea for an infant warmer that looked like a sleeping bag. It could be easily recharged and sanitized and was far less expensive than incubators used in hospitals. Using design-thinking methodologies, the students developed a breakthrough product that saves lives.[10]

Likewise, a Canadian high school student with dual passions for engineering and addressing poverty, Eden Full Goh, began asking herself, "*How might we* create affordable alternative energy for developing countries?" As she tinkered with solar-powered gadgets for science fairs, she struck upon a design that combined a water clock with a solar panel rotator. Using gravity, the device could rotate to follow the sun through the day. Her device produces four liters of clean drinking water, and the movement increases the panel's efficiency by 30%. SunSaluter is now a nonprofit working with partners in several developing countries, teaching local entrepreneurs to make and distribute the solar units to advance economic empowerment.[11]

In South Africa, no one had been able to solve the problem of the poaching of rhinos. Nonprofits asked the question, *how might we* prevent poaching? Whereas most efforts had been focused on intercepting the trespassing poachers and investing in armed security patrols, a radical new idea was, why not relocate the rhinos to a place where the poachers are easier to keep out? Perhaps even outside of the country? I can only imagine the looks of astonishment when that idea was first proposed. But to their credit, they explored the seemingly wild idea. And thus launched the nonprofit Rhinos Without Borders. Pulling off a logistical miracle at the cost of $50,000 each, 87 Rhinos, weighing between two to three tons were safely moved from South Africa to a wilderness area in Botswana, where the herd has since grown to 130.[12]

Andreas Heinecke, a German journalist, was asked by his employer to provide workplace orientation for a new hire who was blind. The experience transformed all previous assumptions he had about loss of sight. He found the experience profound. He asked himself, *how might others* gain this type of experience? By exploring this question, he founded Dialogue in the Dark Foundation, a nonprofit designed to break down barriers between those who are blind and those who are not. Blind guides lead visitors in small groups through different settings in absolute darkness. Visitors learn how to interact without sight by using their other senses, and experience what it is like to be blind.[13]

Circling back to our imaginary nonprofit serving at-risk youth in Pittsburgh you could ask, *how might we* remove or alleviate obstacles and stressors so that the children can truly concentrate in the classroom? The team might brainstorm ideas such as providing services to the whole family, such as GED training, housing and grocery vouchers to the parents, offering stress-management training for the whole family, or counseling services.

Notice that this step of asking, "what's desirable?" engages us in a wide-ranging, creative search for what's possible. And more importantly, it guides us through solution-focused thinking. We are gathering key information, teasing out hidden assumptions, and looking at a difficult social problem from many different angles.

To seek out hidden needs and spur conversations, we can interview stakeholders and ask them about pain points, needs, obstacles, and what they find annoying. We can fearlessly ask "how might we" questions. We can hold focus groups or surveys. We can do field work and site visits. With a client's permission, we can conduct direct observations of clients in their environment or as they receive services. As we design the questions we plan to ask them, we can think about how we might gain insights about overt or hidden motivations and incentives, emotions, or anxieties they are experiencing. We can pay attention. And in the process, discoveries will unfold.

Chapter 3

Stretching the Imagination

While the previous step—"what's desirable?"—helped us to surface hidden needs and form some rough ideas to address those needs, in this step we'll be asking "what's scalable?" to help us stretch the idea and our imaginations a bit further.

Far too often, we sell our ideas short. Instead, we can ask, does a seemingly small idea have larger ramifications?

To illustrate, take a look at the following examples from the Nature Conservancy and Feeding America. What's the difference between each organization's first and second options?

Nature Conservancy

1. Protect and set aside 10,000 acres in Kansas as a tallgrass prairie land reserve. Or,

2. Conserve 650 million hectares of healthy land, 30 million hectares of freshwater, and 4 billion hectares of oceans around the world.

Feeding America

1. Establish a food bank in Phoenix, Arizona, to distribute 275,000 pounds of food to people in need. Or,

2. Create a network of 200 food banks across the country to feed 40 million people at risk of hunger, including 12 million children and 7 million seniors.

If you noticed that the difference is a matter of scale, you are right. Comparatively, the first option represents incremental change, while the second represents exponential change.

Let's also be clear that bigger isn't always the optimal strategy in every case. Let's consider a third example, the Association for Vision Rehabilitation and Employment, Inc. For almost 100 years, this nonprofit has been providing tailored services to those with vision impairment in upstate New York. If you live outside of upstate New York, you have probably never heard of them. But they are very good at innovating and creating opportunities for those with vision impairment to live independently. They provide employment training, support, and opportunities for those they serve. With the nonprofit's help, visually impaired workers operate switchboards, and some do light assembly such as packaging batteries or environmentally friendly cleaning products.[1]

If their team engaged in some "what's scalable?" brainstorming exercises, they might consider becoming a national umbrella organization, expanding their tried-and-true programming to hundreds of state and local chapters across the country or all over the world. Or they might make the equally strategic decision to continue to focus on their local community.

To be clear, each nonprofit should determine its own path based on the unique needs of its beneficiaries, the opportunities before them, their resources, and whether incremental or exponential change is right for them. Even a nonprofit with a smaller scale of change might be right on track given their intent.

Asking "what's scalable?" is a thought exercise to help us explore the *range of possibilities* that social entrepreneurs think through as they craft interventions and approaches.

Incremental change or exponential change are both worthwhile approaches, but note the difference between them. Another way of thinking about it is the difference between 10% change and 10X change, similar to comparing addition and multiplication. A multiplier effect involves great leaps in growth from 1 ▶ 10 ▶ 100 ▶ 1,000.

Exponential change is a vision that requires acceleration, scale, and partners. In the for-profit sector, 10X change might disrupt an industry—for example, how electronic banking disrupted the traditional mailing of invoices through the postal service. In the nonprofit world, 10X change might have a long-term impact on many lives, perhaps legislative or culture change.

But how do nonprofit teams surface what's possible and what's scalable? Is there a set of questions that might help us brainstorm? How did nonprofits like the Nature Conservancy and Feeding America arrive at these models of exponential change? Is there a secret sauce? A mechanism that creates a cascade of value? What takes a nonprofit over the hump from incremental to exponential success? And is it replicable? From my observations of nonprofits that excel at scaling, I find three common factors:

- **Asset mapping**, both within and beyond your four walls, identifying partners and unexpected allies
- Building a coalition and/or acting as a convener, to **Mobilization of a Network**
- Identifying a unique approach or strategy that will create momentum and achieve a **tipping point** for change

Asset Mapping

Before cooking a lavish meal, an experienced cook first takes an inventory of ingredients on hand. Likewise, before starting any endeavor, we in nonprofits first need to know: what tools and resources are we working with? Entrepreneurial nonprofit staff need to have a clear understanding of the nonprofit's unique gifts, strengths, capabilities, its organizational identity, and what it offers to the world, and then we can do some problem solving.

Within our four walls, what are our resources? If we don't have it already, we can draw up a mental or written inventory of our staff, their expertise, volunteers, teams, capabilities, products, software licenses, physical space, budget, and so on. These are important. This is even stronger when our asset mapping includes a description of what makes our nonprofit unique from other organizations—our niche.

We can set aside focused time to think about the ways our organization is unique. We might ask ourselves and our teams the following questions:

- What service or value is our nonprofit uniquely positioned to offer, given our resources (expertise, programming capabilities, and location)?

- Does our nonprofit fill a gap in the market that no one else is serving?

- Are we able to provide a value or produce a service at a lower cost than others?

- Does our nonprofit have a unique, creative approach, compared to others in your field? Consider things such as expertise, track record, brand, unique location, established relationships, and the network in which we operate.

- Are we the first in our marketplace to do what we do, like the first boat to venture into a wide blue ocean? (Blue ocean strategy is about capturing uncontested market space or being the first to enter a new market, making the competition irrelevant. Think of how iTunes was the first to enter the digital music space.)

- Is there a stage in the process of social change in which our nonprofit excels (conception, prototyping/experimenting, execution, coalition building)?

- Is there disagreement or confusion among staff and stakeholders about our niche?

- How do our various audiences perceive our niche and specialization?

- Can other organizations do any of this better than us? Are any of our capabilities and programs redundant with other organizations?

- Are there opportunities to narrow our focus? Are we spread too thin?

As we consider these questions, we might also ask whether ours is the right nonprofit to run a particular program, or would the nonprofit down the street be better suited—thus freeing up our resources for higher goals? One nonprofit might spin off a long-running program to another nonprofit to manage. For example, a scholar who had been successfully managing a research program at my nonprofit left to start his own nonprofit, where he could specialize on his deep expertise of crypto currency policy—it is the entire focus of his research center and what his center is known for, rather than this being one of dozens of other research issues. Considerations for spin-offs would include specialization, brand, and mission alignment.

Or a nonprofit might turn away funding if the proposed new project doesn't fit within what it does best. Being clear about your specialization and niche can be helpful as you think about how to make the best use of your limited resources to achieve social change.

While our description of our nonprofit's niche and comparative advantage might be a fairly long list of traits that change and grow, the list of distinctive capabilities is very short. In fact, it might just be one thing. A distinctive capability is more meta and longer in duration than comparative advantage.

Distinctive capabilities are defined as one or a few special, durable, and broadly applicable organizational attributes that are most important to a nonprofit's long-term success. These are difficult for other organizations to imitate. Distinctive capabilities might take decades to discover and build, through trial and error. For example, Crisis Text Line provides free, 24/7 crisis support from volunteer counselors via text message. A crisis might include anxiety, depression, suicide, school bullying, or abuse. This nonprofit negotiated a deal with major cellphone companies, Verizon, Sprint, T-Mobile, and AT&T to not only waive text messages fees, but also to omit the text from billing records for privacy and safety. This is a distinctive capability that has enabled the exchange of more than 75 million messages with people in crisis.

What are your nonprofit's distinctive capabilities? Think back to the opportunities and social problems we explored when we asked, what's desirable? Are our current capabilities the right ones to address the particular social problem we wish to solve?

As we continue this thought exercise to map our assets, next let's look beyond our four walls.

Stretching the Imagination

A single nonprofit can only achieve so much. On the other hand, nonprofits working with many partners can change the world. If we look at our resources outside of our four walls, we might call this our ecosystem.

If we were to map the ecosystem of Habitat for Humanity, it might look like this:

- The Habitat homeowner and the homeowner's family, friends, employer, neighbors, and community
- Prospective home seekers
- Highly motivated volunteers who donate time
- Prospective volunteers or donors of materials who are not yet a part of the Habitat family
- Sources for volunteer groups: schools, corporations, churches, faith-based organizations
- Social service organizations with whom Habitat partners (job skills training, financial literacy programs for first-time homeowners)
- Corporate partners and construction companies that donate materials or equipment
- Landowners who donate land
- Federal, state, and local decision makers who impact housing, zoning, construction, or mortgage policies
- Journalists and media outlets (local, national, trade journals)
- Network of other Habitat homeowners who pay into Habitat's revolving fund, Habitat headquarters, international network of Habitat affiliates

By mapping its ecosystem and potential allies, an organization like Habitat becomes more aware of its resources. As they make intentional efforts to partner with such organizations, they find themselves far more empowered to dream big and achieve their mission. You too can look beyond your four walls to your larger ecosystem of potential partners and allies. Doing so can open up a world of new possibilities.

Most nonprofits have far more potential partners than you might think. Are your so-called competitors *truly* competitors, or are they potential partners? Nonprofits demonstrate an incredible amount of flexibility and creativity in finding partners and allies, sometimes in the most unexpected ways. For example, the market-oriented Charles Koch Foundation and the liberal ACLU partnered with each other and with others to achieve meaningful criminal justice reforms.[2]

As you make your own mental list of your nonprofit's assets and ecosystem, consider not only people or organizations that currently provide support, but also those around you who might potentially become an asset to your cause. Is there untapped potential in your network? Make an honest evaluation of whether your nonprofit's ecosystem or network that you operate in is clearly identified and understood by the team. Is your ecosystem discussed regularly and incorporated into program strategies and marketing plans? Are you making the most of it?

Mobilization of a Network

A network can be a powerful force for change. Mobilization of a network enables amazing things to happen.

Consider that prior to the 1970s, there was no national 9-1-1 emergency phone system. As Congress was grappling with solutions, a television program, *Emergency!* brought public attention to the heroism of first responders but also the tragic shortcomings of the current system. There was an outcry for change. In 1973, the Robert Woods Johnson Foundation's Emergency Medical Services Program set aside $15 million to make grants to organizations working on finding solutions.

The foundation encouraged its grantees to use a coalition approach to bring health departments, medical schools, public safety agencies, hospitals, police and fire departments together and experiment to solve problems:[3] "We used the way we gave out the money as a means to change the configuration of organizations that might work together on this issue," Robert Blendon recalls. "We essentially required them to form alliances to be eligible for a grant. We let people know they could get money if they formed a coalition."[4]

They funded pilot projects made up of such coalitions in 44 rural communities for emergency medical response. Some tried putting radios in hospitals and ambulances, and some developed a dispatch center, using an 800 number. In time, one of the pilot groups identified the model that would eventually become the national 911 emergency services Americans are familiar with today.[5] Other grantees discovered improved systems for radios in ambulances, interagency communication, as well as training and certification of EMTs.

Partners and coalitions can extend their reach far beyond one organization's grasp. A single nonprofit might achieve outcomes and impact, but it is unlikely to achieve exponential social change. In contrast, a coalition serves as a force multiplier and can surface unexpected ideas. The mobilization of networks allows each member organization to flourish in its own niche and contribute its own specialization to the network.

Likewise, Strive is a consortium of nonprofits that successfully achieved improvement of education outcomes for students in Cincinnati, Ohio. Over 300 local education leaders and stakeholders, from grant makers, local government, school districts, and leaders of education-related nonprofit and advocacy groups participate in the consortium, to powerful effect. At the beginning, member organizations agreed to work on the same set of meta goals, with a holistic approach, but each approaching the goals within their individual specialization and type of activity. Some focused on early childhood education best practices, while others set up regular tutoring sessions for high school students. The members gathered regularly to support each other, share learning, and ensure their efforts were aligned. Strive achieved positive trends across a large swath of indicators, such as improved high school graduation rates, and reading and math scores.[6]

The first woman to win the Nobel Prize in Economics, Elinor Ostrom, had a passion for exploring the many creative ways communities come together to solve complex social problems. Her research suggests that we don't have to solely choose public or private approaches to solving social needs, or rely only on a nonprofit, a government agency, or industry—the problem might require two or even all three of these sectors working together. For example, during Hurricane Katrina, local

Louisiana nonprofits partnered with Walmart for flood relief efforts that had greater effectiveness than FEMA's.[7]

In another example from the aftermath of Hurricane Katrina in 2005, Broadmoor, a socioeconomically and racially diverse neighborhood in New Orleans, was slated to be bulldozed for a city park. These Katrina survivors were the little guys facing down the big guys, fighting for their homes and for the very survival of their community. Broadmoor residents rapidly organized to form the Broadmoor Improvement Association, made up of churches, residents, local for-profit businesses, schools, a library, donors, local and national journalists—and even Harvard's Kennedy School of Government became a partner to aid in community planning. By 2008, based on the combined efforts of this network, 72% of properties were livable or under repair. Due to the power of a consortium of nonprofits and other groups banding together, the city park proposal was nixed.[8]

Or consider a nonprofit-led consortium that successfully restored a polluted watershed area in Virginia. Over a period of 15 years, the Elizabeth River Project engaged more than 100 stakeholders, including city, state, and federal environmental authorities, local businesses, schools, community groups, environmental organizations, and universities. As a result, "more than 1,000 acres of watershed land have been conserved or restored . . . 27 species of fish and oysters are thriving in the restored wetlands, and bald eagles have returned to nest on the shores."[9]

Keeping an open mind about partnerships and institutional complexity can help us find innovative solutions for large-scale problems.

Though there are many benefits of building coalitions, doing so comes with risks and challenges. When a nonprofit engages with partners, its staff must discern how much to accommodate and compromise with others while avoiding the risk of mission creep. There will be push and pull. For example, the many organizations involved in the civil rights movement engaged in frequent disagreement and conflict. Some religious leaders from Black churches opposed the work of the Southern Christian Leadership Conference as too radical and political because they viewed the role of the church as limited to the spiritual. The Black Power movement and public figures like Malcolm X and Stokely Carmichael publicly advocated for a more militant approach and saw nonviolence as weak. As a nonprofit partners with other organizations, a team should give careful thought to how they will navigate such tensions, while maintaining appropriate boundaries, avoiding conflicts of interest, and taking steps to ensure they don't dilute their brand and mission.

Should Your Nonprofit Take the Lead?

Even beyond the need for a coalition, there may be a need to convene your nonprofit's network and strengthen the capacity of allies or partners in your network.

For example, Nonprofit VOTE is a national umbrella organization acting as a convener. They take the lead in their network, providing training, resources, technical assistance, tools, and support to the nonprofit sector to strengthen voter and civic engagement activities. Their approach is to first identify a well-established and credible anchor nonprofit in a state to partner with. The state-based anchor will take a leading role, working with hundreds of statewide nonprofit partners to jointly promote and run voter engagement activities. Other partners include grant makers and foundations. Nonprofit VOTE works with its partners to create state-specific voter engagement training materials, webinars, and email communications, and to address barriers affecting nonprofits and their communities. In 2018, Nonprofit VOTE worked with partners in six states, and the state-based anchors collectively recruited 70 sites that registered or secured pledge-to-vote cards from 14,000 voters.[10]

When a nonprofit steps up to provide leadership as a convener or umbrella organization, it often serves as the movement's backbone that holds many groups together. Conveners might offer some of the following features to a network:

- Serve as an information and networking hub for a movement
- Provide services similar to membership organizations (training, best practices, train the trainer, annual conferences, networking, small working groups or cohorts formed around questions or specialization areas)
- Offer services to their program alumni, help alumni to self-organize[11]

- Have an open-source model (like Linux), give away your model and knowledge so it can be replicated—if your network is stronger, then your nonprofit is stronger
- Create a talent pool pipeline
- Collaborate rather than compete; develop allies and partners, incorporating their unique capabilities, donor base, and particular audiences to strengthen the larger network

Perhaps this kind of leadership already exists in the network in which you work. But if it doesn't, you may want to seize the opportunity to form one. Perhaps your nonprofit is in the right position to be at the forefront.

A misplaced fear is the fallacy that a nonprofit exists in a zero-sum game, where only a fixed pie exists for fundraising, and if we spend our precious resources in strengthening other nonprofits, they will become competitors with us for fundraising dollars. Based on findings from their research on high-impact nonprofits, however, nonprofit experts Leslie Crutchfield and Heather McLeod Grant disagree. They find that successful nonprofits are "more focused on growing the pie for the larger cause than they are on grabbing their own slice . . . [and by] increasing the efficiency and effectiveness of members of their networks, they are able to have more influence."[12]

It may seem hard to believe that partnering organizations aren't ruthlessly trying to steal each other's donors or trade secrets. But nonprofits participating in networkwide efforts have discovered that they are able to expand their services, audience reach, and outcomes by partnering with each other, making the most of each other's respective strengths. Increased effectiveness and strong coalition-based strategies can make a nonprofit more likely to appeal to new donors and grow the pie.

Today, technology makes the work of conveners more possible than ever, and geographical distance matters very little.

Achieve a Tipping Point for Change

As we ask ourselves, "what's scalable?" we can take some advice from best-selling author Malcolm Gladwell. Gladwell popularized the term "tipping point," which he describes as "the moment of critical mass, the threshold, the boiling point" for a desired change.[13] Achieving this kind of momentum is strategic thinking at its best.

One of the best representations of nonprofit strategy I've seen in the movies was inspired by actual events from the civil rights movement. In the movie *Selma*, we see civil rights leaders naming a variety of heartbreaking outrages and injustices, debating the pros and cons of different strategies and weighing the risks. Through their discussion they identified one option that might solve many problems—voting rights. They recognized voting as the single *most important mechanism* that would give them the power to ultimately affect many of the other injustices. It would provide empowerment that over time would create a tipping point for change.

When a social change effort gains enough steam that it begins moving on its own accord, this creates momentum. The civil rights movement had all three elements: asset mapping; they built unexpected allies; and they made a highly strategic bet that they could achieve a tipping point.

A blue ocean strategy is another approach for making a bold, smart bet. It aims to capture uncontested market space, where a nonprofit becomes the first to enter a new sphere, making the competition irrelevant. Most of us are familiar with this in the for-profit world, such as how iTunes was the first to enter the digital music space. We don't hear about blue ocean success stories as often in the nonprofit world, but they are plentiful if we look. Consider the achievement of software engineer Clementine Jacoby, who has a passion for reforming the criminal justice system. She developed an artificial intelligence algorithm to quickly sort through the criminal justice case backlog to identify prisoners who could safely be released.[14] The nonprofit she founded, Recidiviz, brought about the early release of tens of thousands of prisoners in 30 states during COVID, as reported by *Forbes* and *Time Magazine*. Recidiviz found a blue ocean opportunity before anyone else.

There are usually two subtle workplace pathologies that get in the way of stretching our imaginations and asking what's scalable: (1) what we might call the tyranny of the urgent—being too busy to think about the big picture; and (2) silo thinking, or myopic thinking. Both are sneaky. These thought exercises can help us avoid those subtle traps.

We can stretch our imaginations. A nonprofit's limited size and budget should not be a constraint to boldly inspired thinking and setting the world ablaze. The smallest nonprofit may start with nothing more than a spark of an idea and a few passionate volunteers. Now an international powerhouse, Habitat for Humanity began at an impoverished communal farm in rural Georgia with a handful of volunteers and unwanted donated materials.

Let's not sell our good ideas short.

Chapter 4

Stress Testing for Feasibility

We should pursue a bold vision, but at the same time our goals should be realistic and achievable. We don't want to overpromise and underdeliver. Asking what's feasible brings us back to earth.

Consider a cautionary tale of utopianism. Many journalists have written about the failure of an international development initiative from 2005 known as One Laptop Per Child. The idea was to build a low-cost, sturdy laptop for schoolchildren in developing countries around the world. By all appearances, the concept seemed exciting and revolutionary. Press conferences generated buzz. As the effort pressed forward, problems became apparent. There were manufacturing issues, supply chain problems, software bugs, breakages, soaring costs, delivery issues, failure to adapt the features for local cultures, and children weren't using the computers for their intended use.[1] The project was launched with the best of intentions and a sincere desire to make the world a better place. But as we know, energy and enthusiasm are not enough. We must make sure our own good intentions aren't derailed by utopian thinking that isn't grounded in reality.

While we are on the subject of a reality check, we might have 20 great ideas but only the resources to pursue perhaps one or two of them. A former boss of mine, now CEO of a large grantmaking foundation, encourages grantees to "choose the best from the good opportunities." He says this so often I sometimes hear this in my sleep! He is right, of course. Nonprofits don't have limitless resources, and we must say no to things and prioritize. Asking "what's feasible?" also helps us with prioritizing. It brings discipline and helps us do some winnowing.

An old Russian proverb says that if you chase two rabbits, you will not catch either one. But finding our focus is easier said than done. Focus and prioritizing require our hardest thinking yet. The previous two chapters helped us surface many good ideas. But when we have many seemingly fruitful approaches and opportunities, how do we choose? And we don't have perfect information or a crystal ball. How can we be certain we have made the best choices?

This chapter shares three thought exercises designed to help teams think through feasibility; cut through groundless optimism; and focus, narrow, and prioritize:

1. Landscape analysis

2. Surfacing risks, unknowns, and obstacles

3. A two-step SWOT exercise

Landscape Analysis

Sometimes, nonprofits rush in headfirst to throw significant resources at a social problem before having a solid understanding of what efforts are already underway, which experts or groups are already working in that space, what obstacles to prepare for, or what forces or vested interests might be lined up in opposition.

Imagine yourself getting transported back in time. You are a manager of a small nonprofit in the 1950s with a mission to curb teen smoking. You found yourself facing the entire tobacco lobby with its powerful allies, resources, and massive advertising and public relations budget. Before reading further, take a guess at whether public schools, the military, the medical profession and public opinion would be on your side. What do you think?

Here is what the landscape would have looked like:

Medical field: Friends, foes, or neutral? Mixed. In the late 1950s, a medical consensus began forming as research provided evidence of the negative impact of smoking on health. However, despite the fact that they issued medical warnings, individual physicians were slow to adopt a public health approach into their practice, and many doctors were smokers.

Military: Friends, foes, or neutral? Foes. Army surgeons praised cigarettes as relaxing, and cigarettes were part of daily rations during World War I, World War II, and in Vietnam—up until 1976.[2]

Public schools: Friends, foes, or neutral? Neutral. Smoking education in public schools didn't begin until the early 1960s.

TV and movies: Friends, foes, or neutral? Foes. "From the late 1930s through the 1940s, two out of three top . . . movie stars advertised cigarettes while also smoking on screen. In one year alone, tobacco companies agreed to pay stars at least $3.3 million (in today's dollars) for their advertising services."[3]

Public opinion: Friends, foes, or neutral? Mixed. In the 1950s, smoking was perceived by many as seductive and admired, and it even became associated with freedom and equality for women. Some viewed anti-smoking messaging as puritanical social control and overstepping, while others viewed smoking as unhealthy, immoral, and dangerous.

Civil society: Friends, foes, or neutral? Friends. There was a growing number of anti-tobacco nonprofit advocacy groups and grassroots efforts; however, prior to the 1980s these were loosely coordinated, and activists bemoaned duplication of effort, lack of communication, and coordination.

Government and regulatory agencies: Friends, foes, or neutral? Mix of neutral and foes. Most of the nation's chief health policymakers were smokers, often smoking throughout Congressional hearings on the health risks of tobacco.[4]

Tobacco industry: Friends, foes, or neutral? Foes. According to the CDC surgeon general's report, to continue their efforts to promote tobacco to smokers, the well-financed tobacco industry relied on tactics such as intimidation, alliances, front groups, campaign funding, lobbying, legislative action, buying expertise, philanthropy, advertising, and public relations.[5]

Continue imagining yourself as the program manager of this nonprofit during this time. What would you do? How would you approach reforms to curb teen smoking? Considering the obstacles and entrenched interests, this will be an uphill battle. You would have to think long and hard about what programmatic efforts would make meaningful inroads. The way to success would not have been clear at that time. Reform required a coordinated groundswell movement. The lone nonprofit wishing to make this kind of social change would need a long-game strategy, including a movement-building strategy and a legal and public relations campaign compelling enough to overcome the entrenched, powerful forces opposing them.

No matter what field or issues our nonprofit works to address, we must make similar calculations.

Bottom line: any time spent thoughtfully assessing the forces for and against the change you hope to achieve can end up saving substantial time and resources down the road. This kind of analysis can help your nonprofit recognize battles you may not be able to win, as well as uncover opportunities and winning strategies where your time and resources will be better spent.

Surfacing Risks, Obstacles, and Unknowns

Failure happens all the time in the nonprofit world. More than we would like to admit. For example, recall the drug abuse education programs in the 1980s and '90s which relied on education to help young people resist drugs. Millions were spent. However, randomized controlled studies proved that it had no effect on short- and long-term drug use.[6] We will be well served to be mindful of such stories as we design our own interventions; grant makers certainly are.

An experienced grant writer advised that one of the biggest mistakes in grant writing is neglecting to include analysis of risks, or what might cause our efforts to lag or fail. Avoiding any discussion of risk makes a proposal look bad; in fact, it makes us look naive. Grant makers will be skeptical that the program and the proposal have been sufficiently thought through.

What do we mean by risk? A hazard is something that could potentially cause harm, and risk is the degree of likelihood that harm will be caused. Sharing our thinking about vulnerabilities rather than sweeping them under the rug strengthens our planning and proposals.

Take a look at the following grant proposal with an eye for whether this nonprofit surfaced risks.

Cover Letter for a Proposal for Reducing Youth Incarceration[7]

Since our founding 30 years ago, Upward Bound has had the privilege to be involved in the lives of thousands of at-risk young people, to help them regain hope. Our mission is to be a relentless force in disrupting incarceration, poverty, and racism by engaging young adults, police, and systems at the center of urban violence.

Traumatized young people avoid interventions as they are reluctant to trust others. However, we keep showing up and building trust. When a young man is experiencing a crisis, we track him down through his friends, call him, show up at his doorstep, and scout the streets until we find him. For example, we made 112 contacts until a young man in Baltimore joined one of our programs.

Not waiting until he is ready, but while he is dealing with a crisis, we provide tools that help him cope by recognizing negative cycles and taking control of his life. We teach a relatable version of cognitive behavioral theory, which provides a way to understand how situations affect what we think, what we feel, and what we do in response. We provide tailored employment, education, and life skills programs that serve as spaces for young people to change and grow.

We know these approaches work because for 30 years, we have been experimenting, learning and adjusting to find what works. We know that while the state recidivism rate is 52%, only 33% of our program participants recidivated. And four out of five of Upward Bound program participants stop engaging in violent crime.

Our ask: The Magnolia Foundation's support of $10,000 will help change the life trajectory of 10 at-risk young men by providing 80 hours of training in tools that address trauma and providing intensive relationship building with a youth worker. For further details, please see our attached proposal.

Did you notice the descriptions of risks? This nonprofit transparently shares how their target beneficiaries, young men, often avoid their programming and their staff. They describe how these young men are traumatized and distrustful. The proposal doesn't hide this risk but rather acknowledges it and shares how the program directly addresses these obstacles, including up to 112 contacts to reach one young person. As a reader, we sense that Upward Bound is asking the right questions as they design their interventions, recognizing that a trust deficit built over generations wouldn't be simple or easy to solve. This strengthens their credibility with their beneficiaries and with potential supporters and partners.

Being honest about risk in a proposal allows you to show your thinking about how you will mitigate risks, closely monitor known risks, design small experiments to gather more information, or how you'll make the determination that the risks are just too steep and the approach needs to be rethought or dropped. Showing your thinking about risks is smart. It gives you credibility. Incorporating these arguments highlights just how savvy, innovative, and compelling your project is.

There are a variety of risks we can monitor for:

Risk to a nonprofit's brand. In its early days, the global nonprofit now known as Alcoholics Anonymous had not yet discovered the importance of anonymity and confidentiality for alcoholics participating in their meetings. They learned this the hard way. When a national sports figure publicly announced his involvement with the organization and boasted of his newfound success with sobriety, only to very publicly fall off the wagon, the resulting exposure was devastating to their brand, and highly discouraging to members and potential members struggling with alcoholism.

Likewise, the Sackler family provided generous funding to cultural institutions and museums all over the world. Many of these institutions now are dealing with public fallout surrounding the Sackler family's connection with the opioid crisis, including thousands of lawsuits. For example, New York's Metropolitan Museum of Art recently announced it would no longer accept gifts from Sackler family members closely connected to Purdue Pharma and dropped the Sackler family name from its walls.[8]

Risk of unsatisfactory product or service. After standing in the food bank line for an hour and carrying her groceries home on the bus, a mother is dismayed that the bread she brought home for her family is stale. She unhappily shares her experience with others in her community and warns them to go elsewhere. A young pregnant teen who was on a waitlist for months to get an appointment with a pro bono attorney to guide her through medical bankruptcy becomes painfully aware that the counselor is talking down to her and constantly looking at his watch. Or, for nonprofits in the health care profession, a wrong diagnosis or a surgical error can mean life or death.

Financial risks. No matter how big a nonprofit is, it can fail if it does not secure proper funding. The 80-year-old Federal Employment & Guidance Service (FEGS), which ran hundreds of city and state social service programs in New York, with a budget of $250 million, announced it would be filing for bankruptcy in 2015. According to Politico, a "review of the nonprofit's financial disclosure forms and yearly tax returns reveal an agency engaged in risky long-term behavior and slowly drowning in debt."[9]

Risk of failing to differentiate. Grant makers are always on the lookout for clarity of thinking about how you've assessed feasibility, including your understanding of other players in the space. The last thing a grants officer wants to see is a proposal to work on a project that is being addressed successfully by another nonprofit they fund. A nonprofit may come across as uninformed or even arrogant.

Risks of life and limb. Some nonprofit staff and volunteers serve in dangerous conditions. Some are providing disaster relief work, some are helping refugees in war-torn countries, or intervening with gang members to deescalate and prevent violence. Medical workers take risks helping people with contagious diseases. Those advocating for civil rights are often vulnerable to violent attacks by opponents.

Calculated risk means that you have sized up the risk, and **acceptable risk** means you have determined to move forward despite the risk. Helping those who are most at risk and in need is a driving passion for many people working in nonprofits. There is remarkable courage and heart in the nonprofit sector. The mission of Doctors Without Borders is to bring medical assistance to people in distress. Their work often occurs in active conflict zones or in post-conflict environments. The medical professionals and support staff of Doctors Without Borders feel a calling to help and heal vulnerable people, despite the risks. Similarly, nonprofits advancing the education of girls and women in Afghanistan did so at the risk of violence or death by the Taliban.

Similar to surfacing risks, it is also helpful to **surface unknowns**. Meaning, questions we wish we knew the answers to. Being transparent about what we don't know strengthens our credibility in the same way. We can surface them and say that these are things we will continue to monitor. Recall the example of Rhinos Without Borders from Chapter 2. They took the unusual and innovative approach of combating poachers by moving rhinos out of the country. Given the exorbitant cost of such an intervention, there would have been many questions they did not yet know the answer to. For example, could they raise this much money? Could ecotourism be an income generation method they might rely on? Will the rhinos adapt to a new environment? Will their relocation alter the ecosystem in unexpected ways? After the relocation, what new approaches will poachers attempt? Drawing these questions out into the open and putting them in writing strengthens program plans and proposals. This not only strengthens our credibility with stakeholders, but it also strengthens our strategic thinking as we search for answers to these questions.

Risk Can Spur Our Best Thinking

In the words of James Baldwin, "Not everything that is faced can be changed. But nothing can be changed until it is faced."[10] As you identify risks and unknowns facing your nonprofit, you will assess whether or not to take them on, and also brainstorm ways to mitigate those risks. Quite often, this is where some of the best innovation and discovery occurs. Often, the discoveries we make while navigating risk and unknowns puts us at the cutting edge.

Many people may not realize that *Mister Roger's Neighborhood* was created by a nonprofit production company, Family Communications, founded by Fred Rogers. He was attuned to the needs of his young viewers. Weighing heavily on Roger's mind was a risk of causing stress or misunderstandings in the children viewing the show. What his production crew would eventually come to call "speaking Fredish" was a nine-step risk-mitigation method that Rogers developed. He might start with a topic about safety with lines such as, "It is dangerous to play in the street," but his method would identify that as an authoritarian and fear-inducing statement that talked down to children. Through asking a series of questions, by the ninth step, the line was transformed into, "Your favorite grown-ups can tell you where it is safe to play. It is important to try to listen to them. And listening is an important part of growing."[11] Rogers's innovative method earned trust with young viewers, and his method is widely publicized in media and books about parenting and communicating with children.

What risks might your program face? Does your team regularly surface and discuss them?

Prioritizing Our Best Opportunities: Two-Step SWOT Exercise

One of the most popular exercises that teams ask me to facilitate is a SWOT analysis. SWOT stands for **S**trengths, **W**eaknesses, **O**pportunities, **T**hreats. Perhaps this is most in demand because prioritizing is one of the hardest things we in nonprofits grapple with. Let's briefly look at the steps of a team SWOT exercise, and then tease out how and why this can help us prioritize and focus.

How to Conduct a SWOT Analysis

A SWOT can be in person or virtual. The facilitator, or team leader, will welcome participants and explain the purpose, for example: "This is a two-step exercise that will help us prioritize the many options before us. What are the best things we could be working on to achieve our (organization's or team's) mission and vision? How do we ensure we aren't spread too thin? We will update our strategic plan or team road map with our new thinking."

SWOT Part 1

The team leader can send the following homework assignment to participants one week in advance. Ask team members to set aside up to one hour to do some thinking and to prepare 5–10 sticky notes for each category. Perhaps share some sample responses like these:

- Strengths: "We have a very strong brand and perception with our customers."

- Weaknesses: "Our curriculum is too focused on higher education, and we do not offer enough training content for K–12 teachers."

- Opportunities: "Online learning platforms may be a more cost-effective way to offer our services than in-person workshops." Or, "3D printing technology might enable us to build tiny houses for the chronically homeless in our community."[12]

- Threats: "The ABC organization is starting to offer competing services to ours and drawing our target audiences/beneficiaries away."

I recommend including Resources (making it a SWOT-R), which enhances the discussion:

- Resources: "Our team has three full-time staff, 10 volunteers, an annual budget of $500,000." Or "We have many helpful partners such as think tanks."

At the meeting itself, the facilitator (or one person nominated from the team) will ask participants to take turns posting their sticky notes on the whiteboard and explaining their thinking to the larger team. The facilitator continues asking clarifying questions and looking for common themes or outliers. Designate a note taker. During the meeting, group the sticky notes into like-groups to look for patterns: both agreement and outliers. Discuss. After the meeting, circulate notes to give the team time to think through the various ideas.

SWOT Part 2

This is a one-hour follow-up to the first SWOT session. The focus is: what are our best opportunities and what should we prioritize?

Most likely, the team identified many opportunities in part 1 of the SWOT. Narrowing is now needed. This exercise is scheduled on a different day to give the team time to think about what was shared in the last session and to give participants time to prepare their homework.

Homework

Prior to our meeting, participants should set aside up to an hour to identify the top two opportunities the team or organization could be working on. Participants will have the floor for two minutes to make their pitches.

After everyone presents, open the floor for discussion and questions. The team may come to a consensus during the meeting. If not, the facilitator and the team leader can meet one-on-one to discuss what priorities rise to the surface. The leader may then ask the team to build a strategic plan or road map related to the priorities the group identified.

For an example of what this might look like in practice, imagine it is 2005 and you are a team member of a nonprofit that works in advocacy to end discriminatory practices toward members of the

LGBTQ community. Your team conducted part 1 of the SWOT last week, and now team members have gathered and are taking turns making a pitch for the best opportunities.

First, one of your colleagues makes the pitch that our programming should advocate for the rights of those who are gay and lesbian. Another colleague makes a heartfelt case that the focus should be on the broader category of LGBTQ. A third colleague argues for focusing on a specific issue such as marriage equality or transgender rights.

Another team member agrees with the marriage equality idea and builds on that idea. He approaches the whiteboard to write "10/10/10/20 = 50." Noticing the curious expressions in the room, he explains.

First, he describes how same-sex couples and many advocacy groups had been actively pursuing the right to marry through trial and error since the 1970s, but their disparate legal challenges were not making headway. A new approach is needed. Recognizing that opportunities would be different in each state, he proposes that the nonprofit and its allies should aim for "10 states with full marriage, 10 with full civil unions, 10 with some form of relationship-recognition laws, and the remaining 20 with either nondiscrimination laws or significant cultural climate change."[13] This pragmatic approach would mean tailoring approaches to each state, with a mix of professional policy advocacy efforts, building messaging that would persuade people on the sidelines, making headway and nudging where they could, to eventually spur a tipping point nationally.

This actually was a real argument made by Matt Coles of the ACLU[14] that won team members over, and soon after was embraced by a coalition of grassroots and national nonprofits. The strategy proved to be successful when the Supreme Court struck down marriage discrimination in the 2015 case *Obergefell* v. *Hodges*.

The SWOT pulls all of a team's strategic thinking and design thinking together into one place. It is a simple but powerful exercise that teams enjoy, and it helps them focus. Many teams leave value on the table by only doing the first step of SWOT, without realizing the most powerful value of SWOT is taking the second step. Investing the time to thoughtfully sort through many opportunities to select the best opportunity will pay for itself 10 times over.

Notice how the SWOT builds on all of the previous design thinking exercises:

- Resources: You've done much of the thinking for this already (think back to our asset mapping, partners, and ecosystem from Chapter 3).
- Opportunities: consider your thinking from asking, what's desirable and what's scalable, including the tipping point for change.
- Weaknesses and Threats: you've also done much of this thinking from the landscape analysis and surfacing risks, obstacles, and unknowns.

Some teams attach abbreviated SWOT meeting notes to a grant proposal's appendix to share the team's robust strategic thinking.

Innovation can't happen if we aren't being realistic and disciplined in our thinking. Ideation becomes stronger by asking, what's desirable, what's scalable, and then, importantly, what's feasible? We have clarified our thinking about our best opportunities. We have vetted and narrowed from a large list of opportunities to just a few. We have confidence because we have developed the strongest possible arguments behind our choices, which hold up under scrutiny and challenge.

As you think about the many opportunities for your nonprofit, it isn't easy to narrow them down and focus. Yet we must. Of your many options, which of them would have the biggest impact? What risks has your team surfaced? What vested interests will be opposed to the vision and strategy? Is this a battle we can win? Engaging in this thinking helps us consider trade-offs, narrow down our big lists of opportunities, and focus.

Now that we have surfaced our best thinking and ideas, it is time to transform those ideas into action.

Part 2

Transform Innovative Ideas into Action

B ecause we are often building the plane while flying, we can design small experiments, learn, and adjust before scaling.

Based on what we learn, a vision begins to come into focus. Here we will learn about the origin stories of Habitat for Humanity and the Southern Christian Leadership Association. How did the founders go about identifying the social problems they wanted to solve? How did they develop a vision and an approach?

But then we also need to know: Are we engaged in the right action? How do we know if what we are doing is working? Based on stories from the front lines of both innovative and struggling nonprofits, we won't shy away from pointing out evaluation pitfalls. In contrast, we can design commonsense approaches to evaluation that empower learning, innovation, and action.

Chapter 5

Designing Small Experiments

The path to success is never straight. Like the adage about death and taxes, unexpected setbacks and obstacles are also certain. No matter how much thoughtful planning we do, not all risks will be obvious or identified up front. There are unexpected risks, and unknown unknowns.

At the time that this book was being written, we found ourselves adjusting to new circumstances as we dealt in different ways with a worldwide pandemic. Nonprofits in Ukraine found themselves rapidly adjusting in the face of Russia's invasion. Changing cultural attitudes and beliefs, new regulations, technology, or an election turnover can all have a major impact on nonprofit strategies.

WHAT I PLANNED VS. **WHAT HAPPENED**

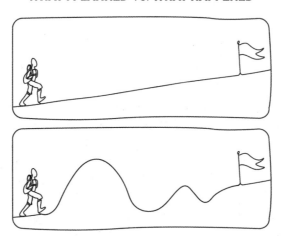

Figure 5.1 Wanchen Zhao

59

One of the best methods for mitigating risk is designing small experiments. Savvy and innovative nonprofits are aware of overly optimistic thinking or going all-in before properly experimenting to find what works, or discover what not to invest further in.

Experiments surface information when there are unknowns or when there are many options, and we aren't sure of the best approach. Another advantage of experimentation is empowerment, when anyone in the nonprofit can make a small bet on what might work and test it. As we will see in these stories, the nonprofit teams that most successfully navigate unknowns and obstacles rely on small experiments to find what works.

Trial and Error

Worldreader is a nonprofit with a mission to bring digital books to disadvantaged children and their families. When the nonprofit launched in 2010, they began an experiment to introduce Amazon Kindle e-readers to a small group of elementary students in Ghana. Yet the devices kept breaking during recess and play. As Worldreader began working directly with Amazon to build a better design for the Kindle devices, mobile technology advanced so significantly that e-reading apps started being developed for phones.

Though unsure if children would adopt the new technology, Worldreader began a second experiment with a mobile reader app and were pleased to find that thousands of users began using it. As a journalist described it, "Only at that point—after the experiment had verified the hypothesis regarding user demand—did Worldreader enter a formal contract with its app developer and begin to make improvements to the mobile-based product. Today, more than 185,000 users read books on the Worldreader mobile platform every month."[1]

The team at Worldreader was savvy enough to spread their bets and start small rather than sinking all its resources into their original idea for a Kindle e-reader device. Though it seemed like a promising approach, going all in on the Kindle would have left them without the resources to develop the better mobile solution.

Sometimes trial and error can be accidental and organic. Years ago, during my time as a US Peace Corps volunteer, I taught computer literacy at a teachers college in Jamaica. For half of my time, my role involved classroom teaching, imparting to Jamaica's future teachers the ability to teach computer literacy. The other half of my time was set aside for teaching the faculty and college instructors so that when I finished my two-year tour of duty, computer literacy training could continue to be taught at the college.

However, I encountered an unexpected problem—the faculty had no intention of learning anything about computers. Weeks went by and not one faculty member showed up to my class. When I asked staff, they would avoid eye contact and politely change the subject. I was baffled. Did they distrust me as a foreigner? Were they anti-technology? Clearly, what I was doing wasn't working.

Next, I tried posting colorful brochures in the teachers' lounge. No response. Then, just in case some felt intimidated by classroom learning, I also offered private one-on-one tutoring. That also had no effect.

Then I tried a completely different experiment. Because I had free time and a perfectly good computer lab sitting empty, I offered classes to the school's ancillary staff of cooks, librarians, and janitors. They were delighted to have a chance to learn skills that would help them with career advancement. My appointment book filled up, I was suddenly in high demand, and they were fast learners. Several times when I was in the school cafeteria lunch line with the other faculty, the cooks would single me out. With a smile and a wink, they always offered me an extra heaping of delicious Jamaican food while letting me know (quite loudly so others could hear) about sending their first email or improving their typing speed. They were proud of what they were learning! This was not lost on the other faculty, and this is what finally led to a few faculty signing up for my class.

As I worked with the first few faculty and gained their trust, in time I finally learned why they had originally refused to participate. The faculty felt overworked. There was no way they would take on any more tasks, including teaching computers—so refusing to come to my classes was actually a labor dispute with the school administration.

The moral of the story is that sometimes experimentation can be deliberate and well structured, based on steps, data collection, or informed hunches, like Worldreader. But other times experimentation is more like a shot in the dark and can be more haphazard without clear steps, like my attempts to recruit Jamaican teachers to my class, or like the 3M chemist-slash-weekend choir singer who accidentally discovered a market for sticky notes. At the beginning you will always face a range of unknowns, but by setting proper parameters, having an idea of what good looks like, persistently continuing the search, and not letting a lukewarm result or failure drag on and on without making an adjustment—your team will discover the right way forward.

Controlled Experiments

In a controlled experiment, we attempt to test one variable by isolating it from other variables.

Nonprofits working in scientific fields, such as medical research at St. Jude's Children's Research Hospital, or at nonprofit hospitals like the Swedish Medical Center in Seattle, rely a lot on controlled experiments, even double-blind control groups where one group receives a placebo and the other receives the actual treatment.

Perhaps a more common example of this in nonprofits is A/B testing in marketing efforts. It might involve isolating a test group of donors, randomly dividing them into two groups, and sending the same email to both groups, with just one tweak. Perhaps the email signer is someone different, or perhaps the email subject line is different. After you see which gets the best results, you send the email blast to your entire group of donors.

But for most of us working in nonprofits, we may not have the appropriate scenarios or the resources to create double-blind control groups, and must find more practical methods of experimentation, such as good old-fashioned trial and error.

Wizard of Oz Tests

Among the many types of experimental designs in lean Six Sigma is the Wizard of Oz test. In this test, you start small and rely on somewhat clunky, inefficient manual labor behind the scenes to deliver a product or service before investing big. In other words, create a prototype or minimum viable product first. The customer likely doesn't know this is happening ("pay no heed to the man behind the curtain"—hence the name). The experiment allows you to gain feedback before building a more efficient, permanent solution.

One such trial was conducted by Marginal Revolution University (MRU), a nonprofit that offers economic education videos for high school and college instructors. A team member thought of a great service for customers: if teachers submitted their course syllabus to MRU via email, then MRU would send tailored, automated emails to the teacher along with relevant videos and instruction materials a few days before they taught a particular aspect of economics. However, building the technology and infrastructure to automate this service would be expensive. So, they started the service with a small test group of subscribers and did all the work manually. Only after they found that the test group liked the service did they automate the service and offer it to all of their thousands of subscribers.

Let's focus for a moment on a big scary word: failure. Venture capitalists accept that 80% of their investments will fail and perhaps only 20% will succeed. They view their investments as experiments that they learn from.

Likewise, we in nonprofits should take risks, design many prototypes, and expect many of them to fail. The key is asking why it failed and learning from it and adjusting. The design thinking process is especially helpful here. It takes you on an exploratory process of vetting ideas and narrowing them, so when you are ready to experiment, you have clarity of thinking about what you are hoping to accomplish. In the words of one strategy consultant, "Small experiments can help us fail fast, fail small, learn, and move on."[2]

As you start seeing results, you'll have a new set of options. If the experiment worked, do we want to repeat it, or perhaps scale it? If it was lukewarm or failed, do we make adjustments with a new experiment? Or wind it down altogether?

That is a key point. Experiments require organizational discipline. It takes time to design an experiment. Staff involved in a programmatic experiment who really like what they are doing may have their favorite role disappear if the experiment doesn't pan out. Creating a culture where experiments are the norm requires setting expectations and being transparent with staff about what might happen. But that discipline pays off. Small experiments mitigate risks. A workplace culture that encourages teams to design small experiments which sometimes fail is motivating and empowering, and helps good ideas bubble up.

According to astronaut Buzz Aldrin, "Failure is not a sign of weakness. It is a sign that you are alive and growing. Get out of your comfort zone and be willing to take some risks as you work on new tasks. Some individuals share an aversion to risks, but it is not foolish to accept a level of risk, as long as the magnitude and worthiness of the goal you are seeking to achieve is commensurate with your risk."[3]

Train yourself to think this way. Start with small experiments, assess, adjust, and then later build momentum and scale. As we in nonprofits grapple with unknowns, small experiments lower the risk and help to surface information. Through small experiments, lessons will leap out at you that you that you never would have expected. That's what innovation is all about.

Chapter 6

Forming a Vision and Theory of Change

Faith is about taking the first step, even when you don't see the whole staircase.

—Martin Luther King, Jr.

How do nonprofits with outsize impact go about identifying the social problem they want to solve? How do they develop a vision and an approach? Can we extrapolate lessons and common themes from the origin stories of successful nonprofits? The answer is an emphatic yes.

Behind every organization is a start-up story. It springs from a problem that, for whatever reason, wasn't being addressed by the private sector or by government. A few individuals decide to respond.

The organization of a nonprofit in its early start-up days conforms to its founders' first steps to deal with a problem. Maybe they didn't succeed right out of the gate. Sometimes they had to learn the hard way and adjust. But they didn't give up. And those of us in mission-oriented nonprofits are also carrying out the vision of the founders into new and perhaps unexpected territories.

The start-up phase of successful innovation involves first seeing what no one else sees. In the same way that a scientist develops a hypothesis, the social change innovator develops a theory to solve a social problem and then undertakes a period of trial and error to test that theory. Doing this involves relentless effort and persistence, requiring founders to be deeply committed.

In the same way that inventors begin, we start to formulate a nonprofit theory of change by asking questions. What is the long-term goal we want to achieve? What conditions or sequential actions must be in place for us to reach the goal? As made clear in the following stories, a theory of change is essential for any nonprofit, whether its focus is criminal justice reform, child nutrition, or civil rights advocacy. It is usually stated in a logic chain—if we do A, we expect B to happen, and if we do C, then D happens, which will lead to a social change outcome. The start-up phase of innovation and discovery requires a theory. A theory must be tested and proven—and it could very well be wrong.

The following stories of Habitat for Humanity and the Southern Christian Leadership Association demonstrate what the start-up phase of innovative nonprofits looks like in practice.

Habitat for Humanity

During my service as a Peace Corps volunteer in Jamaica, I was shocked to witness the tough circumstances that Jamaicans faced. One of the poorest communities, ironically named Majesty Gardens, was built on and around a landfill. Alongside foraging livestock, children in rags would scavenge for recyclable bottles and cans worth pennies.

Across the long island, many people built their homes by hand, doing the best they could with what materials they could buy or find. Often those homes consisted of dirt floors, flimsy zinc siding, no running water, and perhaps an illegally rigged power line for electricity. Homes were open to the elements. Most people did not have access to formal credit or secure land titles and had no choice but to live as illegal squatters.

When tropical storm Isadore hit Jamaica in 2002, the volunteers were sent to assist a rural township where all that was left of a neighborhood was a muddy ravine where homes once stood. Most of the families had huddled for safety in a church shelter, but not all did, and some did not survive. The housing issues were overwhelming. In these dire circumstances, I saw firsthand how Habitat for Humanity provided a way for families to build safe and affordable housing.

Since its founding in 1976, Habitat has helped more than 4 million people construct, rehabilitate, or preserve more than 800,000 homes. Habitat works in local communities across all 50 states in the United States and in 70 countries around the world. For example, volunteers in

Jamaica have built 1,000 homes for families.[1] Habitat gained fame in the 1980s when former president Jimmy Carter and wife, Rosalynn, became active volunteers and ambassadors for Habitat.

Its unique business model is somewhat counterintuitive. Habitat homeowners help design and build the home alongside volunteers. Most of the volunteer workers are not skilled or experienced in construction. One can't help but wonder whether that is the wisest approach. Take my word for it, you would not want to be around when my husband and I are putting IKEA furniture together, let alone a house. Wouldn't it be safer, easier, and more cost-effective if they simply raised money and left it to the experts to build homes? Just think of the liability alone.

Habitat admits they build homes the hard way—and the slow way. Yet what they realized was that in the process of people building a home together, a powerful upswell happens. A sense of community comes into being, as well as a sense of ownership and pride.

Homeowners and volunteers will become immersed in the stories and culture, which they call "Habitatitus." At community meetings you will hear the story of Habitat's founding. How in the late 1960s, self-made millionaires Millard Fuller and his wife, Linda, took a hard look at their lives and made the decision to sell their successful publishing and direct-mail company, give the proceeds to charity, and dedicate their lives to social service. On a spontaneous road trip to visit a friend living in a racially integrated communal farm in the Jim Crow South, they found their calling.

They sat in on community meetings at the farm, listening to their discussions of the farm's vision (self-sufficiency), and their stories of successes and struggles. The community was at a pivot point and members proposed various experiments. One of the experimental programs would focus on building affordable houses for local poor rural families and tenant farmers who were living in substandard shacks. These families had no chance of getting mortgages given discrimination by white-owned banks. The program would rely on volunteer labor and monetary donations. Families would buy their homes with 20-year, no-interest mortgages and the payments would be placed in a revolving fund that would then finance the construction of more houses.

67

Forming a Vision and Theory of Change

This was exactly the kind of need that the Fullers were hoping to dedicate their time and energy to supporting. They stayed on and guided the first four years of the housing program. Given their successes, they next launched a similar experiment in present-day Democratic Republic of Congo. Based on what they learned, they returned to Georgia in 1976 and founded the nonprofit Habitat for Humanity International.[2]

They were interested not in providing a one-time handout but in transforming lives. To Habitat, the program promotes healing, self-sufficiency, and community. It's about "much more than just sheltering people. It's what it does for people on the inside. It's that intangible quality of hope."[3] "'That's my house,' the person will say. 'I helped build it. I spent hundreds of hours building it.'"[4] I experienced this philosophy firsthand as I built Habitat homes alongside families in the mountains of Jamaica. Home ownership provides stability. Home ownership is personally transforming.

Lessons Learned

Habitat identified a social need and, through experimentation and learning, discovered an innovative business model to address those needs. The Fullers wanted to transform the lives of vulnerable people who had poor credit, low income, or faced housing discrimination. Risk of default was high, and in their start-up phase they had to start small, experiment, and learn what worked through trial and error. This model was ambitious and risky, yet it paid off. In the words of President Bill Clinton, Habitat is "the most successful continuous community service project in the history of the United States. It has revolutionized the lives of thousands."[5] According to *Forbes*, Habitat is the eighth-largest nonprofit in the United States.

If we were to diagram Habitat's theory of change, what would it look like? Remember, a theory of change is usually stated in a logic chain, such as, if we do A, we expect B to happen, and if we do C, then D happens, which will lead to a social change outcome. For Habitat, it might look like this:

IF ► Habitat homeowners personally participate in building their house and paying for their mortgage, and IF ► obstacles like unaffordable mortgages and housing discrimination are re-moved, ►THEN homeowners are personally transformed. They gain skills, self-sufficiency, and pride of ownership. They gain credit history and build equity. They gain a sense of commu-nity and a more stable foundation on which to build a life, for themselves and their family.

IF ► volunteers are personally engaged in building houses with their own hands, ►THEN Habitat will create a growing so-cial movement.

IF ► Habitat homeowners pay a mortgage, ►THEN they can support a sustainable revolving fund to build more houses for others.

▲ Social Change vision: Ensure that all people have a decent place to live and eradicate substandard poverty housing.

Notice how a theory of change takes a far-off vision, perhaps 10 years or more in the future, and provides a theory for how that vision could be achieved. It makes underlying thinking and assumptions ex-plicit, which then serves as a guide in making better-informed decisions about on-the-ground strategy and daily activities.

Vision Versus Mission Confusion

As a theory of change begins to come into focus for your nonprofit, this is also a good time to consider your vision and mission. Allow yourself to imagine that your organization or program is so wildly successful that it no longer needs to exist. If you were to receive a postcard from that future, say 30–50 years from now, how would it describe what the world looks like? This is your vision. Consider these examples:

- "A hunger free America."—Feeding America
- "A world without Alzheimer's disease."—Alzheimer's Association

A vision statement should rally people and be compelling. If you feel stuck, sometimes it helps to define the social problem you want to solve, and then write its opposite—as if it is solved.

Many nonprofits mistakenly call their mission their vision. Notice the difference between the vision and mission of Habitat for Humanity:

- Vision (seeing a future state): "A world where everyone has a decent place to live."

- Mission (doing): "Seeking to put God's love into action, Habitat for Humanity brings people together to build homes, communities, and hope."

Is a vision statement realistic? Are we overpromising and under-delivering? A vision statement is aspirational, it's about direction, where you are headed toward. It's the "why" of what you do. Likewise, your mission describes *what* you do, and your strategy and theory of change are how you plan to get there.

Taking a close look at how Habitat innovated during their start-up phase, social entrepreneurs might take away ideas such as their revolving fund model and their philosophy of personal empowerment.

Habitat was hardly the first nonprofit to innovate with a revolving fund business model. For example, in his will Benjamin Franklin created philanthropic foundations in Philadelphia and Boston with seed money of $2,000 each. They were revolving funds, providing low-interest loans to help deserving poor young couples get started in life. As the couples repaid the low-interest loans and the fund grew, Franklin designated the excess funds to be used for new borrowers and for public works. The foundation wound down after 200 years in 1991—with $6.5 million.[6]

Likewise, when Habitat homeowners put "sweat equity" hours into building their home, and when they pay a monthly mortgage that helps build the next house, they have "skin in the game." That means having a personal stake in something. The saying was popularized by financier Warren Buffett, referring to when company leaders use their own money to buy stock in the company they are running. It changes incentives and commitment.

Homeownership provides stability. Homeowners put down roots in their community. Homeownership is personally transforming because it enables a person to build credit history and home equity, which in turn enables them to get loans to buy a car, finance their education, make home improvements, or start a small business. All of this has a healing effect, enabling people to offer more of their gifts to the world.

Perhaps they were inspired by the words of author C. S. Lewis: "The proper aim of giving is to put the recipients in a state where they no longer need our gifts." As Millard Fuller explains, "Hope and pride of ownership change everything. Give a person some dignity, hope, and gratitude—then stand back and see the positive results. We must look at the housing problem this way. Instead of attempting to ignore the poor, it is only common sense and in the enlightened self-interest for the community to help its own. But that help must be administered in a way that is uplifting, empowering, and strengthening—not demeaning. There's a big difference."[7]

Southern Christian Leadership Conference

The history and development of nonprofits wouldn't be complete without organizations that fought against formidable political and legal challenges. Nowhere is this more apparent than in the civil rights movement of the 1950s and 1960s.

Imagine that you are an African American living in Selma, Alabama, in the 1950s, and you wish to vote. Every obstacle imaginable would be blocking your way. You must pay a poll tax. You need to study and pass a rigged "literacy test." Your family members in the next county need to find a currently registered voter willing to personally vouch for them in order to register—and no white voter will do so.

These tactics and others were meant to ensure that segregationist whites stayed in control of the local and county government, and the tactics worked. In Selma and the surrounding county, of the 15,000 African Americans eligible to vote, fewer than 350 were registered.[8]

These were the brutal realities facing many American citizens, including Rosa Parks, who in 1955 was arrested in Montgomery for refusing to give up her seat in the "colored section" of a segregated bus for a white male passenger. She said she was simply tired of giving in.

Local pastor Martin Luther King Jr. provided the use of his church for a meeting of Montgomery's church and civic leaders. The group proposed a bold experiment, a boycott of the buses. They called themselves the Montgomery Improvement Association and elected King as their leader. The organizers had no idea how many locals would participate in the boycott, and they knew that there would be violent repercussions from whites.

On the first morning, the city buses were empty—most of Montgomery's 40,000 African American workers chose to walk to work. Thousands came to the mass meeting, and King passionately spoke about the principles of nonviolent resistance. They discovered that a national movement was being born.

In the following weeks, segregationists reacted to the boycotters in full force. Black churches were burned. Numerous movement members' homes, including King's, were bombed.[9] Carloads of Klansmen drove through African American neighborhoods at night. Many boycotters lost their jobs, including Rosa Parks and her husband. The city created ordinances to stop non-licensed volunteers from offering rides to the boycotters. Many were jailed, including King. But the determined protesters stayed the course, drawing national attention. When in the months to come, Rosa Parks's attorney took the issue of segregation on public transit systems to a federal district court, the court would declare racial segregation laws to be unconstitutional. The bold experiment had worked.

Immediately following the Montgomery Bus Boycott victory, black ministers and leaders met in Atlanta to form the Southern Christian Leadership Conference (SCLC), with the aim of scaling the lessons from Montgomery across the south. SCLC elected King as its first president, and organized as an organization of affiliates, many of which were churches or local organizations similar to the Montgomery Improvement Association. Despite economic retaliation, arson, and bombings, the movement continued to grow, and its passionate members were determined to achieve justice.

The Southern Christian Leadership Conference would provide the necessary leadership for the American Civil Rights Movement's many achievements. As King described, "Its fever boiled in nearly one thousand cities, and by the time it had passed its peak, many thousands of lunch counters, hotels, parks, and other places of public accommodation had become integrated."[10] SCLC movement organizers led one of the largest political rallies for human rights in US history, which helped to bring about the Civil Rights Act of 1964. Movement protesters sought the right to vote in Selma, which led to the Voting Rights Act (1965). King would also win the Nobel Prize (1968).

Lessons Learned

What made the American Civil Rights Movement so effective? Are there lessons that nonprofits can learn from and replicate?

Though the SCLC and civil rights leaders at that time didn't call it a theory of change, (the term "theory of change" didn't become formalized until the 1990s), the movement certainly had one. A theory of change is a hypothesis, or set of assumptions about the expected steps needed to achieve a specific societal change. A diagram of the movement's theory of change might have looked like this:

- IF ► there is a shared and internalized underlying philosophy (nonviolent resistance); IF ► there is motivation and sense of urgency; IF ► individuals are willing to face jail, harassment, and physical injury, ► THEN there is a community of mutual support and a movement that will become too large to be stopped.

- IF ► the movement could surface hidden injustice and oppression in the national media, ► THEN this would garner public sympathy and support and impel neutral people off the sidelines.

- IF ► participants did not return violence, ► THEN the opponent would make a mistake (racists unleashing violence against them), and Americans of good conscience in the name of decency would demand federal intervention and legislation.

▲ Social Change vision: the administration, under mass pressure, initiates measures of immediate intervention and supports remedial legislation to end discriminatory and unjust Jim Crow laws nationwide.

If we explore the theory of change in more detail, the Civil Rights Movement includes the following elements:

Ideas. A shared and internalized underlying philosophy, namely, non-violent resistance. The movement held well-defined assumptions about human nature and power, including the important belief that the powerful won't give up their privileges without strong resistance.

Motivation and sense of urgency. Intolerable injustice motivated courageous individuals to be willing to face jail, harassment, and physical injury for the sake of doing the right thing. "We had expected violence, even death."[11] Participants had to be trained as soldiers of a sort and learn to become fearless and disciplined to avoid falling into the trap of retaliation. Protesters prepared for lunch counter sit-ins by role-playing difficult encounters in anticipation of the violent tactics of the white segregationists.

Unity. The movement garnered strength from a community of mutual support, including individual activists, church groups, the Student Nonviolent Coordinating Committee, the Regional Council of Negro Leadership, the National Association for the Advancement of Colored People, and many others. "It is no wonder that the movement couldn't be stopped. It was too large to be stopped. Its links were too well bound together in a powerfully effective chain. There is amazing power in unity."[12]

Experiment, learn, and adjust. In time, the movement learned to carefully select an experimental test case, learn from mistakes, and determine whether to kill the program, adjust it, or scale it. For example, a failed experiment in Albany informed future campaigns.

Incite neutral observers off the sidelines. The movement learned how to earn national media coverage of hidden injustices and oppression, which garnered public sympathy and support.

Wait for the opponent to make a strategic mistake. In the words of King, "Long years of experience indicated to us that Negroes could achieve this goal when four things occurred: nonviolent demonstrators go into the streets to exercise their constitutional rights; *racists resist by unleashing violence against them*; Americans of good conscience in the name of decency demand federal intervention and legislation; the administration, under mass pressure, initiates measures of immediate intervention and supports remedial legislation."[13]

Have a specific goal with a step-change escalation plan. The movement learned to focus on a specific, achievable issue, like desegregating lunch counters or advancing voting rights, rather than a broad issue or sentiment, like ending racism.[14] They would then negotiate with the local or state government to change laws for that specific issue, and then if necessary, challenge the laws by taking it to the courts and the federal level.

Despite enormous pressures from within the Civil Rights Movement and violence from without, King and other leaders maintained cohesiveness, relying on a clear vision and theory of change. Holding the course required moral courage and power of conviction.

The Southern Christian Leadership Conference is a case study of innovation and social change achievements. As seen in the earliest moments of the start-up phase, the SCLC leadership saw something that no one else saw, and they asked themselves what their long-term goal was. They began asking what conditions or sequential actions must be in place to reach that goal. Their hypothesis was the roots of a theory of change, which they began to test and adjust, until they eventually gained clarity and cohesiveness and formed a powerful movement that changed the cultural and legal landscape of a nation.

The origin stories of Habitat for Humanity and the Southern Christian Leadership Association demonstrate how social entrepreneurs can accomplish bold breakthroughs for the social good. They found creative ways to advance the important causes of freedom, dignity, healing, empowerment, and self-determination. They were not hampered by the status quo but rather created unique approaches and highly innovative theories of change.

Forming a Vision and Theory of Change

What else did the two case studies have in common? They saw what no one else saw. The founders of these nonprofits had deep firsthand knowledge of a social problem they felt compelled to solve. To them, the cause was personal. They had a relentless commitment to chisel away at the problem despite uncertainty, risks, and setbacks. They showed a willingness to listen, experiment, learn, and adjust as they discovered the model that worked best. And in the process, their commitment and passion inspired others to join the cause.

And for us, how do we ensure that we're effective in serving the people we want to help most? How do we tinker, experiment, and—yes—innovate for their good? For the common good? Considering the goals of your nonprofit or team, what is your theory of change? What are the assumptions behind how your team plans to achieve your goals? What does the "if-then" sequence look like?

Stories like these—and yours—will propel us forward, bolstering the knowledge that the work we do is meaningful and ultimately life changing. We want to succeed because, for us, it's personal.

Chapter 7

Evaluating, Learning, and Adjusting

Something is wrong in the state of Denmark. Often, when I hear how teams talk and think about program evaluation and performance metrics, something is amiss. It's common to hear team members sigh and say, "Let's just get this out of the way and move on to more important work."

But evaluation, when done right, is really about empowerment, creativity, learning, and sparking innovation. It is how we build a feedback loop that informs trial and error, iterating and learning, as we search for better outcomes for the people we serve.

I suspect one of the culprits lurking behind the confusion is as follows. Because evaluation is required in grant proposals or reports, many teams approach evaluation as a dry, annoying obligation. I can certainly agree when teams sense that *poorly conceived* evaluation serves little purpose. We are busy. Wasted time, irritation, and unnecessary bureaucratic hurdles are not going to help nonprofit staff achieve the mission.

Perhaps there is a difference between what evaluation should be (a meaningful, empowering feedback loop that drives action) versus the approach that many nonprofits take in practice (bureaucracy).

Perhaps another of the culprits is that for nonprofits, information can be hard to come by. To assess how they are doing, business leaders have access to rapidly unfolding quantitative information like profit, prices, and sales. But before we get too envious of their "wealth" of hard data, consider that business leaders must rely on imprecise judgment for how to interpret and act on the information. As we in nonprofits seek information so we can make better decisions, the road is foggy for us too. Our results aren't immediate—sometimes the impact we seek can take years, or even decades. How do we surface information that can help us without creating costly and inefficient processes and tracking systems?

Let's untangle the bureaucracy and ensure that our evaluation approach actually helps us make decisions, helps us innovate, and is designed with thoughtful pragmatism.

How to Recognize "Evaluation" Practices That Stifle Innovation

First, we can empower team members to recognize worst practices and call them out when they see them.

To set a tone for having this kind of conversation with teams, I will share an image of an inept detective bungling the evidence of a case—someone like Sherlock Holmes as played by Will Ferrell. I'll post the picture where participants can see it, and alongside it will write the following question on the whiteboard as the theme for the discussion: "Measurement and evaluation—what could possibly go wrong?" And on another nearby whiteboard: "Can we get away without evaluation and metrics?"

We start with the first question. I ask them to share any positive or negative experiences, and I will write their responses on the whiteboard. I encourage them to be candid and reassure them that they can't shock or offend. If participants are reluctant, share your own worst experience with an evaluation gone wrong. By setting this tone, participants sense they can speak their minds. Some may be relieved to have the opportunity to vent—so let them. You might hear things like:

"The focus on numbers has gone too far."

"With all of this pressure on evidence, it feels like management doesn't trust us."

"One of our major funders asked us to track and report 'prestige metrics' such as the rankings of the undergraduate institutions of students participating in our PhD fellowship program. But this data is meaningless to us."

"The focus on exam results comes at the expense of student learning."

There tends to be a lot of frustration regarding evaluation; draw this out. As they warm up to the exercise, I usually notice patterns. Their examples of what could go wrong may likely include:

- Measuring the wrong thing
- Measuring the easy thing
- Overemphasizing short-term goals at the expense of long-term outcomes
- Gaming the system, incentivizing the wrong thing, or creating unintended consequences
- Collecting data that doesn't guide action or decision making

If participants identified some or all of these, congratulate them for their savvy observations and tell them they are right! Thank them for candidly sharing their experiences, which we should learn from and make sure not to repeat.

Reassure them they are not alone. These problems are also identified in the book *The Tyranny of Metrics*, where historian Jerry Muller demonstrates how metrics can go terribly wrong. Driving his points home, he uses compelling examples from policing and education from the HBO series *The Wire*. For example, he shares the story of when the mayor's office pressures the police to reduce major crimes by 5%, which created incentives for the police to overlook actual crimes.[1] We face similar problems in nonprofits as we struggle to evaluate success and be accountable for results. How can we be on guard for these pitfalls? Let's start with some real-world examples.

Measuring the Wrong Thing

It is easy to get caught up in the work that is right in front of us. Evaluation systems often reflect a focus on the immediate, perhaps because it is easier to measure. Yet that might take us down the wrong path or draw our attention to activities and outputs rather than outcomes.

People doing the nonprofit's work on the ground can design far more meaningful evaluation approaches than executives from afar. Why? They are closest to the information and have better context.

Evaluating, Learning, and Adjusting

One such example comes from alternative charter schools that design education programs for students who are at high risk. Some are economically disadvantaged, homeless, or require English as a Second Language training. Others have learning difficulties, suffer from trauma, emotional disorders, or substance abuse. The children often hardest to reach are serving sentences in the juvenile justice system.

Holding those schools to the same standards as traditional schools might be measuring the wrong thing. Those measures might be irrelevant or, worse, counterproductive. The wrong metrics might make a nonprofit look like they are failing, when they could be performing well in light of the difficulties they are addressing.

To address this, the National Association of Charter School Authorizers created a working group of people employed in charter schools to study the problem and make recommendations. The group recommended that alternative charter schools design evaluation and accountability frameworks that show evidence of progress and take their unique mission, circumstances, and population into account.

The working group's recommendations included a wider range of instruments and measures geared for these specific schools. These included:

- Monitoring and reporting reengagement with dropouts
- Providing continuing education to students who did not meet standards for a diploma
- Addressing recidivism
- Ensuring job readiness
- Assessing student growth and progress compared to their previous year
- Closely monitoring attendance and truancy, which serves as an early warning system for risks[2]

Those metrics were deemed more appropriate because they could provide evidence that the students are making measurable progress. They rightfully raised the challenge of, Are we asking the right questions? We can learn from their example.

Similarly, LifeWorks, a nonprofit focusing on at-risk youth in Austin, Texas, was dissatisfied with the lukewarm results of their programming. Through a series of strategy discussions, team members asked themselves, what is the ultimate problem we are trying to solve? They determined that all of their work should be laser-focused to help each client become self-sufficient. They then asked hard questions about each of their 17 programs—do they put us on a path to that goal?

They faced the uncomfortable truth that many of their programs were not aligned to that goal. Programs were disjointed; each had its own intake process and metrics that were funder driven.

They began to look more closely at their intake data and think about the specific challenges and needs of their clients. They developed a standardized intake process to better understand their clients in a more holistic fashion. They began to analyze the data and ask specific questions such as, How does trauma impact a young person's performance in workforce training? They realized their programming, such as classroom-based trainings, interview practice, and on-the-job skills training, was designed for traditional clients and adults, rather than for young people wrestling with trauma. The workforce training program was failing because it was misaligned with the client's needs. They looked to models of workforce development trainings in the mental health field for a better fit and created new programming. Within a year, results improved—for example, job retention was measurably increasing. In time, teams designed a self-sufficiency matrix, a more holistic framework for assessing if their efforts and programming were helping an individual young person become more self-sufficient.

As described by Susan McDowell, executive director of LifeWorks, "It was a journey of curiosity, asking, how do we get better for our clients?"[3] Their evaluation efforts paid off in terms of better results for their stakeholders, which also gained donor attention and trust.

Similarly, Pratham is a nonprofit with a mission to improve literacy of children in India. One of its efforts pairing volunteer tutors with children appeared to be performing well; children participating in the program did indeed show increased literacy. But Pratham teams were concerned they might be measuring the easy thing. When they undertook randomized controlled trials in the localities in which they worked, and looked at the data, they learned that there was no change in reading levels in the aggregate population they served.

Dr. Madhav Chaven, cofounder of Pratham explained, "We discovered that the volunteers were not sufficiently targeting the kids who needed the most help. Rather, the volunteers were teaching kids of high-income, educated parents who have some literacy themselves and are engaged. These kids would learn to read anyway at some point. The volunteer had no way of knowing that; the volunteer was just teaching. What was happening was that the data that we were seeing on monitoring was saying that the kids were learning and our intervention was creating improvements, but when we were looking at the state level, [we found that] the volunteers were teaching the kids who were going to learn to read eventually, even without the intervention."[4] They altered their model to target the young people most in need of literacy interventions.

We can mistakenly be patting ourselves on the back for our perceived successes, when in fact we are measuring the easy thing, or the wrong thing. Keeping our evaluation focused on the long-term vision and analyzing whether we are making progress in the right direction makes us far more likely to innovate.

Collecting Data That Doesn't Guide Action

Sometimes an organization collects data and doesn't know what to do with it. Evaluators should think through the costs and benefits of collecting data, and they should make sure the data is not just unnecessary detail and distracting noise.

One issue advocacy nonprofit wanted to know if their ideas were gaining public attention, and tracked all media mentions of their nonprofit in their database. This included tagging every media placement record in their database as either a positive, neutral, or negative story about the organization or their ideas. This involved reading every story and then manually filling in data for thousands of records each year. But after examining the data closely, the team found hardly any negative stories. In other words, categorizing the data drove no action. Rather, it just filled up the database with noise and took up the team's time. After checking with stakeholders, they eliminated the field altogether. The data was never missed because it wasn't useful.

A Commonsense, Pragmatic Approach

Designing an ideal evaluation system that captures everything we would like to know would be impossibly expensive. Most nonprofits, for instance, don't have the budget to conduct double-blind control group studies or nationwide polling. And because some outcomes won't happen for 10 or 15 years or longer, tracking long-term outcomes can seem formidable. As stated by the Kellogg Foundation, nonprofits "operate in complex environments where the scientific certainty of 'proof' is seldom attainable."[5]

An evaluation system for a nongovernment organization with a $100 million budget is going to be very different from one for a small animal shelter run by volunteers with a $500,000 budget. Therefore, we need to be pragmatic and consider the cost benefit of collecting data.

On the one hand, we shouldn't simply wink at our donors and hope they trust us. Whenever we can, we try to capture evidence. Evidence helps us counter unjustified optimism and faulty assumptions. On the other hand, gathering evidence may be impossible or too costly. Evaluators must determine whether they have enough knowledge, evidence, and information to guide decisions and investments in programming and resources. In the absence of hard evidence, ask whether you can instead explain the logic of your decision to your stakeholders. Can you provide cues, indicators, or the assumptions underlying your programmatic investments and the bets you are making? Is your logic transparent and does it hold up to scrutiny? Nonprofit staff must rely on pragmatic and thoughtful discernment to navigate the best approach.

Nonprofit philanthropist Mario Morino has extensive experience as both a donor and an evaluator. Here is his commonsense advice: "Let's decide jointly on a simple, coherent, user-friendly system to which we can both pay attention, which will prevail over bureaucratic [requirements] . . . and which will feed into a serious body of knowledge."[6]

Economist and nonprofit CEO Emily Chamlee-Wright echoes that sentiment and recommends a pragmatic approach:

Casual observation seems to suggest that many nonprofits have access to a rich source of local knowledge that serves as a *meaningful guide to action*. A mother looks for cues that her son's involvement in high school sports is contributing to or inhibiting the development of other life skills. The director of a domestic violence center tries to understand the particular reasons some clients return to their abusive spouse and others do not. She may adjust the center's programs in response and watch to see whether the changes make a difference.[7]

A commonsense, pragmatic approach to evaluation will serve us best. It will likely be a mix of hard data, qualitative evidence, trial-and-error experimentation, and professional judgment, all serving to help your team answer the question: How do we know if what we are doing is working?

Nonprofit staff work far too hard to be buried under a mountain of poorly conceived and counterproductive evaluation practices. Make sure members of the team know they not only have permission but are encouraged to point out data collection that isn't useful or, worse, gets in the way of innovation. Make sure your evaluation system is worth your team's valuable time. Plus, by talking openly with staff about evaluation practices, you are empowering them and creating trust, as together the team builds the right kind of system that spurs innovation.

What Are the Questions We Should Be Asking?

Now back to our second whiteboard question, where we ask team members, "Can we get away without evaluation and metrics?" Write their responses down. The team will probably share comments like, we need to be held accountable in some way, we need to agree up front about what good looks like, and we need evidence to know whether what we are doing is working. It can be good when we are all using the same yardstick, and we want to be rewarded for successes. We need to surface information that can help us make better decisions.

This is an important exercise, because we want teams to understand the underlying purpose, so they feel empowered and creative in making sure evaluation is designed to truly achieve its ends and challenge the process when it doesn't.

Building on this, ask the team, what is it we want to know or to learn? For example:

- How do we know if what we are doing is working?
- Did we achieve our intended outcomes? How did our beneficiaries fare?
- Processes—how did we do?
- Structures—how well did we organize our efforts?[8]
- Comparison of approaches—which worked best?
- What are we learning from our experiments?

Evaluation, done right, helps teams answer these questions. It can help us identify problems, such as cutting waste or lukewarm programs, as well as opportunities, like discovering better tactics and strategies for continuous improvement. Better information might help prevent overly optimistic thinking about something that isn't working. We might have barn-sized blind spots. We might have status quo bias. Evidence and information can help us overcome these common and very human biases.

Evaluation should lead to action or decisions. Take the Cincinnati Children's Hospital, which has a strategic effort for infection prevention. They began to closely track how many patients developed infections after surgery and assess how the infections were developing. The effort helped them identify ways to reduce the number of infections by half.[9]

Discovery is a process of asking questions, testing, learning, adjusting, and iterating. Just think of the tenacity required for the discovery of the lightbulb, and for the discovery of, well, anything! All innovators worth their salt know that their first steps involve curiosity and identifying a theory. Then the theory needs to be tested.

Evaluation and metrics must be meaningful and actionable. They should help you decide if a program is worth pursuing. They should help you test your theories and learn from experiments. I make a point of calling metrics "strategy-based metrics" because they should be based

Evaluating, Learning, and Adjusting

on a program or organization's strategic plan and help staff make decisions about the strategy.

Clarity of intent, and being explicit about strategy and goals, is the essential first step of evaluation. In fact, make this your mantra: strategy always comes first. Then and only then can we figure out how we should evaluate.

Evaluation Should Be Actionable

Nonprofit teams that write a fixed, inflexible plan are in for disappointment. If the plan gathers dust on a shelf, then we have wasted our time.

Evaluation is the lynchpin that makes strategy a meaningful, living process, not a lifeless, unused piece of paper.

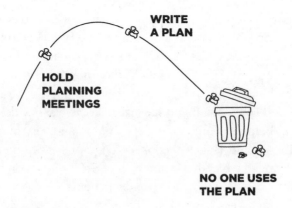

WRITE A PLAN

HOLD PLANNING MEETINGS

NO ONE USES THE PLAN

Figure 7.1   Wanchen Zhao

Nonprofits need a clear road map for how to achieve their aims. Nonprofit strategy should be a flexible process so that the team can constantly adjust as new opportunities come to light.

A well-designed evaluation system supports continuous learning. It is a dynamic feedback loop. It addresses the question: How do we know if what we are doing is working? If an evaluation system isn't helping teams answer that question, then it is of no use. Leadership consultant Paddy Miller refers to this continuous learning as "tweak."

Figure 7.2   Wanchen Zhao

Evaluation helps people to "test and challenge their ideas constantly, exposing them to frequent feedback and promoting a culture of rapid learning and experimentation."[10]

Michael Marquardt's *Building the Learning Organization* describes this process as action learning, comparing it to how sports teams and orchestras work and learn together. He writes:

> Asking the right questions when everything is uncertain and nobody knows what to do next encourages outside-the-box creativity . . . shaking up our underlying assumptions, opening us up to greater learning, developing listening skills and thus more caring and trust among group members, enhancing creativity, empowering each team member, developing new mental models, and attaining an elevated level of discernment and understanding that will lead to better reflection and more effective action. Action-learning programs provide the time and space we need to stand back and reflect, unfreeze our thoughts, rise above everyday problems, and develop a common perspective.[11]

The innovative nonprofits mentioned throughout this book regularly asked themselves these questions. For example, Martin Luther King Jr.

described how civil rights leaders and volunteers learned from their mistakes in Albany, Georgia:

> The mistake I made there was to protest against segregation generally rather than against a single and distinct facet of it. Our protest was so vague that we got nothing, and the people were left very depressed and in despair. It would have been much better to have concentrated upon integrating the buses or the lunch counters. One victory of this kind would have been symbolic, would have galvanized support and boosted morale. . . . When we planned our strategy for Birmingham months later, *we spent many hours assessing Albany and trying to learn from its errors.* Our appraisals not only helped to make our subsequent tactics more effective but revealed that Albany was far from an unqualified failure."[12]

Failure can lead us to valuable new insights. A wise board of directors will advise nonprofit teams that it is OK to fail, as long as they can demonstrate how they are experimenting, learning, and adjusting.

Evaluation of Programs

Teams often express frustration with planning. Nonprofit staff frequently tell me they are perplexed. "How can we evaluate program strategies that cover a very long time horizon? How can we design a long-term system that gives us flexibility to adapt and adjust without being rigid or bureaucratic? Why do we need strategy anyway?" Perhaps the world of sports can help us with these questions.

Think of your favorite football team. Could the team get away without being intentional? Without having any goals? What if the quarterback doesn't call any plays? Perhaps the occasional unplanned miracle might happen based on luck or talent, but I wouldn't count on it.

While a manager for a professional football team may have a five-year goal to build a team that wins the Super Bowl accomplishing that long-term goal requires intentionality, discipline, interim milestone goals and metrics to assess progress. Similarly, social change strategies can take years to accomplish—and sometimes decades.

While you shouldn't attempt to plan for every contingency, and you want to leave room for people on the field to make on-the-spot decisions given changing circumstances, you certainly do want to define your big-picture expectations. Then you can define interim markers along the way and collect information to help you know when you are off target or need to course-correct.

Multiyear efforts will change over time based on learning and new information. Programming and approaches should change when they aren't working, and plans should adapt to fast-moving opportunities. On the one hand, you need flexibility in your plan so that you aren't rigidly locked in, but you must also articulate your current thinking to internal and external stakeholders. Your long-term vision serves as your North Star and won't change frequently, but your short-term experiments probably will change more often as you evaluate, learn, and adjust. When you need to course-correct, you merely need to be transparent and explain the rationale behind the change.

Well-designed program evaluation should be flexible, too.

Evaluation over a long-term horizon will include strategy-based metrics that provide information to help you assess whether you are moving in the right direction. As you design an evaluation system that makes sense for your program, remember that strategy and evaluation work as a living system and feedback loop to help you assess if what you are doing is working.

Having well-defined outcomes is critical for this system to work. Outcomes are meaningful external change in the world; they are either a sustained change, a change in conditions or behavior, or a measurable change in people's lives. Outcomes break up a nonprofit's distant vision into achievable chunks. Outcomes play out over a longer period than a tactic or activity like publishing a study or running an event.

Let's take a look at what a flexible program evaluation might look like over a long time horizon.

Recall St. Benedict's Prep School. How might a similar school go about evaluating the long-term change they hope to achieve?

Evaluating, Learning, and Adjusting

Figure 7.3 Wanchen Zhao

We would start by zeroing in and asking the program team some preliminary homework questions such as:

Q. Who is your target audience?

A. Middle school and high school students within a 10-mile radius, whether they are prospects or currently enrolled students. A large percentage are at-risk youth.

Q. Do you break that audience into segments for different types of program delivery or messaging?

A. We assess each student individually and make a customized achievement plan.

Q. What actions do you want students to take?

A. We want our students to meet and exceed standards for attendance, grades, participation in the community, sports and activities, demonstrate personal growth and transformation, and develop leadership skills. Students should also gain mastery of the skills needed to overcome risks and obstacles in their lives. We want our students to choose these options rather than recidivating or turning to drugs and gangs.

Q. How will you craft your message to them?

A. We will train students by traditional classroom instruction, daily morning convocation, small discussion groups, counseling, and individual mentoring by faculty as well as by senior student mentors.

Next ask the team to brainstorm: Given the audiences you have defined, what would be some appropriate metrics? Remember the examples of Lifeworks where the team asked, how do we know if what we are doing is working? What evidence might fill in pieces of the puzzle to give us a complete picture?

Q. What would provide evidence that your target audience is *interested* in your services or programming?

A. Their answers might be: application rates signal competitiveness; gathering information about the applicants, including demographics and risk factors; attendance and participation rates; surveys; exit interviews; and focus groups.

Q. What would provide evidence that your target audience is *using* your services or programming in their lives?

A. Their answers might be: pre- and post-tests to demonstrate learning; assessment of students' progress per their personal achievement plan; conducting a phone survey of alumni to gather such information as graduation rates and college enrollment and completion compared to local statistics; evidence of stability and whether students have overcome the challenges of their community (for example, poverty, drugs, gangs, recidivism, lethargy, and ignorance).

Now let's apply the thinking from the preliminary homework to design an evaluation approach. At the 30,000-foot level, the **strategy** can be diagrammed like this:

IF ► the school staff deeply listen to the needs of their students and immerse themselves in the lives of the students to better understand the students' obstacles, ►THEN they can design a school model that addresses those needs and removes or diminishes those obstacles.

IF ► the students gain the opportunity to demonstrate leadership and form bonds of community, ►THEN they experience personal transformation, and they will gain self-respect, confidence, and the interior strength to meet and overcome the challenges of their community (for example, poverty, drugs, gangs, lethargy, and ignorance).

OUTCOME ▲ Students and alumni have skills to be active members of their community, raise their own families, lead fulfilled lives, and break the cycle of poverty.

How might the school design methods to evaluate whether it is accomplishing the above? A facilitator would encourage a team to brainstorm starting with the preceding questions, and then group the metrics into categories of short-term, interim, and long-term goals. Their list of metrics might look this:

Short-term (tactical) metrics (good):

- Assess brand and perception of the school via web analytics, local media coverage, and application rates.

- Track information about the applicants the program is attracting, their demographics, preferences, needs, obstacles, and risk factors.

- Conduct surveys and focus groups with students and parents to assess their feedback about quality of school programming. Conduct exit interviews of students and parents.

- Assess whether alumni recommend programming to their own network of friends and family. Why or why not?

- Demonstrate analysis of the external landscape; for example, how is programming adapting to external changes like the economic and fundraising climate, online education, changing student demographics, or increasing or declining enrollments?

Keep in mind that while short-term metrics like these are important for a nonprofit to track, this is only one very limited piece of the puzzle. They tell us something about efficiency and whether our tactics are working, but they don't tell us anything about our impact. For the organization to know whether it is making progress toward its mission, we must gather evidence about how our target beneficiaries are affected or changed in some meaningful way, based on the nonprofit's efforts and programming. You will notice that the following interim and long-term metrics provide progressively stronger evidence and help the organization assess whether it is achieving its mission.

Interim metrics (better):

- Evaluations of student learning through pre- and post-learning assessments and grading.
- For each student, identify obstacles and risks and work with student to develop a plan to overcome those risks. For example, risks might include family issues, trauma, recidivism, or substance abuse. Evaluate the student's progress according to that plan, including academic achievement, attendance, activities and personal relationships, mentoring time, and assessment by mentor. Track completion of tactics, activities.
- Identify early warning systems (truancy, lower grades) and action that will be taken.
- Track evidence of whether student has formed bonds of community, built social skills, developed conflict-resolution skills, demonstrated leadership, and completed the capstone hike.
- Assess completion of college applications, financial aid applications, college prep tests, and track college admissions.
- Track student's ability to build credentials, such as work study, volunteerism, internship, and job offerings.

Filling in a bit more of our puzzle, notice how the interim metrics are more closely related to what is happening with external audiences. They help the nonprofit assess whether students are making milestone steps that will eventually lead to long-term outcomes.

Long-term metrics (best):

- Compare graduation rates and college enrollment and completion to local statistics and comparable school system data. What can we learn from the data?

- Periodically survey alumni to capture information including demographics, evidence of stability, and whether they have overcome the challenges of their community (for example, poverty, drugs, gangs, lethargy, and ignorance). If the data is available, compare alumni to local non-alumni with similar demographics.

- Track alumni involvement with the school, such as donating, mentoring, and volunteering.

- Perform a multiyear case study that assesses the school's effectiveness over time, including successes, lukewarm results, and failure analysis. What has the school's impact on the local community been? For dropouts, are there any trends to learn from?

Notice that the long-term metrics provide far stronger evidence and a more complete picture because they help us assess whether the program is achieving meaningful external change. Also notice how these metrics are measured further out in time. Though the long-term data tends to be more difficult and expensive to capture, these metrics help inform whether the program strategies are working and on track, they help us make decisions about adjusting, and they enable powerful storytelling for donors and external stakeholders who want to know whether their donations are making a difference in the world.

Once the team has defined how they will evaluate, the next step is determining the right intervals to hold periodic check-in sessions or debriefs. For some programs this might occur quarterly, while for others twice per year is sufficient. This is when the team asks tough questions about their performance to assess progress toward their stated goals. See the following facilitator's guide as an example.

How to Conduct a Debrief

The facilitator or team leader explains the purpose of the debrief to participants. For example: "The debrief helps us learn from our performance on a specific project, share and teach best practices, identify what works, and for efforts that aren't working as well as we would like, we can discuss adjusting our strategies and tactics. We will then update our (strategic plan, project plan, or team road map) based on our new thinking."

These exercises can be in person or virtual.

The fundamental problem with most debriefs is that they are too long, too personal, not actionable, and demotivational. Get everyone to agree to these rules up front:

1. **Keep it short.** Two-hour meetings are always a fail because you never want to repeat them. Try to keep these discussions focused and aim for an hour.

2. **Keep it professional.** The moderator may have to enforce professionalism brutally but agreeing to this rule helps keep a meeting from escalating into an argument.

3. **Keep it actionable.** Too many debriefs get lost in the minutiae. The goal of the debrief is to come out of it with targets you can change, not just a list of what went wrong and whose fault it was.

4. **Sticky notes are your friend.** It is too easy to kill conversation. Whenever someone raises something irrelevant, list it on a sticky note and put it to the side. Never lose an idea or ignore feedback.

5. **There are no seniors.** In a debrief, everyone is equal. Don't allow seniority, expertise, or personality to allow someone to dominate the conversation or detract from team learning. Have the most senior person speak last.

Four Phases of the Debrief

1. **Expectations.** Briefly describe the project's planned strategies or target outcomes as originally planned. Explain how they advance the mission.

2. **Timeline.** Recap what happened. Both right and wrong, describe the story of the project. Share any feedback about the project (can be both from your own and other perspectives: external customer or stakeholder, other team members).

3. Assess:

a. Consider assigning some homework or asking team members to come prepared, for example, "bring three wins, one luke-warm result, and one or two things we should learn from and adjust." Or, if the project we are assessing is large or multiyear, consider sending a pre-meeting survey or conducting one-on-one background discussions to prepare for the debrief. This may make the best use of everyone's time and allow the facilitator to resolve sensitive issues behind closed doors rather than put participants on the spot.

b. Hand out sticky notes to each person and ask them to list every issue they can think of associated with the project (include multiple perspectives: external customers, team members).

c. Keep it from being personal: not "Doug let the servers go down" but "server uptime."

d. Assist in grouping the issues (challenges, technical issues, process issues).

e. Stress that we are here to challenge. Even if a project is yielding "good" results, is it good enough?

f. Prompt discussion with project-specific questions as needed.

4. Actions.
For each issue identified in step 3, associate an action item or agreed-upon solution. Actions should be SMART (specific, measurable, achievable, relevant, timely). Assign someone to check on action items in a month.

At the end of every meeting, you should always know if the meeting has been valuable. So, close off by focusing on wins, not just fails. While the purpose of the debrief is to learn from mistakes, a meeting spent talking only about mistakes for an hour is demotivational. End with the wins and successes to remind your team that while things went wrong, failures aren't the whole story.

Some additional discussion questions that the meeting facilitator might raise:

- If there is an outcome, or evidence of external change, what does it mean in the lives of those we are serving? Would our "win" pass the "so what?" test with skeptical stakeholders? Does it measurably advance our mission, or are we just patting ourselves on the back? If it is a small win, does it have ramifications for future wins? (The questions are meant to draw out whether we are underselling or overselling our success.)

- Likewise, what are we learning from our results so far? Would we say this is a wild success, a lukewarm achievement, or a failing result?

- When claiming credit for results, can we say "but for our efforts" this wouldn't have happened? Were we a voice in a choir of many other organizations? Absent our efforts, would the result have occurred anyway?

- What were high-value interactions leading up to the outcome? What are the motivations behind the external actor's interest in these efforts?

- Does this quarter reinforce our strategy, or do we need to rethink it? What would constitute a complete failure? What would prompt a scaling up or winding down of this effort?

- What would we do differently or the same? What was unexpected? What was unique?

- How should we adjust or update our written strategy, based on what we have learned?

Check-in sessions or debriefs should include tough love. Catching a problem internally is far better than producing a less-effective outcome for a client. At the same time, success stories should be highlighted in all-staff meetings and in marketing materials to donors and stakeholders, and they should be discussed and rewarded in team budget decisions and in individual performance reviews.

After the debrief, the team leader or program manager might use the notes or outline from the session to create a program report that contains results, analysis, learning, and storytelling. The report can be

Evaluating, Learning, and Adjusting

shared with whichever stakeholders find it useful, such as the executive level or the fundraising team, or it can be made available to the rest of the organization. Typically, based on the program's strength of strategies and track record of results, it should have an impact on internal budgeting and resource decisions.

This kind of thinking is very helpful to assess programs and to encourage a healthy culture of robust challenge and learning.

Evaluation of the Organization as a Whole

Should we evaluate our organization as a whole? How can staff be confident that the organization's efforts are on track?

Consider the example of the nonprofit Freedom Forum, the primary funder of the Newseum in Washington, DC, that spent $477 million to build the building on Pennsylvania Avenue. Newseum executives garnered shockingly large salaries. Projected visitor numbers fell short each year, perhaps related to the high admission fee of $25. Although Freedom Forum continued putting in large sums of money, the concept was clearly not working. A professor who often brought his students to the museum commented, "They are a good resource for journalism education. Maybe they can come up with something new that doesn't have to do with a dazzling building in the middle of Washington."[13] Within 10 years of its opening, the Newseum closed its doors and sold the building to Johns Hopkins University.

Or consider the tragic example of one of the most famous nonprofits in history.

Founded in 1889 as a settlement house for immigrants, Hull House was a Chicago institution for 122 years. Hull House was considered a model for innovative social and educational programs. Founder Jane Addams described the mission of Hull House and the settlement house movement as "close cooperation with the neighborhood people, scientific study of the causes of poverty and dependence, communication of these facts to the public, and persistent pressure for [legislative and social] reform."[14] Hull House achieved reforms such as improved labor laws, sanitation services, and public spaces for poor neighborhoods. By 1920, almost 500 settlement houses nationally had modeled themselves after Hull House, and by 1931, Addams was the first American woman to receive the Nobel Peace Prize.

So, when the legendary nonprofit unexpectedly closed its doors in 2012, the Chicago community was in shock. The nonprofit's leadership provided one week's notice to its 60,000 clients, its staff of 300, and the local community. Op-eds and angry letters to the editor ensued in the wake of the closing. What happened?

Some scholars surmise that Hull House gradually lost sight of their mission and identity. Over time, they slowly shifted their fundraising model away from a passionate base of local donors who were personally committed. Instead, they sought grants from the federal government, which expanded over time to become their main funding source. Though perhaps not deliberate, this led their programming to shift so that Hull House "became not a political challenger seeking social change but instead a political instrument implementing government programs."[15] As they drifted, Hull House's effectiveness became watered down.

There are many cautionary tales of good intentions gone wrong in international development work, similar to the story of a failed trash cleanup day shared in Chapter 2. When we neglect important cultural, legal, or institutional considerations, our efforts, no matter how well intentioned, are unlikely to produce their intended effect. These are usually stories of well-intentioned top-down solutions that miss the mark or have unintended consequences.

During my time in Jamaica, I was shocked to take in the on-the-ground reality that land titles and property rights don't always exist in developing countries. Because of this, many Jamaicans couldn't legally own their land and homes and had no choice but to be illegal squatters. Very few charities, many of which were headquartered in highly developed economies, were focused on resolving this fundamental issue. If this issue could be addressed, it has the potential to empower families with the security of truly owning their home and building equity and credit history. To me, this was a barn-sized blind spot. I observed NGOs and charities providing handouts, which are generous, well intended, and needed, but serve only as a temporary fix and fail to address something deeper and more structural that could have a far greater impact. Perhaps part of the equation is that providing handouts is simpler than disentangling a massive, national legal quandary. After finishing my tour of duty in Jamaica and heading off to graduate school, I made this the topic of my master's thesis.[16] Similarly, journalists have reported how exporting clothing donations from developed countries can end up harming small textile businesses in developing countries.[17] If your organization is involved in international efforts, or where there's a considerable gap between your efforts and local knowledge, then you will want to be sure that you're keenly aware of the cautionary tales and analysis offered by people like William Easterly, Chris Coyne, Gary Haugen, and Peter Greer.[18]

So how do we ensure we don't fall into these traps? Imagine that you were a manager at Hull House, a Jamaican NGO, or at the Newseum, what might you have done to address these organizational blind spots? What troubleshooting or diagnostic questions would you ask? Perhaps something like:

- Does the organization and its programs have a clearly articulated theory of change, strategy, and outcomes? Do they hold up under scrutiny?

- Is the organization's efforts addressing an underlying root cause of a social problem, or serving as a band aid? Do the organization's efforts truly empower people?

- Does the organization have clear parameters for making decisions about when to invest in capabilities and programs, versus when to wind them down?

- Via surveys and focus groups, how do beneficiaries, donors, and other stakeholders perceive the value that we provide? How do they suggest we can improve?

- Does the organization regularly gather information about its changing eternal landscape? For example, changing preferences and attitudes, new technologies, new competitors, or new regulations?

- Does every team member understand the organization's vision, identity, and comparative advantage? Does that understanding inform resource decisions and program design, and what opportunities are turned down?

This kind of organizational health assessment would also include questions about the nonprofit's fundraising health, its mission integrity versus mission creep, its programmatic capabilities, brand, and legal compliance. In addition, a board of directors and executive leadership would be well served to ensure that this kind of assessment occurs every few years.

If Hull House had asked itself tough questions like these, it might still be serving the Chicago community today.

Leaders can share cautionary tales like these with teams and encourage and reward team members for challenging the status quo. Go out of your way to praise a team member for a time when they spoke up and challenged the status quo. Make sure they know they are expected to do this.

Thoughtful evaluation practices like these can help us assess our experiments and can support learning and innovation. They can help ensure that our nonprofit doesn't become irrelevant.

Negotiate with Stakeholders Regarding Evaluation Approaches

We shouldn't tolerate any practices carried out in the name of evaluation that stifle innovation. An evaluation system should provide credibility to donors and at the same time help the nonprofit make meaningful decisions. To accomplish that, an evaluation system should contain these three elements:

- *Logic*: what are we trying to accomplish, and how will we get there?
- *Evidence*: qualitative stories or quantitative data gathered via an evaluation system
- *A culture that embraces organizational learning*: openness, humility, and a track record of challenging the status quo

Donors are looking for evidence of effectiveness, and so are you. Donors are on guard for a dog and pony show. Instead, show them that the system you have designed is meaningful for informing your strategies and resource decisions. Make sure that your fundraising team has a strong understanding of your evaluation system, and then walk them through your strategies and metrics so that they can convey this information in the best way to donors.

When preparing for these conversations, it helps to know, Is the particular donor looking for compelling storytelling or hard evidence? Consider these two perspectives. Helen Keller believed, "The best and most beautiful things in this world cannot be seen or even heard—they must be felt with the heart." In contrast, Isaac Asimov said, "I believe in evidence. I believe in observation, measurement, and reasoning, confirmed by independent observers. I'll believe anything, no matter how wild and ridiculous, if there is evidence for it. The wilder and more ridiculous something is, however, the firmer and more solid the evidence will have to be."

Are your donors more like Helen Keller or Isaac Asimov? Are they looking for compelling storytelling or hard evidence? Or both? Which approach you use depends on the donor and the context. Know your audience, and tailor your communication and negotiation talking points accordingly. All the while, remain mindful that it is those working on the front lines who are the most important users of the information—in order to learn, adjust and take action.

The good news is that you can design an evaluation system that works for your nonprofit *and* meets the needs of your donors. By demonstrating accountability, transparency, and results, a nonprofit will create trust with grantmakers and over time increase that trust and financial support.

Evaluation, when done right, is a way of asking, How do we know if what we are doing is working? Evaluation can encourage innovation. It can empower staff to be creative. When things are murky, evaluation can surface information to help us make decisions. Evaluation requires us to seek evidence, test our assumptions, and ask tough questions of ourselves as we go about the daily business of making the world a better place.

Part 3

Build Innovation into Our Organizational DNA

Does workplace culture matter? Does culture affect innovation? Non-profit powerhouse Mayo Clinic built an innovation culture that any size nonprofit can learn from. We will explore how they encourage creative collaborations and build trust among colleagues and ensure team members of all ranks walk the talk.

What is the organization's role in supporting innovators? To get an idea across the finish line, the idea will need resources and perhaps approvals from decision makers. The idea may need support from downstream teams. It is important that our work be high quality and on time. We may find ourselves navigating organizational structures and processes that we like, or dislike.

Heavy-handed or bad organizational design can stifle creativity, decrease efficiency, create bottlenecks, and increase mistakes. On the other hand, good organizational design helps teams to be their entrepreneurial best, constructively solve problems together, and achieve the best possible outcomes. Who gets to make decisions? Should it be bottom-up or top-down? Can we leave room for play and discovery? What's more, when is the best design in fact no design at all?

As we think about building an ecosystem for innovation, what specific role do donors play related to a nonprofit's ability to innovate? Can they help or hinder innovation? How do nonprofits navigate donor partnerships—both opportunities and pitfalls—so that teams are empowered to innovate?

Chapter 8

Encourage Creative Collaboration

Let's imagine what a culture of innovation looks like in the nonprofit workplace. At 6:00 a.m. on a Monday, Lashawn's alarm clock rings. Thinking about the day ahead, she feels good about her work at the community food bank. At her morning team meeting, she will present a proposal for improving the food bank's partnerships with local grocery stores. She knows already that her colleagues' feedback will make her proposal stronger. She feels emotionally connected to her work and enjoys problem-solving with her colleagues. She expects her workday to be productive and fulfilling.

At the same time across town, Joe's alarm goes off. With a sense of dread, he remembers the infighting and finger-pointing that happened last week. He has some ideas about improving the legal aid clinic's intake process for new clients, but the last time he made a suggestion, his boss and colleagues were outright dismissive. It's not worth the drama, he decides. He thinks about calling his boss to take a sick day, and he practices a fake cough. As he reluctantly gets out of bed, he decides to update his résumé during his lunch hour.

While an atmosphere like Joe's is toxic for all involved, Lashawn's workplace culture encourages everyone to be entrepreneurial, which benefits team members, clients, and stakeholders alike. Workplace culture has a significant impact on our ability to be innovative.

How does a positive culture develop? Is it spontaneous and unplanned or intentionally designed?

Yes, and yes. Organizations *aspire* to a culture, but people's behaviors *create* the culture. Workplace culture combines intentionally designed top-down rules and bottom-up informal norms. Culture embodies how people expect to work together and get things done. How they interact and relate to one another. It is expressed in the language they use with each other and how they process their tasks. Overall, it consists of a shared understanding of acceptable norms, social cues, expectations, and perspectives.

As an example of an *intentionally* designed aspect of workplace culture, many organizations have well-defined, official organizational principles or values like "respect" or "customer service." Those values can then be rewarded by financial incentives or bonuses.

But culture also springs up *spontaneously* out of the personalities of your people. Consider an example of a public policy nonprofit. The staff is largely made up of economists who are endearingly passionate about ideas and societal patterns. They tend to drop nerdy economic lingo into everyday workplace conversation. If you were hanging out with them at the watercooler, you would hear them talk about "opportunity cost" and "the invisible hand"—even when they are discussing such mundane matters as Valentine's Day gifts, office parking space allocations, or keeping the office kitchenette clean. If you were to ask team members about this aspect of their culture, they would not be even consciously aware of doing it. In fact, one person was taken off guard when I asked. She replied, "I don't even think about it. Economics is just the air we breathe here." This reminds me of the story of a fish swimming by another fish and calling out, "How's the water?" The other fish responds, "What's water?" People immersed in a workplace culture may not be aware of the cultural nuances that make their workplace unique.

Cultural norms can be positive and constructive, but they can also be toxic. For example, promising bonuses based on fundraising targets might unintentionally create incentives to hoard information rather than collaborate. One need only recall the national headlines a few years ago when Wells Fargo Bank rewarded staff for the average number of their products held by a customer, leading to the creation of millions of fraudulent savings and checking accounts on behalf of clients without their consent. Unfortunately, this happens in the nonprofit world, too. If a supervisor regularly limits pay increases for team members whose experiments failed, this might lead to the unintended consequences of suppressing experimentation and learning. Though the intention is to create excellence, the practice creates the opposite effect by fostering a culture of fear and backstabbing—not innovation or collaboration.

Common Workplace Problems That Get in the Way of Innovation

Stop to think about your own nonprofit experiences. What aspects of your workplace culture support innovation? What aspects get in the way?

- **Is there myopia or silo vision?** The organization or team might be so overly focused on itself and its internal operations that it fails to focus on external customers or the changing landscape. A symptom might be weak, vague, or nonexistent marketing plans. Does the organization miss opportunities to work with partners and build coalitions? Is there a culture of "stay in your own lane"?

- **Is there a lack of vision, focus, and clarity?** Are teams rowing in different directions or even redundant in their efforts? Is there clear guidance for prioritizing, winding down projects, or saying no to things? Do team members feel spread too thin and over-worked? Is there evidence of mission creep? Do team members focus on tactics and the tyranny of the urgent rather than the big picture or meaningful change? Strategies aren't clear and transparent so there is no buy-in or alignment. Staff and donors are uninspired; they aren't confident in how decisions are made about resources and priorities.

- **No excitement or creative energy?** Are results lukewarm or middling? Perhaps team members keep doing the same old things. There is a failure of imagination. Team members are complacent, don't ask hard questions, or face up to problems. Things are being done, but fruitlessly. Are there incentives to be creative, experiment, and take risks?

- **Bottlenecks, missed deadlines, and opportunities?** Do all parties have clear expectations for deadlines and deliverables? How are teams prioritizing conflicting priorities? Is needless bureaucracy in the way? Do too many layers of approval or mis-guided systems slow people down? Do certain practices waste precious staff time and resources, like data collection or reports that no one uses? Are antiquated technology and processes slowing things down? Is there demoralizing micromanagement? Alternatively, does too much democratic decision making create bottlenecks?

- **Crickets?** At team meetings, people don't really speak up or take the initiative. Despite plenty of entrepreneurs in the organization, they keep their heads down and stay under the radar. Why is that? Is there a culture of fear? Are team members rewarded or penalized for speaking up?

- **Are there many unresolved conflicts?** Do team members have a process for working through healthy disagreements? Are roles and responsibilities clear, or is there confusion and tension about who does what? Instead of collaboratively solving problems, are people pointing fingers at each other? Do team members feel management has one set of standards, but frontline workers have another? Is there high turnover?

Workplace culture challenges like these can undermine the causes that we love and the beneficiaries that we serve. They make us less effective. If some of these challenges hit close to home, you aren't alone. All nonprofits struggle with such organizational challenges.

When something seems amiss in our workplace, all too often we might shrug off a problem as an individual's fault, when in fact the "system" or incentives or rules might be the culprit. Workflow, procedures, budget processes, the handoff between teams, or clarity about who has authority to make a decision, can all have an impact on how easy or difficult it is for people and teams to collaborate and succeed.

Four key practices strike me as the cornerstone of a workplace culture of innovation, and these practices are readily applicable to any nonprofit:

- Creative collaborations and strong trust among colleagues
- Organizational values and principles that set the right tone

- Not just empty platitudes—values and principles are incorporated into everyday practice
- Team leaders who create an environment for innovation . . . and walk the talk

Creative Collaborations and Strong Trust

For the last 27 years, nonprofit Mayo Clinic has maintained a position at or near the top of hospital rankings.[1] Their world-class reputation attracts clients from all over the globe. Innovations include over 2,500 patents and the discovery of cortisone, for which Mayo Clinic doctors were awarded the 1950 Nobel Prize in medicine.

Scores of books, journal articles, and films document the special qualities of the clinic and the remarkable breakthroughs for patients accomplished by Mayo Clinic teams.

As Nurse Lori Plate observed, "Patients who would never have survived where I had worked before went home to live normal lives. The patient really did come first . . . I called [Mayo] "Disneyland for Nurses" because finally, after 17 years of nursing, I could be the nurse I always wanted to be."[2] Testimonials like this are plentiful, from patients and team members alike.

What is it that Mayo Clinic does to inspire testimonials like this, and to encourage everyday innovations, both big and small?

For one, team members at Mayo excel at creative collaborations for the benefit of patients and to achieve clinical breakthroughs. Clinicians, specialists, and laboratory workers collaborate to focus on the particular needs of a patient and then reconfigure differently for the needs of the next patient. As described by a Mayo physician, "It's like you are working in an organism; you are not a single cell when you are out there practicing. As a generalist, I have access to the best minds on any topic, any disease or problem I come up with and they're one phone call away."[3]

Likewise, in another part of the nonprofit universe, consider a coalition of nonprofits, foundations, and for-profit businesses that are committed to expanding hiring and advancement practices for people with criminal records. These very different organizations bring their expertise and perspectives to design pilots and programs. The Second Chance Business Coalition (SCBC) is composed of nonprofits and foundations like Dave's Killer Bread Foundation, the Stand Together Foundation, the Georgetown University McDonough School of Business Pivot Program, and the Society for Human Resource Management (SHRM) as well as businesses such as Bank of America, Home Depot, GM, Cisco, JP Morgan Chase, Microsoft, Walmart, Target, and others. Together, they bring together their respective expertise and share best practices for what works and for developing pilot programs.[4]

Considering your nonprofit culture, do team members feel a strong sense of trust among each other? Do people freely collaborate and share expertise and ideas?

Organizational Principles Set a Tone

In interviews, team members of Mayo Clinic say that good patient outcomes come about from the nonprofit's values, such as, "the needs of the patient come first" and "unsurpassed collaboration."[5]

By all accounts, team members model and prioritize these values when they are in the midst of high-stakes decisions. Mayo Clinic's team members seek to treat patients with dignity and give them confidence that their time at the clinic will result in a good health outcome. These values are built into the aesthetics of Mayo, from the architecture, art, soft lighting, and the music of the grand piano in the lobby to the bedside manners of nurses and doctors who take extra time to listen. As employees are hired based on alignment of values, much trust is vested in individuals and in small teams empowered to make decisions. These values became part of their workplace culture, guiding all decisions, big or small. Out of concern for how noise can affect a patient's peace of mind and how lack of sleep can disrupt the healing process, team members conducted noise studies that led to designing quieter flooring, quieter wheels on carts, and lower decibels for overhead paging.[6]

There are endless variations of how different nonprofits define their core values. For example, a nonprofit based in Washington, DC, emphasizes a core value of "freedom." Their leadership team made the decision

110

that the organization would have no official vacation or time-off policy. As long as the work gets done, team members can negotiate work commitments with their supervisor. Team members use their own judgment about working remotely if they have no meetings or because of adverse weather. How does this work in practice? Team members often mention the policy as a motivating factor that they deeply value. This core value of freedom attracts potential hires as well, making the organization more competitive when recruiting talented people. The leadership team describes the concept as: treat people as adults and they will respond accordingly. And team members describe the policy as liberating. No one is micromanaging your time or looking over your shoulder about what time you come to work. Friends and family of the employees will incredulously ask, don't people take advantage of so much freedom? Amazingly, they don't. Team members value this policy so highly that they brag about it, and they take time off thoughtfully because they don't want to risk losing this benefit.

Principles are too important to get wrong. They can combat common organizational learning disabilities that get in the way of innovation— like finger-pointing, silos, turf, disgruntled team members, human foibles, or egos.

What unique core values would advance your nonprofit's mission and benefit your internal and external stakeholders?

Not Just Empty Platitudes

Core values are a powerful tool when they are specific, proactively communicated, and put into daily practice. To be meaningful, we need to regularly teach values and reward team members who model them. That starts with hiring team members who understand and live these values.

The Mercatus Center at George Mason University, where I work, is highly selective when hiring applicants, thoughtfully designing interview questions to find candidates who embody their organizational values. For any open position, candidates are screened by HR and the hiring team until the pool is narrowed to four candidates who will visit for a 90-minute panel interview. The nonprofit's leadership has come to believe that competency can be learned, but values are often inherent and only slowly altered. Therefore, candidates are asked carefully about their behavior in different situations.

My colleagues at Mercatus believe that virtues trump skills and experience. Who you bring into the organization affects the culture. One rotten apple can ruin the bunch, as they say.

For your nonprofit, interview questions might be structured to find out how a potential hire lines up with your core values. Does the person have a track record of drama wherever they go, or do they de-escalate? When describing problem solving, do they throw everyone else under the bus, or do they take responsibility for the outcomes of their decisions?

When screening for new hires, interview questions can be designed to filter for candidates who have track records of demonstrating these principles in practice. "Can you tell me about a time when you challenged the status quo?" How the candidate presents the scenario, whether with arrogance, humility, respect, and taking ownership or blaming others, matters. Hiring mistakes can prove as painful as being stuck in a bad marriage, because each significantly affects culture and morale.

Once a new hire is brought on board at Mercatus, they are immersed in its 40-year history, culture, and values as part of the onboarding process. They participate in follow-up presentations every few months. New hires regularly review and discuss the organizational principles. Onboarding and continuous learning plans are customized given each employee's role and interests. During brief, weekly all-staff meetings, team members share key projects they are working on, tied to the mission and values of the organization.

To further incentivize collaboration, all team members are reviewed by peers in a 360-degree review process. For example, let's imagine that Diego is up for his annual peer review. The organization's principles, such as respect, are already included in Diego's job description as an expectation. His work performance is assessed by three or four peers with whom he has worked most closely that year. His peers provide feedback and answer questions such as, "How did Diego demonstrate 'respect' or 'customer service' in his interactions with you this year? Provide specific examples." Diego's supervisor shares a summary of the peer feedback (without naming names) with him and considers the feedback in decisions about compensation.

When an organization encourages and rewards these values, and specifically recruits for entrepreneurial people who model these values, then a culture forms where team members are innovating and learning from each other.

Employee surveys and focus groups are helpful tools for assessing or reinforcing culture. These might take the form of employee engagement and job satisfaction surveys. Exit interviews are another way to gather information. When individuals leave the organization, exit interview or exit survey questions might include, "In your time here, did you find that colleagues demonstrated the principles in daily practice? Where were teams strong or weak?"

When exit interview data indicate that a nonprofit is not living up to one of its core principles, the executive director must take swift action. A task force could be assigned to investigate and recommend solutions. The task force can design a survey to gather feedback, and then conduct a listening tour of small, diverse focus groups. The focus groups lead to three outcomes: (1) a list of actionable improvements; (2) employees feel "heard" as valuable contributors; and (3) the employees' perception of how the organization lives up to its core principles in question is measurably improved.

Clear values that are internalized by team members can also mean that individuals are empowered or deputized to make on-the-spot decisions to put those values into practice. For example, at Mayo, "If the employee's choices are either getting back to work on time or taking 10 minutes to get a wheelchair for a patient who seems unsteady, the patient will most likely get a wheelchair. Exceptional service frequently results when employees invoke values-based authority."[7]

How does your nonprofit ensure that your organizational values are not just empty platitudes, but are put into daily practice?

Team Leaders Walk the Talk

A workplace culture where people feel safe enough to challenge the status quo and engage in uncomfortable conversations does not happen by accident. How can individuals be entrepreneurial if they don't feel safe, or if the culture provides no way to constructively disagree and collaborate on solutions? When a team leader welcomes challenge, models openness, and provides a mix of constructive feedback, team members know they are safe to speak up.

A safe workplace culture can be the difference in whether challenging the status quo and learning is the everyday norm. When Tina Postel was newly hired to manage a YCMA in Billings, Montana, she was invited to a retreat with other newly hired managers. She described the onboarding retreat as typical and forgettable, full of "rah-rah" and "we are excited that you are here." But one workshop was different. The head of the YMCA retirement fund asked participants about the risky debt load each local office was carrying and challenged participants to be frank about organizational problems rather than hide them. She found his candor refreshing, and she described this moment as the thing she remembers most from the retreat. It inspired and motivated her to be a responsible executive, and she resolved to create this kind of atmosphere in her workplace. "As a leader, don't be afraid to surround yourself with people who are smarter than you . . . that you can have frank and honest conversations with." Years later, in her subsequent role as CEO of a food bank, Loaves & Fishes, she continued to create a workplace culture where people can be frank. This culture enabled the team to rapidly reinvent themselves in 2020 during the COVID-19 pandemic from a model that had worked well for over 40 years. They closed 41 brick-and-mortar food bank locations and invested their resources in mobile food banks and doorstep delivery, allowing them to feed 80,000 people in North Carolina that year.[8]

An innovative nonprofit requires a workplace culture that encourages openness, intellectual humility, respect, and integrity, and does not shy away from uncomfortable truths, healthy disagreement, or analysis of failures. Every nonprofit is already overflowing with social entrepreneurs—they just need to feel the assurance they can stick their neck out and share their ideas. Team leaders can help create this environment.

One junior employee at a nonprofit said, "My supervisor will say things like, 'Here is what I am thinking, but challenge me on this. What information am I missing?' She might say, 'My experience has been different from what you are describing, but tell me more . . .' And she really does want to hear our ideas. She'll change her position if someone provides a good argument, and she'll thank them."

A team leader holds more power than their team members. They can easily quash good ideas and stifle people's innate abilities. Conversely, like a good coach, they can empower team members, draw out the best in them, and help them realize their potential.

Team leaders should be mindful of the courage it takes for someone to come forward. They must express appreciation for that person's initiative. Team leaders should be mindful that their seniority can be intimidating.

To mitigate that standing, a team leader should regularly let the team know they are receptive to challenges and use language that encourages honest feedback. Showing that you heard and understood a person's point is validating to team members. Even if you have doubts, as the leader, you do not always have to be the one to disagree. Practice such messages as:

- "Team, here's my perspective on ABC, but I'm looking for you all to challenge my assumptions. Am I missing key information?"

- "I'm looking for some hard challenges from you all. Give me your best arguments for our trade-offs. Let's hear the pros and then the cons."

- "I'd rather have this idea crash and burn here with you all than to have it crash and burn with our clients. What risks or problems should we anticipate?"

- "Jane, it sounds like you are concerned that if we schedule the event next week, we run the risk of no-shows due to a conflicting event at the same time. Jane raises an interesting challenge. What does everyone think?"

Team leaders should regularly seek feedback from the team. Set ground rules at the beginning of the conversation that we are all among equals. At least weekly, whether in group or one-on-one settings, ask team members about obstacles, frustrations, and challenges. Recognize who the introverts are or those who may be reluctant to share and assure them that your team is a safe environment where they can come up with fresh ideas. Find ways to draw them out. Introverts will especially appreciate seeing a proposal in advance and having time to think about it, rather than being asked on the spot. Be mindful of the loudest voices in the room becoming too dominant. "Do you mind if I hold you back for a moment? I want to make sure Janine has finished and then I'll come back to you."

When you tap the potential, spirit, and ideas of the people doing the work, you empower them to freely collaborate. In contrast, the "my way or the highway" mentality runs the danger of consistently missing out on key information. This kind of top-down organization will underperform.

When appropriate, teams can use surveys, focus groups, or "listening sessions" to gather evidence when dealing with difficult problems or unknowns. A leader at Big Brothers Big Sisters of Eastern Missouri, Ms. James-Hatter, advises that blunt feedback isn't always easy for people in leadership positions. "Charities that seek employee opinions need to make sure they're ready to make changes based on what they hear—and that they can handle potential criticism."[9] Her nonprofit issues staff surveys several times per year. One such survey uncovered that team members whose jobs mostly entailed procedures were feeling like cogs in a machine. They described feeling like they were losing sight of the organization's mission. Based on what they learned from the survey, the leadership made some organizational changes that would free team members to spend more time interacting directly with beneficiaries.

Usually, the best ideas with the biggest impact will not be obvious or come from someone in an executive role. Frontline expertise is hard to come by for someone who is far removed from the action. That is why an innovative organization should encourage all team members to share ideas and remain open to hearing each other out.

Team leaders can use another method for reducing fear: encourage right thinking about risk taking, experiments, and failure. Remind team members that experimentation and risk taking are OK. They can make bets and even fail. That's how innovation happens! Of course, encourage teams to fail small before failing big or to fail early rather than fail late.

Nonprofits might learn by the example of Pixar, where teams are expected to give "brutal" feedback to each other. A Pixar executive says that they assume, "early on, all of our movies suck" and the job of the creative feedback process is to get the movie "from suck to not-suck." Shocking, right? Importantly, however, "Everyone in the room knows that the questions raised must be in the spirit of making the creative product as good as it can possibly be."[10] Without the manager setting the tone as a safe space, this kind of tough-love feedback process would never get off the ground.

Pixar's approach is similar to that of the collaborative medicine approach at Mayo Clinic. Dr. Lynn Hartmann, a medical oncologist, reviews the tests of a 65-year-old man with a possible kidney tumor, and she assembles a team of five other medical experts: two oncologists, a nurse, and a resident. They debate among themselves and ultimately end up challenging Hartmann's original proposed approach. Hartmann hears them out and ends up agreeing with the group's advice. "I take great comfort in the proximity of expertise," Hartmann says. "I feel much more confident in the accuracy of my diagnosis because I've got some very, very smart people right next to me who have expertise that I don't have."[11]

The doctors who are attracted to practicing this kind of transparent and collaborative medicine at Mayo believe that this model of accountability simply makes for better science and better outcomes for the patient. Similar to Pixar's process, Mayo team members call their approach "an institutional personality trait of self-criticism."[12]

A project owner should not walk away feeling utterly devastated or that they lost all control of their project. The intention is to help a project owner think differently or get unstuck. Setting a ground rule to pose questions rather than state forceful opinions can sooth fears. Again, the manager is the one who can set this tone during brainstorming sessions.

I have seen some nonprofits teams together write team culture norms that describe the desired culture specific to that particular team, the culture in which they want to work. For example, a team may agree to create a "no drama" rule and instead always look for ways to de-escalate. Perhaps the team creates a "no gossip" rule. This document might then become a part of annual performance reviews, discussed at annual team retreat sessions, or used for onboarding new members of the team. I have also seen nonprofit teams hold discussions of books related to a workplace culture of openness, using discussion questions to spur thinking and sharing about how these values can be put into daily practice.

As a team leader, anticipate likely sources of tension within the team to prevent it. For example, one of the biggest culprits that get in the way of innovation and lead to tension is turf wars. Clear roles and responsibilities can help prevent unnecessary frustration and distrust within the team.

Thinking of your nonprofit, do team members have high trust and encourage each other to ask uncomfortable questions and push each other higher? Are team leaders and colleagues open to looking at situations from different vantage points? Do team leaders create a safe environment where team members feel free to challenge assumptions and ideate?

Bottom line, creative and collaborative work cultures matter, for better outcomes and even to save lives. Consider the creative workplace culture that led to the invention of cortisone, destination medicine, or the design of quieter wheels on hospital carts. Workplace culture is a mix of top-down *organizational* systems and bottom-up norms that come about through *individuals*. Seek out and employ the many practical ways that nonprofits can create an entrepreneurial workplace culture.

What is more exciting than building a workplace culture that unleashes people's creativity and inspires bottom-up innovation? Amazing things can happen as a result.

Chapter 9

Optimize Organizational Design for Innovators

In nonprofits, we often manage complexity. To ensure that a service or product is not slipshod, organizational design can help us. That involves taking intentional steps to direct policies, processes, rules, and workflow, assigning clear roles and responsibilities. This may not sound very sexy, but the stories in this chapter reflect ninja-caliber management techniques. These are tools that serve us, helping us to be more innovative, make better decisions, improve efficiency or speed, make staff transitions smoother, and reduce the likelihood of mistakes.

What is the organization's role in supporting innovators? To get an idea across the finish line, teams need the freedom to be creative. The idea will need resources and perhaps approvals from decision makers. You will need support from other team members, and that support needs to be high quality and on time.

For example, what if no one remembered to arrange for catering for next weekend's conference? What if the fundraising team forgot to call and thank a new six-figure donor who supported your project? How comfortable would you be if the accounting team deducted the wrong amount of payroll taxes from your team members' paychecks? Would you feel more confident if these teams were well-prepared and following an intentional process?

Good organizational design can give our nonprofit an edge over the competition. But savvy managers must also be on guard for how heavy-handed or bad organizational design can stifle creativity, decrease efficiency, create bottlenecks, and increase mistakes. In other words, we should make sure that our organizational efforts don't squelch innovation. Organizational design that supports it strikes a balance.

Nobel Laureate Friedrich Hayek, who was well known for his warnings of the dangers of bureaucracy, was also known for saying that organization is one of the most powerful tools human reason can employ.[1] We must strike the right balance. And, as a nonprofit grows, organization becomes more important. We must thoughtfully discern our way through these questions.

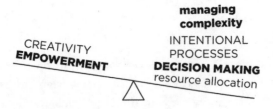

Figure 9.1   Wanchen Zhao

As social entrepreneurs, our job is to keep an open mind and ask, Under what conditions would adding intentional organization be a good or bad idea? This chapter explores four key design considerations that can help social entrepreneurs:

1. How might we empower colleagues and teams to be entrepreneurial? Can we build ownership and incentives into the design of roles, agreements, project plans, and performance check-ins?

2. Who should be empowered to make decisions? Under what circumstances is top-down decision making or bottom-up empowerment preferred?

3. As we strive to make the most of our scarce resources, can our budgeting and decision-making processes empower innovative thinking?

4. When is the best organizational design . . . no design at all? Can we leave room for experiment and play, spontaneity and discovery, rather than creating barriers?

The answers to these questions can give us confidence and spur ideas for how we might design the optimal structures (or no structure)

Innovation for Social Change

to advance our mission effectively, without imposing unnecessary bureaucracy.

Empower Colleagues and Teams

People need freedom to be creative. When my roles and responsibilities are clearly defined, when I know what the guardrails are, then I can take the ball and run with it. I can feel ownership and pride in what I have accomplished. I feel like an empowered entrepreneur.

The single biggest cause of conflict in the workplace stems from unclear ownership. Sometimes no one was ever directly assigned to a decision or process, leaving gaps or unfinished steps to fulfill it. I have observed situations where two individuals separately thought they were in charge of a decision, leading to awkward misunderstandings, finger-pointing, hurt feelings, and wasted effort. Clarifying roles up front can prevent those conflicts in the first place.

We can intentionally design structures that help us designate what gets done by whom. A necessary first step involves conversations and negotiation. Agreements can take many forms. A verbal agreement and a handshake might be perfectly fine. For an individual team member, they might be given a written performance agreement or job description. At the team level, they might decide on a team road map with deliverables, or a program strategy with defined outcomes and milestones. For a contractor, this might mean a written contract with service level agreements. For multiple teams or organizations entering an agreement, a memorandum of understanding might define who will do what, when. And there should be agreed-upon mechanisms for reviewing, updating, or reinforcing those agreements. Circumstances change rapidly on the ground, and you may need to check in with a colleague sometimes to ask, "Which of us is accountable for X?"

Buy-In

When President John F. Kennedy made a visit to NASA during the era of the US/Soviet space race, he stopped to talk with a janitor who was sweeping the floor. Kennedy asked him what his job was. The janitor replied, "I'm putting a man on the moon." He wasn't thinking in terms of his own work silo or even the immediate task at hand. He was thinking like a visionary entrepreneur.

Think about your nonprofit. Can every team member articulate how their role ties into the overall vision? And do they feel empowered to speak up about problems that jeopardize the mission, even if it falls outside their role? For ownership and entrepreneurship to work in practice, people must not only be aligned and bought into the vision but must also be empowered to respectfully challenge and escalate.

Incentives

Poorly designed organizations can often create incentives with unintended consequences. For example, do monthly quotas for traffic fines serve as deterrents to unsafe driving, or revenue generation for police departments? Thinking creatively, the city of Stockholm in Sweden experimented with a traffic violation lottery. Cameras captured safe drivers and speeding drivers. The speeding drivers paid a fine that went into a lottery. Safe drivers were entered into that same lottery for a chance to win. Unsafe drivers were paying the safe drivers, not the police department. The average speed limit was reduced from 32 kmh to 25 kmh.[2] This prompts the question, Would these new incentives transform the behavior of police departments and also improve how they are perceived by members of the local community they serve?

When well designed, incentives can spur innovation. Nonprofit Cleveland Clinic established a policy that net proceeds from any commercial licenses created by a staff member will be split. Inventors receive 40%, and the remaining 60% is divided between the inventor's clinical institute of origin, Cleveland Clinic Innovations, and Cleveland Clinic's Lerner Research Institute.[3] This not only encourages and rewards individual team members to innovate, but it also encourages their department and colleagues to support them (rather than compete with them or hoard knowledge). A portion goes to their internal incubator for experiments and innovative new ideas. Incentives like this help keep The Cleveland Clinic at the cutting edge, with such breakthroughs as coronary angiography, coronary artery bypass grafting, the artificial kidney, cadaver kidney transplant, and a near-total face transplant.[4]

Recognizing the power of incentives, state and local governments are increasingly experimenting with performance-based contracting with nonprofits delivering social services.[5] Consider the story of Courtney, shared in the book *What Matters: Investing in Results to Build Strong, Vibrant Communities.*

Courtney arrived at Frontline Services, a nonprofit organization that helps citizens in Cleveland, Ohio, when she was 28 years old. She was living in a shelter for homeless women, struggling with mental health and substance abuse issues, and parenting three young children who were in custody of the county. Courtney had just about given up hope that she would ever be able to care for her children on her own. Until then, the county caseworker assigned to her family had little incentive to reunite mother and children, as the caseworker's primary job was to protect the children. Living with a birth parent is almost always better for a child's development than foster care, as long as the home environment is safe and healthy. However, before entering Frontline Services, Courtney had few options to change the trajectory of her children's lives. What Courtney didn't know when she arrived at Frontline that day (and likely will never know) was that she was walking into a social services experiment—one of only seven other similar experiments across the country at the time.[6]

The county and the nonprofit had jointly entered into a performance-based contract which changed the incentives. The nonprofit's pay was based on reuniting families successfully. This meant that a caseworker would be dedicated to Courtney to look at her particular circumstances and work with her to create a tailored plan and mix of services to help her turn her life around with the end goal of reuniting her with her children as quickly as possible.

There are a variety of types of pay-for-performance contracts. Some pay only for meeting certain performance standards, while others are a hybrid, meaning a portion of contract payments are cost-based and the remainder are performance-based. In Courtney's example, the incentives helped reunite her family.

As another example of how incentives can be structured in organizations, try using a 360-degree peer review process. This means that several times during the year, a handful of a team member's peers provide feedback on Leslie's performance, which her supervisor, Jamal, compiles and shares with her. While the supervisor knows who provided the feedback, he does not disclose the identity when sharing the feedback with Leslie. Knowing that her peers hold her accountable incentivizes Leslie to not only care about making her supervisor happy, but also to provide excellent service to her colleagues. Nor does she need to fear that her colleagues are incentivized to compete rather than collaborate with her, because she is providing peer feedback on their performance as well.

The right incentives can help to smooth over human foibles. For example, we might have an irrational impulse to cling to our own ideas rather than give others' ideas a fair hearing. It is human nature to be competitive and ambitious, but if ambition is taken too far, it can lead to territorialism, kingdom-building, or budget-hoarding. Likewise, we are inclined to think first of our team silos. Taking an enterprise-wide view may not be the first thing that comes to our minds. As another example, fear can lead people to avoid risk rather than making a risky decision.

If you notice some of these very human foibles getting in the way of innovation in your workplace, think about ways to overcome or prevent them by creating incentives, and then build them into your organizational design. Here are some methods that can help:

- **Ownership.** Set expectations in job description agreements, project plans, program strategies, and memorandums of understanding. Ownership means that the individual is rewarded for an outcome and also held accountable for it. For example, specific questions can be built into the performance review process, after-action reviews, debriefs, or program effectiveness check-ins.

- **Specificity.** Agreements can include specifics about stretch goals or outcomes. Define what would be evidence that the individual or team is on track toward meeting the goal.

- **Incentives.** Identify what matters most to individuals, whether it is compensation, time off, flex time, remote work, expanded responsibilities, or an increased budget or resources.

- **At-risk compensation.** Incentives might include adding compensation. For example, a team member might get a 5% bonus for completing a report by a specific date.

- **Communication.** The desired outcome can be emphasized and reinforced through private conversations, training, repetition, shout-outs, and kudos (carrots), or when not meeting the mark—corrective action plans (sticks).

Who Should Be Empowered to Make Decisions?

How many people should be consulted before a decision is made? How many layers of approval should be demanded? What about teams, departments, or handoffs between teams? Under what circumstances should decision-making authority be top-down versus bottom-up? Making the right organizational design choices will affect whether teams can be free to exercise their entrepreneurial spirit, constructively solve problems together, and achieve the best possible outcomes.

When we want to optimize decision making, a five-point test can be helpful:

1. **Efficiency.** How quickly does the decision need to be made? How much input or deliberation will lead to a better decision versus a bottleneck?

2. **Knowledge.** Who is closest to the information? Who has the best knowledge to make a good decision?

3. **Consequences.** Who will be impacted by the decision? What are the risks of being wrong? Does the decision maker have any skin in the game? (Having skin in the game means having a personal stake in something. The saying was popularized by financier Warren Buffett, referring to when company leaders use their own money to buy stock in the company they are running. It changes incentives and commitment.)

4. **Accountability.** Will the decision maker be held accountable for a good versus bad outcome? If someone makes a bad decision, can the majority, or a board, hold them accountable? Are checks and balances in place?

Optimize Organizational Design for Innovators

5. **Incentives.** What are the decision maker's incentives? Will they act in the best interest of a team or silo, or in the best interest of the organization?

Decision makers will weigh these five points differently depending on the nature of the decision, such as the costs associated with making the wrong decision (risk), or deliberation costs (time).[7]

Organizations that respect the dispersed, specialized knowledge of people doing the hands-on work tend to be the most successful and innovative organizations. But is bottom-up decision making right in every case? Let's explore the trade-offs of either approach, and how each can impact innovation.

When Are Bottom-Up Decisions Optimal?

"I perform better under strict micromanagement," said no employee ever! So, when should executive leadership and managers get out of the way? The right answer, in my humble opinion, is most of the time.

At the nonprofit where I work, Executive Director Dan Rothschild shared a story about a time when a program manager pitched the idea of a new podcast. Rothschild had seen other podcast efforts unimpressively fizzle, so he had his doubts, but he got out of the way.

Sometimes people want to make a bet, and I may not agree with the analysis, but I will tell them to go ahead and try it. For instance, the director of our monetary policy program wanted to start a macro policy podcast. I thought, who would listen? Would David have the right skills to produce a steady stream of quality content, or to be a good interviewer? But he agreed to start small, and he sought a lot of advice. Now the Macro Musings podcast has 5,000 people listening, which is comparatively small, but we are reaching the right target audience for our strategies. He's got a huge listenership at the Federal Reserve, for instance. The handful of journalists who specialize in this field and who matter listen! So David had identified the gap in the marketplace, knew his theory of social change, and he wanted to reach the 2,000 people who matter most to achieve the strategy.[8]

Likewise, nonprofit Cleveland Clinic holds to the maxim that innovation is likely to originate from any team member in the organization. When two staff members noticed the time and cost of frequently laundering the heavy, unwieldy privacy curtains that separated emergency room bays, they were empowered to act. They asked for equipment to check the entire curtain for bacterial counts and found that bacteria were negligible, except for a narrow section frequently touched as people pulled it aside to enter and exit. They brainstormed a better solution: a new detachable vinyl panel that is easily disinfected. Hundreds of emergency departments throughout the Cleveland Clinic system installed the new curtains, resulting in cost savings and freeing up staff time to focus on other patient needs.[9]

When frontline teams are free to experiment, amazing things happen.

A good principle is to encourage bottom-up decision making and empower small experiments wherever possible, taking advantage of the specialized knowledge of the people on the front line doing the work. These practices reflect ninja-caliber management at its best. It takes restraint, humility, and discipline to avoid the temptation to micromanage, to embrace complexity, and to allow for messiness and failure—that is where innovation happens. Making mistakes is how people figure out the best path forward.

Empowering frontline workers to make decisions is essential because they must navigate the unexpected, and they have the best knowledge of the on-the-ground situation. For example, the headquarters of an international development agency shipped mosquito nets to families in malaria-infected areas. To their surprise, the intended beneficiaries used the mosquito nets not on their beds but as fishing nets. The frontline workers, given their relationships with locals, might have anticipated this, or would have had the best knowledge for resolving the issue, perhaps through training, messaging, or designing a different intervention altogether.

When Are Top-Down Decisions by Executives Optimal?

I have deep respect for nonprofit leaders. At times they have the unenviable task of making a hard choice, or an unpopular choice, such as: Do we stop accepting money from a major donor who is taking a controversial position in public? Do we continue the relationship at the risk of alienating other supporters and risks to our brand? On top of this, leaders often wear many hats, especially in smaller nonprofits. They may be under significant pressure to fundraise.

In nonprofits, senior leaders are often held accountable for functions like:

- Mission integrity
- The fiscal health of the organization; fundraising effectiveness
- Legal and regulatory compliance
- A stable, long-term institution
- Organizational health, effectiveness, and accountability
- A strong organizational brand
- Appropriately adapting to changes in the external landscape (for example, regulatory changes, new competitors)

Why is an executive often charged with these responsibilities instead of a frontline worker? Thinking back to our five-point test, a common thread in the above list is risk, where consequences and accountability are very important. When the stakes are high, poor performance or a bad decision could put the entire nonprofit in jeopardy. There would be no entrepreneurial staff or programs, for example, if the organization closes its doors due to legal jeopardy or loss of funding. If the executive makes good decisions in such cases, this will have an empowering effect on the rest of the organization.

An effective board of directors should (ideally) hold a nonprofit's executive leader accountable for these responsibilities. The leader may delegate some of these tasks, and may seek input from others, but the bottom line remains the same. If the board fails to hold the executive accountable, then sooner or later, forces of competition will. Team members who are dissatisfied or lose confidence in their leadership will likely leave to go to work for better firms, and donors will invest elsewhere.

While each team may naturally be focused on their particular strategies, the executive leader, perhaps with the help of others, must make the right resource-allocation decisions across departments and ensure the organization has the right capabilities to best advance the mission.

With the big picture in mind, executive leadership should be alert to gaps and opportunities. On the flip side, leaders must recognize when existing capabilities are no longer necessary, or where resources may be put to better use elsewhere. Teams may pitch 150 great ideas, but the organization may be able to act on only 10 of them. The executive leader may put a team together to make recommendations for these types of decisions. This requires creative, big-picture thinking, active listening, navigating competing requests, and holding sensitive, even tense conversations. Resource decisions should be made based on proven results or strong justifications or strategies.

It is perfectly appropriate for leadership and managers to pose provocative questions, but then get out of the way. The executive director of Loaves & Fishes Food Bank, Tina Postel, takes the right approach, stating, "I like to call myself a lovingly disruptive leader . . . asking questions such as, why do we do it this way? Can we feed more people if we do things differently?"[10]

In addition, executive nonprofit leaders are building long-term institutions. This means thinking not just in terms of what programming activities the organization focuses on for the next three months but thinking in terms of decades. For example, by year 2 we will build a media capability; by year 3 we will grow fundraising by 20%; by year 8 we will need a capital campaign to build a new wing of our hospital. Long-term organizational health and stability matter for current and future staff. A good executive leader is not looking through binoculars but through a telescope.

A savvy executive won't try to do everything, but instead has a healthy awareness of who has the best information to make a decision. Depending on the type of question at hand, the response might be, "I'm not the right person to make that call. This is a marketing team decision; you'll want to talk to Kate." The leader will have a good sense of the big picture, but knows they can depend on teams and staff for carrying out the work based on their expertise and local knowledge. In another example, board members should not be choosing the wall color and office furniture (sadly, this really has happened).

As novelist and essayist David Foster Wallace put it, "A leader's real 'authority' is a power you voluntarily give him, and you grant him this authority not with resentment or resignation but happily."[11] An executive who values innovation will encourage decision making to be as bottom-up as possible, and will have earned the credibility and trust of the people they lead.

When Are Top-Down Decisions by Managers Optimal?

For years at a Virginia nonprofit, the freedom to choose communications software like Slack, Asana, Trello, or Google was left to each team. Based on the principle of encouraging people to make their own entrepreneurial decisions, teams were free to use whatever software worked best for them. The culture prided itself on being bottom-up. But as the organization grew and more people were working with multiple cross-functional teams, they found that this was not working well. No one wanted to learn how to use four different communication tools. The murmuring eventually swelled into a roar, and teams approached IT: "We would like to empower you to make a centralized decision for the organization. Let's choose one communication software for all teams across the board." This was an unusual case of a bottom-up demand for a top-down decision. Thinking back to our five-point checklist, the teams prioritized efficiency.

Likewise, an executive leader may grant wide decision-making authority to managers to make centralized decisions in certain situations. The human resources manager can be granted authority related to legal compliance and preventing lawsuits. IT can be granted authority related to security policies in the face of cybercrime. Per our five-point test, this kind of decision-making latitude is usually related to organizational effectiveness, risk, and specialized knowledge.

Managers are held accountable for the performance of their teams. A manager should be empowered to drop the hammer when it is appropriate, coaching and correcting problematic performance, and sometimes parting ways. On the other hand, the supervised individuals are also empowered to respectfully challenge, negotiate, and escalate, or even become whistle-blowers, when appropriate.

We should acknowledge that organizational design will never make everyone 100% happy. We should of course do our best to listen and build buy-in, but we won't please everyone. And organizational design is all about balancing trade-offs to optimize as best you can. In the words of economist Thomas Sowell, "There are no solutions, only trade-offs."[12]

When Is Close Supervision and Verification Appropriate?

No one enjoys micromanagement. But are there occasions when close supervision and layers of approval are needed? Teams working at non-profit hospitals, for instance, work in a high-risk field; lives are at stake. Given the low tolerance for error, the appropriate organizational design might include rigorous processes, checklists, and perhaps tasking another team member to provide verification that a critical procedure was done properly.

For example, a research center that regularly publishes books has a double-check system called "read back," where two copy editors take turns reading a text out loud to each other to ensure they didn't miss any errors. Though time-consuming, the team feels this step is essential to maintaining quality.

Or consider a new employee who doesn't know the ropes and needs hand-holding in the first months on the job. Tight supervision might be appropriate. Decision-making latitude might only be granted after the new team member earns it.

That said, tight supervision has ramifications for morale and trust, as pointed out by nationally syndicated parental advice columnist John Rosemond. "Invariably, micromanaging results in four problems: deceit, disloyalty, conflict, and communication problems."[13] Similarly, W. Edwards Deming, considered the father of quality systems, warns, "A bad system will beat a good person every time."[14] Leaders who hoard decision-making authority can stifle innovation and create decision-making bottlenecks. Wherever possible, give team members room to make mistakes and learn.

Referring back to our five-point test, teams might develop risk-related or quality-related justifications for tight supervision. But balanced with concerns about risk, when might tight supervision go a step too far, replicating efforts, slowing things down, or squelching creativity? We probably all have cringeworthy stories of being micromanaged. Remember that we should consider the five criteria and strike the right balance, depending on the circumstances.

Optimize Organizational Design for Innovators

Hybrid Team Configurations

Surfacing information and expertise from various specialists can provide real value and support collaborative innovation. There are a variety of creative team configurations for joint decision making.

More and more frequently, we hear about **matrix-style teams** or cross-business teams. People on a matrix team are pulled from other departments in the organization. An example is a matrix team that focuses on homeless policy advocacy. The team might pull in specialists with a clinical background, specialists from a media department, from the policy research department, and specialists with Capitol Hill advocacy expertise and relationships, and from fundraising, all of whom work together to advance a strategy. Each member of the matrix team has multiple bosses: their regular boss and a boss on the matrix team.

Is a matrix-style team an appropriate design for your organization? Consider the trade-offs. Having two bosses brings new challenges, such as conflicting directives to resolve, but it can be managed. Matrix-style teams might mean some redundancy or duplication of efforts. But the benefits might outweigh the costs.

Ad hoc **issue teams** are created to solve a one-time or short-term problem. Like a focus group, they are granted authority to work on a particular problem. Perhaps someone from the executive committee assembles the team and provides a scope of the problem to be solved. Mayo Clinic does this often, for example, assigning a troubleshooting team to examine a business unit's multiyear loss of millions and propose solutions. An organization may ask an ad hoc issue team to propose a better onboarding process for new hires, or a remote work policy during a pandemic.

Sometimes it makes sense to grant decision-making authority to **a centralized or shared service**, like HR, payroll, or IT. Following are some questions to help determine if a function should be centralized or decentralized:

- Does the task require specialized local knowledge? Is there a high or low learning curve?
- How many hours per week will this task require?

- Is the same task needed by multiple teams?

- Are multiple teams providing the same service now in a redundant fashion? Would centralizing the service save costs?

- Will centralization of a task make costs less transparent? Is it best to keep the incentives within the team for this task so they can judge budgetary trade-offs?

- Is the task a nice-to-have or essential? What is the worst that would happen if this task didn't get done? Can we experiment for a short time without offering this service to see if anyone complains?

- Will the person or team performing the task be held accountable?

- Who will be impacted by the decision? What are the risks of being wrong?

- Other factors to consider: volume, speed/nimble, quality, price, and economies of scale.

How Many People Should Be Consulted?

Is the decision complex, with many unknowns, where surfacing information from different people is helpful? Is it a controversial decision that requires wider input and buy-in?

Consider Southend Community Services, a multiservice nonprofit whose mission was to promote independence and economic success through innovative programs and services in the greater Hartford, Connecticut, area. They offered a mix of programming that provided social services to local youth and to the elderly. In a theory of change workshop, participating team members recognized that their elderly services were legacy programs and not what they did best. They proposed adopting a revised mission: "Helping urban youth become successful adults," which would narrow their focus. However, this would mean uncomfortable, even painful conversations with the rest of the staff. It would mean cutting programs for the elderly. Some team members were quite reluctant. Through a series of meetings, the staff came to a compromise of keeping a few small experimental programs that tied youth job training with services for the elderly. They would closely monitor the results. In time, they observed weak results, and then the whole staff agreed to completely cut those programs and apply resources to better use. They continued to refine their model, focusing on youth.[15]

As another example, an organization may recognize that it makes sense to have only one central intake process for new clients, rather than 20 different intake forms for its 20 different social service programs. Can they all agree on one format? This decision will affect many team members, so buy-in and openness to each team member's feedback and expertise will be important.

If the impact of the decision doesn't fall so much on the decision maker, but primarily affects others, then exerting extra effort to gain buy-in might be well worth the time. For example, an accounting team may be assessing whether to purchase a new software app that enables fundraising team members who frequently travel to upload receipts by taking a picture of the receipt with a smartphone. Though the accounting team has the authority to make the software decision due to their specialized knowledge in financial security and legal compliance, they aren't actually the end users of the product. As this proposed system aims to make life easier for the end users, their feedback will be critical. If the team members who are often on the road do not like the product and continue scanning and uploading receipts the old manual way, then the accounting team has wasted their time on a failed project.

In that case, a representative from the accounting team might make presentations to the frequent travelers about the various options, sharing the options under consideration, the trade-offs, and risks. Or they might survey affected teams for feedback and concerns. This person should communicate that the accounting team remains open to hearing challenges and exceptions and make improvements to the product after it is launched.

Listening and empathy is helpful for buy-in. That said, not many decisions in an organization should be put to a democratic vote, as nothing would ever get done. Ultimately, someone must make a decision. Everyone isn't going to be happy every time, and that should also be a consideration when weighing trade-offs. Per our five-point test, dispersed knowledge and who is affected are prioritized in this situation.

Author Tim Brown describes the optimal approach as a balance, "a judicious blend of bottom-up experimentation and guidance from above." He also advises not letting "the results of bottom-up experimentation dissipate into unstructured ideas and unresolved plans."[16]

Budgeting and Trade-Off Thinking Fuels Innovation

Recently, I was surprised to learn that the recipe for spaghetti carbonara was created during the food shortages of World War II. American GIs would offer their daily ration of eggs and bacon to villagers in Italy, who invented the recipe.

Likewise, the COVID pandemic has forced many in-person events to shift to virtual, and in many cases, we have been surprised that such events are better, less expensive, more convenient for participants, and can attract diverse audiences from wider geographic areas than ever before.

Or consider the work of conservation efforts. In the 1980s, poaching had reduced Kenya's rhino population from around 20,000 animals in 1960 to fewer than 500. The dire circumstances and necessity led to some new ideas and transformation. In 1995, as wildlife-based tourism was generating considerable income and was operating in conjunction with livestock production, elders from the community set up a community conservancy. Conservancies give marginalized indigenous communities a framework and incentives to protect the wildlife they share the landscape with, manage rangelands and fisheries more sustainably, and improve regional peace and security.

Necessity is the mother of invention. Constraints force discipline, trade-offs, and creativity that can inspire the best innovations. We can apply this concept to our thinking for how we design our internal processes.

According to organizational design expert Jay Galbraith, "Limits and boundaries can be likened to brakes on a car: their primary function is not to slow down the car, but rather to allow it to go fast. Just as brakes give a driver confidence that the car can be slowed down when required, clearly articulated design limits and boundaries empower people to make decisions and act."[17] Embracing scarcity means understanding that we must create guardrails and say no to more far-flung ideas, which helps us focus and excel.

Following are two types of internal processes that embrace the "necessity is the mother of invention" philosophy:

- Sorting. We can't say yes to everything, but we can create tools that help us sort and identify our best opportunities
- Budgeting. We can design a budgeting process that inspires creative thinking to help us make the best use of our limited resources

Both of these tools surface information and preferences to help us make an optimal, rational decision, and they help us identify our *best* option from a multitude of options.

Sorting—to Find Our Best Opportunities

We are often faced with having more opportunities than we can green light. How do we decide? How do we prioritize? Can we identify standards? The good news is that certain tools can help us extract key information so we can make comparisons and better decisions.

In the same way that a hospital triages patients, or scholarship committees use criteria for sorting through many applications, nonprofits can also create decision-making methods that help us sort through our opportunities.

Figure 9.2 Wanchen Zhao

Let's look at how asking the right questions can winnow down the number of new ideas. How can a leadership team choose the best ones? They might develop a decision-making rubric that looks like the following.

- Does the proposal include a compelling case for mission impact?
- Credibility? Past performance, previous results, and track record of the team (or if the team is brand new, does their proposal cite lessons from others working in this space)?
- Well-defined outcomes and a plan for gathering evidence to evaluate the program?
- Analysis of risks, feasibility, and what failure looks like? Is the plan realistic? An exit strategy for winding down the program if it is failing?
- An analysis of who else is working in this space and how this effort provides a unique contribution? An analysis of partnerships, coalition building, or spin-off opportunities?
- A theory of change?
- Arguments for how the project makes the most of the organization's comparative advantage and capabilities?
- A timeline for results? Is it a short-term or long-term strategy?
- Clearly defined target audiences, messaging approaches, and definable actions we hope the audiences will take?
- An approach relying on small experiments, learning, and adjusting, before scaling?

Based on the answers, it becomes easier to rank or score the proposals and the best opportunities will become apparent.

For example, from my own experience on grant selection committees, I have seen the best and worst of proposals and presentations. I recall a passionate, energetic scholar presenting an idea for new research, but when a committee member asked the fifth question from the preceding list—tell us about other scholars or organizations who are doing related research—he didn't know. People on the committee with less expertise quickly mentioned the work of others in his field. Needless to say, other proposals outshined his, and he did not make a good impression or win the grant.

Here's another real-life example. Events are expensive. Let's say an events team gets an average of 15 requests per year from different teams, but only has the budget and staffing to run five events. How do they decide which events they will support? They might develop a decision-making rubric that includes questions like these:

- Has the program team provided a compelling justification, including how the event advances the mission? Does it include a reasonable assessment of the costs compared with the benefits?
- What would we lose if we don't host this event?
- What will success look like? What will a failure look like?
- What do we want the audience to know or do as a result of participating in the event?
- Could the team achieve the desired outcomes through other means, such as relationship-building or marketing?
- Does the event need to be held by a particular date to be effective? Is there adequate lead time to plan the event?

Another significant benefit of a decision-making rubric is the perception of fairness and transparency. Asking questions shows that the events team isn't playing favorites and that all requests are filtered through the same criteria.

In yet another example, let's say that a nonprofit IT team gets an average of 80 requests per year, but only has the budget and staffing resources to work on 30 projects. How do they decide what to work on? How do they prioritize? An IT team might entrepreneurially develop a decision-making rubric that defines their key criteria, with questions like these:

- Does this request affect key organizational risks, such as security or legal compliance?

- If we don't act, what is the risk? What would be lost? Will this disrupt people's work?
- Will it affect our brand or relationship with an external stakeholder, such as a donor or beneficiary?
- Has the team provided a justification that provides a cost/benefit (how it advances the mission, time saved, efficiencies gained)?
- How many people or teams will the project affect?
- Is there a temporary or non-technical work-around?
- Is there a phased approach or minimum viable product?
- Would the team be willing to expend resources from its own budget to outsource the project to contractors?

The IT team might ask teams to build this information into their requests and then assess which of the projects they should prioritize.

Budgeting—to Find Our Best Opportunities

We face many decisions throughout our lives where we must rely on trade-off thinking. For example, I have a young nephew who loves to read. One day, I told him I would treat him to a shopping spree at a bookstore. To my surprise, after perusing the aisles, he approached me with 10 hardcover books in his arms. I soon realized my mistake, and quickly said, "That's great! Buy anything you want within $50." His expression turned thoughtful, and then he began thinking through his trade-offs, replacing most of the hardcovers with paperbacks.

Most nonprofits must do the hard work of raising their annual budget from scratch every year. Unless your nonprofit is Harvard, you probably do not have the luxury of a large endowment. Raising an annual budget from scratch each year means that a nonprofit must be lean and mean, must make hard trade-off decisions with its resources, and in a competitive landscape, must continuously make a strong case to potential supporters that it is an effective organization. And we should be conscientious with our donors' money and make the best use of their generosity.

In our daily work, we make decisions about the best use of our limited resources. If I do X, I can't do Y, so I have to give something up. Is X better than the next best thing the organization could do with the same resources? We must wrestle with short-term thinking and long-term thinking. There are seen and unseen consequences of our decisions.

This is what economists call considering our opportunity costs. Andrea Caceres-Santamaria, senior economic education specialist at the St. Louis Fed, advises putting on our magic "economist glasses" and asking ourselves three questions:

- How much do I value this?
- What am I giving up now to have this?
- What am I giving up in the future to have this now?[18]

The budgeting process is a tool that can stretch our imaginations. Without a crystal ball, we make projections and imagine scenarios. In a well-designed and well-communicated budgeting process, teams are aware that they are competing for organizational resources. Teams must make their best pitch to convince decision makers that they have thought through their options and that their program strategy or team road map is more compelling than other options. This is the time to show off their strategic thinking, demonstrating that the team has rigorously stress-tested the proposal and it holds up to tough questions. This is the time for each team member to bring his or her A game sales pitch.

Think of the budgeting process as a resource to help us compare and think through our options. It should help us make trade-offs. It should spark conversations and imaginations.

Having an approved budget empowers entrepreneurial teams to make long-term plans. But if a better opportunity comes along outside your budget, there should be an avenue for discussion. The likeliest first question is: "Looking at your own internal budget, what would you give up to pursue this new possibility?" The director making the decision will want to know how much you believe in the initiative, and what you would be willing to sacrifice.

Always remember that the budget process is a tool that serves you and your entrepreneurial creativity. Never feel your hands are tied by a quarterly or annual budgeting time window. It is simply a snapshot in time when you made an educated guess to predict the future, which might well change. In reality, you are making cost-based decisions all year long and new information will arise. As one nonprofit CFO put it, "Budgets are projections, not permission."[19]

The world around us is always changing, and as we gain new information, an item we already have budget approval for may no longer be the best use of our resources. Or maybe we have spotted a new opportunity that we did not yet get budget approval for, and it's in the middle of our fiscal year—should that constrain us from making the pitch? Absolutely not. Don't let budgeting time windows prevent you from making a pitch for the resources that you need, any time of year. Budgets should be malleable, not written in stone.

For an even higher level of entrepreneurship, team members should have an enterprise view rather than a silo view. For example, I might release money out of my team's budget that can be put to an exciting, higher-value use on another team, and I expect budget managers on other teams to do the same. If we are territorial and siloed, then we lose opportunities for advancing our mission. To encourage this kind of thinking, budget owners can be evaluated in their performance reviews with questions like, "Describe one or two hard trade-off decisions you made this year. In which cases did you take an enterprise view over a team/silo point of view?" And compensate the team member accordingly. Give them kudos in staff meetings.

When teams make their budget proposals, the process might include questions such as:

1. Succinctly, how will your proposal/program/project advance your nonprofit's mission and vision?

2. What would you do differently with 20% less?

3. What would you do with 20% more?

4. Be audacious. What moonshots would your team accomplish if it had significantly more resources? How might you scale your efforts?

Optimize Organizational Design for Innovators

Your answer to question four might lead to a brainstorming opportunity with the fundraising team. They might know of a donor looking for a passion project and willing to provide seed money. Notice that these are questions meant to spark entrepreneurial conversations and stretch imaginations. What are your best ideas?

Let's circle back to question two, what would you do with 20% less? This might seem like a jarring question at first. Maybe all of your current efforts *seem* like they are doing OK, but . . .

Consider the Otto Schiff Housing Association (OSHA), a London-based nonprofit that served survivors of the Holocaust and their families. In 2001, they made the difficult determination to close after 25 years. After a two-year assessment, with dwindling numbers of residents and high costs of buildings, they determined that they could have a greater impact if they liquidated their assets and distributed the money to other nonprofits that also serve Holocaust survivors and Jewish refugees. The Otto Schiff Housing Association transformed into the Six Point Foundation, a grant-making organization that provides financial assistance to Holocaust survivors.[20]

Likewise, a Washington, DC, think tank had been researching a specific trade policy issue for five years. Senator John McCain was very interested in the research, and the think tank expected him to be a champion for the issue. However, upon the senator's death, and given that no other congressional policy champion stepped forward, the team made the hard decision to sunset the program and reassign resources elsewhere.

There are many stories of nonprofits that should have been overhauled much earlier, like the abstinence education programs in the 1980s and 90s. It turned out that students who received the training were as likely to be sexually active as students who did not.[21]

It shouldn't take a crisis or a nonprofit folding to jolt us out of complacency and spur us to ask if there is waste or a lukewarm program that should be ended. Discipline and constraints force us to optimize and to imagine different scenarios. When a budgeting process is well designed, it should spur our creativity and imaginations.

Creativity and budgets in the same sentence? You bet. If your nonprofit's budgeting process is an uninspired, bureaucratic box-checking exercise, if it doesn't stretch your imagination or help you think through trade-offs, then your nonprofit is not doing it right.

We should be kind to ourselves and acknowledge that cutting programs is hard to do. We might consider some advice from tidying and decluttering expert Marie Kondo:

> When you come across something that you cannot part with, think carefully about its true purpose in your life. You'll be surprised at how many of the things you possess have already fulfilled their role. By acknowledging their contribution and letting them go with gratitude, you will be able to truly put the things you own, and your life, in order. In the end, all that will remain are the things that you really treasure.[22]

We can apply her advice to how we think about our nonprofit programs and projects. We can take the lead and not allow failed or stagnating projects to become forever projects that keep sucking up resources.

Following are some simple practices that can help us surface faulty assumptions, complacency, or initiatives we might have killed off long ago:

Share stories with the teams about how the organization has entrepreneurially launched, overhauled, and sunset programs. I was struck by a presentation by a CEO at a think tank, which included a graphic he had created of a timeline spanning decades, showing the birth and death of various organizational programs at his nonprofit through the years. He would periodically present it in all staff meetings, speaking of his own beloved programs that had been sunset, while explaining how doing so was the right step. He made sure to explain that killing off lukewarm programs didn't mean he was fired. He shifted to other teams and projects that were likely to have better impact.

This CEO felt it is critical for teams to internalize this ongoing process, because in his view, any nonprofit's biggest risk is getting too comfortable with the status quo and continuing to operate while becoming irrelevant. He called this creative destruction. Communicating in this way helps teams internalize that making tough decisions and hard trade-offs is normal—this is how we do business—and that projects, teams, or individuals aren't being unfairly singled out. When leaders model killing off their own beloved projects, they provide credibility and set an example.

Another way of removing fear of risk taking is to focus on what was learned. For example, the Hewlett Foundation created a prize for grants officers for "the worst grant from which you learned the most."[23] One team member can share their earlier thinking for why they invested in a project, how they made their bets, assumptions, and unknowns, and how they came to learn that it was not working. Other team members can learn from this, and also see that people won't get fired for risks and experiments, as long as they learn and adjust.

Astronaut Buzz Aldrin said,

> Some people don't like to admit that they have failed or that they have not yet achieved their goals or lived up to their own expectations. But failure is not a sign of weakness. It is a sign that you are alive and growing. Get out of your comfort zone and be willing to take some risks as you work on new tasks. Some individuals share an aversion to risks, but it is not foolish to accept a level of risk, as long as the magnitude and worthiness of the goal you are seeking to achieve is commensurate with your risk.[24]

Proposals for new programs or projects can speculate about what an **exit strategy** would look like, and under what circumstances the team would wind down the program.

Don't automatically assume people need all of your work— **occasionally test your assumptions**. You might experiment with not sharing a regular report to see if anyone misses it or asks for it. Similarly, wait a while before rehiring for a role. See how people innovate and how work patterns emerge.[25] Don't assume you are in the right job— occasionally reimagine your own role.

Create incentives to encourage team members to demonstrate creative destruction or make difficult trade-offs. Reward people for thinking entrepreneurially. For example, include a question in performance reviews such as, "Share an example of winding down or radically adjusting a program that was underperforming." And compensate people accordingly.

Just because your nonprofit isn't the right home for a project doesn't mean it is a bad idea. Nonprofits can encourage teams to think about **spin-offs or partnerships**.

To **alleviate fears**, communicate that people can shift into other roles when programs wind down. Communicate that the organization values entrepreneurs and is confident they will find new and better ways to apply their talents toward the mission.

Getting Out of Innovation's Way

What is impressive about Alcoholics Anonymous is that it has transformed so many lives with a radically decentralized model. Today, dozens of groups that focus on addictions, compulsive behaviors, or mental health issues are modeled on AA's 12 steps. The US Surgeon General's 2016 Report on Alcohol, Drugs, and Health states, "Well-supported scientific evidence demonstrates the effectiveness of 12-step mutual aid groups focused on alcohol and 12-step facilitation interventions."[26] AA was also instrumental in the medical profession accepting the concept that alcoholism is a disease.[27]

AA identifies as a mutual aid fellowship. Leaders rotate. There are no rules, fees, or dues. A centralized office provides services, written principles, and steps. But each group is autonomous and self-supporting, and no outside donations are accepted. What can we learn from this radically decentralized model? How did it come about?

In the 1950s, the medical profession did not have any helpful answers for those suffering from the nightmare of alcoholism or for their loved ones. Treatment might mean being committed repeatedly to hospitals for "drying out" or worse, a forced lobotomy. Alcoholism was regarded as a vice and stigmatized. Doctors would tell desperate patients that their plight was hopeless. This was in fact the dark prognosis for the two men who were to found AA, Bill Wilson (or Bill W., respecting AA's anonymity conventions) and Dr. Robert Holbrook Smith (or Dr. Bob).

Bill W.'s first drink was at a casual mixer when he was a lieutenant during World War I. Alcoholism would ravage his life. It would lead to the loss of his Wall Street job, alienation of friends, and strain on his marriage and his health. He committed himself to drying-out programs with no success.

Optimize Organizational Design for Innovators

In the midst of these struggles, Bill W. faced a letdown when traveling to an out-of-state business opportunity in Akron, Ohio, which didn't pan out. He found himself alone in a strange city, fearful of succumbing to a drink in the hotel's bar. He instinctively sensed that he might overcome the desire to drink if only he could find another alcoholic to talk to and perhaps help. He dialed phone numbers until a mutual friend put him in touch with Dr. Bob Smith, an Akron surgeon on the brink of losing his job because his hands shook from alcoholism. The doctor reluctantly agreed to meet with Bill W., but only for five minutes.

At their meeting, Bill W. earnestly shared his experiences with alcohol—the ups, the downs, and his doctor's prognosis of hopelessness. Dr. Bob found himself listening intently and the five minutes turned into an hour. A later account stated, "This stranger from New York had been there. He didn't ask questions and he didn't preach. He had felt the obsession of craving, the terrors of withdrawal, the self-hatred over failure—all of the things that he himself had experienced and was experiencing even as he listened."[28] The meeting was a powerful turning point for both. Bill W. extended his stay in Akron so they could continue meeting and helping each other toward sobriety. A way out of darkness began to emerge.

After Bill W. returned home to New York City, the two men stayed in regular contact. In their respective communities, both men began helping others through similar conversations and meetings. These small communities often learned the hard way through failed experiments, learning and adjusting until they found what works. Within four years, to their surprise, they had helped 100 alcoholics and grown to three groups in Akron and New York. They realized they had stumbled on a model that could help people.

They weren't sure exactly how to scale the program, and they sought feedback from the members. In his spare time, Bill W. began putting the group's practices down on paper and running draft chapters by the members for feedback.

Members kept debating, learning, and evolving in a decentralized, organic fashion. In time, the group came to see itself as a fellowship more than a structured organization. As described by a biographer,

"From the beginning, Wilson and Smith openly showed willingness to accept in their program changes based on successful experience equal to or greater than their own."[29] As membership grew, letters poured in with questions about theory, practice, or procedure, to which Bill W. replied with humility and openness. His responses would usually be formulated along these lines: "I understand your issue as X, and here is what we've seen or tried, with this result. Please write back to let us know what you try and how it turns out."

Navigating questions like these, over time, through direct one-on-one experience, openness, learning, radical honesty, and internal debate, the group came to a profound understanding of the nature of addiction and what is needed for an individual to become and stay sober. Over the years 1935 to 1955, the members created the name Alcoholics Anonymous and published two books that outlined the now well-known Twelve Steps and later the Twelve Traditions.[30]

If we were to diagram AA's theory of change, it might look like this:

IF ► alcoholics engage in the 12 steps, including an admission of alcoholism rather than denial, and through the practice of one alcoholic talking to another, ►THEN the alcoholic stops their harmful denial and begins to form much-needed bonds of community and trust. The sponsor and sponsee begin to form a relationship that provides a healing effect, and the alcoholic takes their first steps toward recovery.

IF ► AA's organization structure remains a decentralized, bottom-up, mutual-aid fellowship, ►THEN learning will come from direct one-on-one authentic and lived experience, and addicts can engage in radical honesty with each other, which is when healing occurs.

IF ► members are anonymous, ►THEN confidentiality is respected, and stigma is avoided.

▲ Social Change vision: the alcoholic achieves sobriety and has the tools to be free of their suffering in the long term. Lives are healed and transformed.

Optimize Organizational Design for Innovators

Today, according to AA's fact file, they estimate current membership at two million members with 61,000 groups in the United States and more groups internationally. Since its founding in 1934, AA continues to grow and inspire many other programs that have copied its 12-step model. But AA's model of anonymity creates challenges when trying to provide evidence of its effectiveness. And true to Bill W.'s tradition of experimentation, openness, and learning, they appear to welcome debates and criticisms of the program.[31]

The AA model might be a tough pill to swallow for micromanagers or those accustomed to top-down hierarchical organizational structures. During AA's start-up phase, some critics saw their decentralized model as anarchic and lacking the capacity to assign responsibility. Despite feeling pressure toward more rigid organization, the founders held the course with a simple, bottom-up model. And AA is thriving.

The moral of the AA story is that social entrepreneurs shouldn't be afraid to experiment with decentralized decision making. The results might be transformative.

We might conclude that perhaps at times the best organizational design is—no design at all.

Consider a different nonprofit example. One evening several years ago I attended an orientation for new volunteers at a nonprofit that provided mentoring and job coaching services to inmates of the county jail. Five minutes into the orientation, I found my interest in working with this nonprofit waning. The presenter was a senior executive, and the tone of the orientation was very top-down. The executive overwhelmed his group of potential volunteers by talking at length about restrictions, structure, and limits. His emphasis on this sucked all of the creative energy out of the room. I suspect I wasn't the only prospective volunteer who, overwhelmed by the sense of bureaucracy, didn't go back.

At times we run the risk of overdesigning in the workplace. Some rules and structures turn out to be red tape that stifles creativity. Sometimes the better approach is for managers to forgo the temptation to organize and instead simply get out of the way. When given the freedom, people might surprise us—doing an unstructured task more effectively, more creatively, and with more buy-in.

Open-Source Business Models

With open-source software, the original source code is freely available, allowing end users to contribute as co-developers, and empowering users to adapt the software to fit their personal needs. In contrast to holding information close to the vest, as with a trade secret, an open-source business model is when an organization freely gives away its practices or expert knowledge with the aim that others will use it, adapt it to their own scenarios, or build on it and improve it. As nonprofits embrace this model, innovation can flourish in unexpected ways.

One such nonprofit brings together individual volunteers from across the globe to share designs for 3D-printed prosthetics, often for children and even for injured animals. The nonprofit's name, e-NABLE, is short for "Enabling the Future." It started in 2011 with a carpenter in South Africa who had lost several of his fingers in a woodworking accident and found the $10,000 cost of a prosthetic out of reach. He ran across a YouTube video by Seattle artist and puppetry designers Ivan and Jen Owen, who had used 3D printing to make giant mechanical hands that they wore at a weekend cosplay event. He emailed them to ask if they would be willing to apply the same technology to design prosthetic fingers for him. Intrigued, they began prototyping and, in less than a year, had a successful design and shipped it to the carpenter. As the Owenses blogged about the experience, this generated interest and led to more requests. Rather than profit from the design, the Owenses opted to make it open-source and launched a nonprofit. With the open-source approach, the community has since grown to 30,000 volunteers, 140 chapters, and hundreds of schools that have designed and gifted approximately 7,000 3D-printed hands and arms in over 100 countries.[32]

Or consider the Nightscout Foundation, which is a group of parents who use open-source tools to help create better insulin monitoring and delivery technologies for people with Type 1 diabetes. The open-source technology enables parents to keep track of glucose levels whether the child is "at school, at daycare, playing sports, at a sleepover, or while traveling overseas."[33] The foundation encourages citizen scientists to find solutions through "the exploration and creation of open-source technology projects that enhance the lives of people with T1D and those who love them."[34]

These open-source nonprofits let go of the temptation to be top-down and in full control. They are highly unstructured while pooling knowledge and creativity from all over the world to advance their missions. With organizational design, sometimes less is more.

Dedicating Time and Resources for R&D

What if no one in our nonprofit's network, or even on the planet, has yet developed the knowledge for a social problem we are trying to solve? If your nonprofit or program is venturing into uncharted territory, you can set aside some time and resources so team members can experiment, play, and let discovery unfold. Nonprofits do this in a variety of ways.

For example, similar to a small business start-up incubator, some foundations invest in creative individuals. They provide open-ended grants with no strings attached. This is common for artists, musicians, scholars, and scientists. For example, nonprofit Emergent Ventures provided this type of grant to Angad Daryani, a 22-year-old social entrepreneur and engineering student from Mumbai. His goal is to develop a low-cost, filter-less air purification system that can capture air pollution and turn it into something else.[35]

Nonprofits working in the health care industry like St. Jude's Children's Research Hospital regularly engage in R&D. In fact, it may be a significant portion of their annual budget.

Some nonprofits are experimenting with allowing a percentage of paid time for team members to pursue personal projects that they think will benefit the nonprofit's mission. I am a prime example of this, as my nonprofit allowed me to spend 20% of my time writing this book! The concept is inspired by the 20% Project at Google that led to the creation of Gmail.[36] Some nonprofits only grant this freedom to certain team members with a proven track record. Some organizations treat it as a six-month trial run. Some schools have replicated this for students in the classroom, giving them the freedom to pursue their own learning agenda.

Similarly, though they don't call it R&D, nonprofits working in public policy research set aside a designated "discovery" phase. For a number of months, scholars are allocated a percentage of unstructured time for exploring a research question or hypothesis. The organization holds off on requiring the usual accountability standards and does not yet require them to articulate a theory of change, intended outcomes, or metrics, recognizing that it is too early in the process.

This same kind of discovery phase can be applied to other challenges or opportunities that a nonprofit might be wrestling with. For example:

- Would our donors respond positively to a fundraising video rather than a mailed fundraising letter?
- Would our charter school's students have different learning outcomes if a portion of the class was virtual rather than in person?
- If our food bank's client intake process were to offer a web-based form, in addition to our current phone intake system, would they be likely to use it?
- Would our new podcast idea attract listeners?
- For our workforce training program for at-risk youth, could we emulate or learn from models in the mental health field?

During the discovery phase, the nonprofit might gather research around this question, talking with stakeholders, conducting focus groups, or designing small experiments.

Other Unstructured Approaches

When nonprofits have an organizational principle that **emphasizes openness and humility,** this can lead to discoveries from unexpected sources. Aravind Eye Hospital in India wanted to reach the poorest of the poor with eye care services, even offering free services, but the poorest in India wouldn't come to the clinic. Not until a small elderly woman in an Aravind waiting room told the doctors that the poorest people living in faraway rural communities didn't have the means to travel to the city did the clinic realize it would need to travel to them. The clinic then created traveling eye care "camps," which was the breakthrough they had been searching for that allowed them to reach their target clients.

Nonprofit teams that embrace and practice openness and humility recognize that a nonprofit's beneficiaries might find the solution to problems before our experienced staff or "experts" will. People are an endless well of new ideas, and circumstances on the ground are always changing.

Not everything can be prescribed or known in advance. So, a practice of providing optional guides rather than mandates **leaves the door open for new and better ideas**.

For example, at a nonprofit psychiatric hospital, Cedarcrest Regional Hospital in Connecticut, team members identified an urgent need to reduce patients' violence toward themselves and others. They designed a pilot project in which staff researched and created a rating tool to guide risk assessment regarding which patients should have less or more freedom (such as going to the bathroom unaccompanied or trial trips away from the hospital). The rating tool became standard practice, with instructions that it be considered only as guidance to be used with judgment—not as a top-down mandate. Given complexity and nuances, the staff was empowered to pair their clinical judgment with the matrix. The new process reduced violent incidents by 80%, and the team continues to improve the matrix based on experience and learning.[37]

Nonprofits can encourage teams to **state any unknowns** in program strategies or proposals. "We don't yet know X, and we are benchmarking with others and will continue monitoring for solutions. We may need to wait for the person with the right talent to step forward." By not trying to hide what we don't know, by being transparent and sharing the unknowns with more people or even with funders, we may find someone will step forward with ideas or information.

In survey design, it can be helpful to include **open-ended questions**. We might acquire feedback we never would have anticipated. For example, a typical closed-ended survey question that a refugee resettlement service might ask would be, "Please rate our services on a 1–5 scale." However, they might also ask open-ended questions such as,

"What are the biggest needs facing your family?" Responses might be typical and expected, such as "I need transportation to get to my new job," "I need a suit for job interviews," or "My daughter needs a back-pack and school supplies." Other responses might be unexpected, such as: "I am feeling loneliness and depression. I don't know anyone in this new country, and I miss my family and community back in Afghanistan." The nonprofit might then consider developing programming to help address the isolation felt by new immigrants.

Nonprofits are experimenting more with **unstructured conferences**, which are sometimes called unconferences or world cafes. In them, the participants decide on the agenda and topics. Participants gather and begin with some icebreakers, and then they answer some initial questions on a whiteboard, such as what topics they came to learn about, or what expertise they have that they are willing to teach. Participants then vote on the topics and create a loose agenda for the day. Designated areas are set up where people can go to teach, learn, or discuss that particular topic. Compared to lecture-style presentations and planned workshops, this method is more spontaneous and flexible, and prioritizes cooperative knowledge and interactions.

Rather than overdesigning with processes and formal structures, sometimes the better approach is for managers to forgo the temptation to organize and instead simply get out of the way of entrepreneurial people, as we see in the example of the decentralized model of AA.

Making the right organizational design choices affects whether teams can achieve their entrepreneurial best, constructively solve problems together, and accomplish the best possible outcomes. This is an art. My hope is that the examples in this chapter will help you creatively discover the right structures to advance your mission, make better decisions, and balance intentionally structured design while leaving room for flexibility, experimentation, and iteration.

Chapter 10

Attract Donor-Partners Who Fuel Social Change Breakthroughs

We can thank the vision and generosity of donors for breakthroughs like hospice care, public libraries, the discovery of insulin to treat diabetes, the 911 phone emergency system, and even the painted lines on highway shoulders to prevent accidents.[1] Translated from ancient Greek, the word *philanthropy* means "love of humanity." The individual donor who embodies that spirit of caring and generosity brings many gifts to the table—heart, life experience, selflessness, vision, time, money, ideas, and passion for a cause. Donors inspire those of us carrying out the work in nonprofits to strive even higher. We owe a debt of gratitude to these generous souls who are our essential partners.

Donors are a key part of our ecosystem. We certainly can't build an innovative nonprofit without the generous support of donor-partners who share our passion for our vision and mission. As we go about building innovation into our nonprofit's organizational DNA, where do donor-partners fit? As I researched this book, I sought answers to two questions:

1. What can donor-nonprofit partnerships teach us about innovation?

2. How do nonprofits navigate donor partnerships—both opportunities and pitfalls—so that teams are empowered to innovate?

What Can Donor-Nonprofit Partnerships Teach Us About Innovation?

The following examples showcase ways that donors and grantees work creatively together to solve seemingly insurmountable social problems. These partnership models include unrestricted generational operating support, de-risking, incentives, prizes, and large-scale coalitions. We will look at the pros and cons of each, and the examples might spark ideas for exploratory conversations with your donors.

Long-Term Partnerships and Innovation

NBA superstar LeBron James closely identifies with the at-risk youth in his hometown of Akron, Ohio. He is personally committed to removing obstacles in the way of their education and upward mobility. To accomplish this, the Lebron James Family Foundation entered into a multiyear partnership with the Akron public school system.

The school system and the foundation innovate together. The foundation provides additional operational support for a single (already existing) elementary school targeting at-risk students. With the extra funding, students enrolled in the IPromise School can participate in an unusual public school experience. The STEM-based and trauma-informed curriculum puts them in classes year-round from 9 to 5. The school provides wraparound services, which include support for the student's extended family such as job and career services, legal aid, medical and vision care, financial literacy programming, and mental health assistance. Students' parents can apply for support while pursuing a GED. A food pantry for the whole family is provided, as well as transitional housing and transportation. Early measurement results show IPromise students narrowing the achievement gap,[2] and James has pledged up to $2 million annually in support.[3]

Partners willing to help a nonprofit build a long-term institution and provide multiyear meat-and-potatoes support are special finds indeed. This kind of funding provides certainty for long-term planning and hiring and gives a nonprofit the latitude to experiment and innovate. Most nonprofits must do the hard work of raising their annual budget from scratch every year. That's why they find it challenging to commit to any long-term planning. But happily, long-term committed partnerships like these do exist. During the twentieth century, long-term support helped build nonprofit institutions such as the Council on Foreign Relations, the Brookings Institute, American Enterprise Institute, the Carnegie Endowment for International Peace, university research centers, hospitals, and many others.[4]

Committed long-term relationships between nonprofits and donors can be highly fruitful as we go all-in and work on a common vision together. Over time both parties will experience ups and downs, adjust per lessons learned, celebrate wins together, and build trust, a body of knowledge, and a common language.

Funders may be concerned that if they commit to multiyear operational support, the nonprofit will take the money for granted and become complacent. To address their concern, donors and nonprofits can establish clear, agreed-upon outcomes. The arrangement can specify what would suffice as evidence of progress, and general operating support will be renewed only if the nonprofit achieves those targets.[5] As an example, Cleveland's Mandel Foundation provides "evergreen" funding to a small number of grantees, contingent upon an annual review.[6] Similarly, the Fund for Global Human Rights and the Ford and MacArthur Foundations provide a mix of multiyear operational support in addition to restricted funding for specific projects.[7]

Keep in mind that providing unrestricted generational operating support to keep the lights on is not a sexy aspect from a donor's perspective. If you are preparing to make this kind of pitch, be aware that major donors often would rather contribute restricted funding than general operating expenses. Donors may feel more vested in providing essential seed funding for launching new nonprofits or new programs. Restricted funding provides targeted support to specific programming or objectives, where results can be reported and donors can feel that their money is making a difference. For example, to fund a small fledgling program, transform it, and feel like they have been an essential partner.

To convince this kind of supporter, emphasize building a long-term institution. Walk the donor through a bird's-eye view of the multiyear phases necessary to build the nonprofit: from seed funding to the startup phase, to describing what capabilities you plan to build over the years (for example, a communications/media capability by year 2, a podcast and educational video capability by year 2, three more major donors by year 3). Help donors see the vision and how their long-term support can build an institution, in contrast to a short-term investment in a program or project.

157

Incentives and Innovation

Most of us are familiar with organizations that offer cash prizes, of which the Nobel Prize is the most famous. While we may be familiar with the story of how Charles Lindbergh was the first to fly nonstop from New York to Paris in 1927, many may not know that this was prompted by a $25,000 prize offered by a New York City hotel owner, Raymond Orteig, who wanted to support innovations in aviation.[8]

Similarly, the nonprofit XPRIZE Foundation often makes headlines, offering large cash prizes for solving complex problems such as lunar exploration, oil spill cleanup, adult literacy, water abundance, or women's safety. In recent years, the nonprofits Learning Upgrade and People for Words split the $7 million XPRIZE for developing free mobile apps with songs, video games, and rewards that measurably improved adult literacy during a 12-month testing period.

The number of nonprofits with a prize or competition model is growing; a McKinsey study reported that since 2000, more than 200 philanthropic prizes of over $100,000 have been offered.[9]

Should your nonprofit consider applying for prizes, or partnering with donors to offer philanthropic prizes to others? Following are some considerations from the perspective of both nonprofits and philanthropists.

Applying for prizes. Because prizes involve risk, a nonprofit team might spend seven years researching water abundance—and not win. On the other hand, grants provide more certainty to help with financial resources and support for program activities. Given the cost to operate, nonprofits interested in applying for prizes often pursue grants as well.

Awarding prizes. How do nonprofits and foundations think about offering grants versus prizes? Grantmaking requires the infrastructure for soliciting and refereeing proposals as well as judging what grant seekers are capable of achieving. Yet there is no guarantee that the grant will lead to the outcomes donors hope to achieve.

What nonprofits and foundations like about the prize model is that it provides incentives for creating new ideas and solutions. There usually is a precisely defined goal (for example, create a device that extracts a minimum of 2,000 liters of water per day from the atmosphere at a cost of no more than two cents per liter). How to solve the goal is up to the creativity of the prize applicants.

Publicity and crowdsourcing are key aspects of how prizes work: to surface ideas from unexpected places. The organization offering the prize may have no idea where the best ideas will come from, which may be easier than having to identify and vet potential grantees, as required in grantmaking. And in contrast to grants, prizes only pay out for a success, changing a philanthropist's or grantmaker's risk calculation.

Prize models are not limited to billionaires or large foundations. For example, some small nonprofits launch essay contests for high school students, offering cash prizes or partial college scholarships.

Within a month of the COVID-19 outbreak, the Mercatus Center at George Mason University, where I work, rapidly mobilized funders and resources to create FastGrants, offering prizes for COVID science. Funders include tech innovators like Elon Musk and Patrick Collison, founder of Stripe. FastGrants encourages speed and innovation, with an application form that can be filled out in less than an hour, and funding decisions made within 48 hours. The nonprofit reached out to its network and beyond, rapidly raised $10 million, and gave 200 grants over the course of seven months for vaccines, immunology, and genetic testing. In the ensuing months, they raised $50 million.[10]

As an example of impact, FastGrants helped fund a team at Yale which created Saliva Direct, a spit test with rapid results, used by the NBA and now used in labs across America. FastGrants stood apart from other traditional funding models that required months to fill out lengthy applications and additional months to review.

Nonprofits considering offering prizes should realize that they may be acting as a middleman. You will need to ensure that staff has knowledge of tax rules and have administrative processes in place for coordinating the money coming in and quickly going out. You may keep a small portion for overhead, but the end result may not be that lucrative, since you are giving most of the money away. That said, the nonprofit may attract a lot of publicity and build its brand as an innovative nonprofit that helps bring partners and resources together to solve big societal problems.

Some social problems are so big that they can only be overcome by many organizations coming together and inspiring others to join the cause. The HIV epidemic in Africa at first seemed overwhelming and insurmountable. For example, Botswana lost 17% of its health care workforce to HIV between 1999 and 2005.[11] In response, nations, charities, civil society organizations, and national and international organizations formed partnerships to combat HIV.[12] These partnerships have made an impact; new HIV infections declined by 14% between 2010 and 2015 in Eastern and Southern Africa, the world's most affected region, and by 8% in West and Central Africa.[13]

For decades animal rights groups made few inroads as they worked independently on a wide variety of issues such as encouraging veganism or opposing fur coats or zoos. But in 2005, farm animal advocacy groups and funders came together to focus on a single issue: the cruel treatment of hens. To this end, they worked together, building social media awareness campaigns, targeting advertising to consumers and investors, organizing street protests at restaurants, including celebrities, and making clear asks of companies to implement cage-free practices.[14]

Many of these joint efforts have a regional or local focus. The Gates, Dell, and the Community Foundation of Texas provided combined donations of $130 million to invest in the Texas High School Project to boost college readiness for underperforming high schools.[15]

Should my nonprofit consider participating in a coalition-based funding model? Advantages of this funding approach include stronger financial resources, broader constituencies, and joint learning. These efforts usually include a common vision, common goals, and common metrics, but with each nonprofit specializing within its niche, working in a coordinated fashion to achieve the shared vision.

A nonprofit participating in a coalition should also be aware of risks. A group of funders may go all in and make big bets, but what if funders are applying all of these resources using the wrong approach? What if they use their leverage and influence to take an uninformed top-down approach rather than a bottom-up approach based on what works? Or in a coalition of many organizations, will some of them try to push their weight around? Will there be infighting? Disagreements over strategy? The realistic answer is, of course there will be. But a nonprofit can enter coalition efforts with eyes wide open about the potential pros and cons. The pros may far outweigh the cons, given the social problem that is at stake.

To reduce such risks, do some sleuthing and research. You can share your concerns about these risks directly with funders or talk with several grant recipients about their experience with the funders. Did they find an attitude of arrogance or humility? You might try to find out whether the group of funders spread their bets and encourage experiments to find what works before scaling.

Depending on the size of the social problem, consider what happens when we act alone. We run a higher risk that efforts might be insufficient, uncoordinated, spread too thin, or redundant.

Innovative Financing and De-risking

Social entrepreneurs are good at finding ways when there is no way. Sometimes when there is a good social outcome, but the costs or the risks seem too high, foundations and nonprofits step in to develop innovative solutions.

We may not use the term "public goods" in our everyday conversation, but this economic concept is at the heart of what we do in nonprofits. Typical examples of a public good would be the national defense, lighthouses, roads, and dams. An individual can't simply purchase one unit of a lighthouse or of the national defense. For-profit businesses don't have an efficient or simple way to package and sell a public good because there is a free-rider problem, so they tend to focus on what they do best: selling private goods to be consumed by the purchaser, such as shoes or electronics, or a service such as a car wash or a massage. Closely related is what economists call the "the commons," such as shared natural resources like the air we breathe, grazing lands, or bodies of water where there are risks like overfishing or pollution. In the case of public goods or the commons, this is typically where philanthropy or government steps in to play an active role. But as we'll see in the following examples, multisector partnerships are

Attract Donor-Partners Who Fuel Social Change Breakthroughs

becoming increasingly creative, sophisticated, and adaptable, rising to meet complex problems and societal needs.

In this arena, we can observe creative partnerships at work, often involving innovative financial arrangements or de-risking.

Consider a public good like clean air. When solutions are over-whelmingly cost-prohibitive, sometimes foundations and partners create "blended finance" scenarios. In this model, philanthropic grants are not used to fund projects directly but are instead used to "de-risk" private investment. For example, the Hewlett Foundation implemented a blended finance approach to jump-start the clean energy sector in developing countries.[16] The thinking behind this approach is that by strategically injecting funds into high-potential but high-risk projects, the private sector will be less hesitant to invest.

Or consider the example of loans for individuals with low credit scores, where a typical for-profit bank or credit union would be uncomfortable with taking on the risk of providing a loan. Some nonprofits provide low-interest mortgages. The Neighborhood Assistance Corporation of America is a nonprofit that provides home loans based not on credit scores but on payment history. A family of five in Baltimore that was paying $650 a month to rent a one-bedroom basement apartment applied for a loan at 2.7% interest, and now pays $531 a month for their three-bedroom rowhouse. Now the family is in a position to build a credit history and home equity.[17]

Another de-risking approach is to use a hybrid funding model. This is when the service offered by a nonprofit is partially subsidized by the non-profit's donors, and the balance is then partially paid by the beneficiary/customer on a discounted or pay-as-you-can model. For example, clinical treatment for eating disorders can be prohibitively expensive for many people. It may involve a lengthy residential treatment program, costly medical treatments, or long-term counseling, while at the same time the participant runs the risk of losing the ability to work or handle daily activities and responsibilities. The nonprofit Rock Recovery offers treatment on a sliding scale, focused on "removing the barriers of stigma, cost, and accessibility and by connecting people to clinical community and quality care."[18]

Another de-risking approach is an incentive structure known as Pay for Success. Grantmakers, as well as state or local governments, instead of awarding grants, enter into contracts with nonprofits that deliver social services. The contract specifies that the nonprofit will only get paid if they can provide evidence of progress on predefined outcomes. This might include reducing homelessness or measurably improving learning outcomes for at-risk youth.[19]

Oklahoma-based George Kaiser Family Foundation is committed to its local community, improving quality of life and addressing local poverty issues. They saw an opportunity during COVID to attract virtual workers to increase the local tax base, offering them $10,000 to relocate to Tulsa, a year of free co-working space, workshops, and networking events to help them feel like a part of a community. This is a highly innovative way to de-risk an out-of-state move for virtual workers. In the first two years of the experiment, the program attracted 1,300 virtual workers. One estimate calculates that these new relocated workers contributed $62 million in new labor income to the local economy in 2021.[20]

Are you familiar with recoverable grants? These allow people to loan money to a good cause rather than donate it, thus keeping their principal savings intact.

The nonprofit Kiva has created an online platform that enables anyone to act as a lender. Its website features stories of people who, working to escape poverty, are starting small businesses and need modest start-up loans. You might decide to provide a low-interest microloan, alongside others, by providing $25 of the $500 needed so a farmer in Kyrgyzstan can buy a dairy cow. As the farmer repays the loan, you get your initial loan amount back. You can use it to provide another loan through Kiva or opt to have your money refunded. This is a clever way of de-risking for individual donors who may be hesitant about giving. In the Kiva funding model, you are a lender—not a donor. Yet Kiva is a nonprofit, and the low interest of its loans is what finances its general operating expenses.

Similarly, the Vanguard Charitable recoverable grant program offers a range of options to investors. It seeks to change the world through

Attract Donor-Partners Who Fuel Social Change Breakthroughs

long-term, strategic charitable giving, including offering flexible financing to nonprofits. One such loan might go to a minority entrepreneur whose kitchen provides meals to frontline workers at the Detroit Health Department and the Henry Ford Hospital.[21]

Should my nonprofit consider seeking recoverable grants as a source of funding? If your program model is similar to the examples above, where you can project a financial return on investment, then this model may be right for you.

Should a donor consider recoverable grants? A benefit to donors is that it frees up their money to later invest in other charitable opportunities. Donors, however, would be well advised to consider that the loan may or may not be repaid. Some of these loans involve a reasonable risk; for example, Kiva's repayment rate is 96%.[22] Donors should thoughtfully review the nonprofit's track record and their own risk tolerance, to make sure they are comfortable with the loan.

These examples, such as de-risking, incentives, and prizes, and large-scale coalitions, represent creative thinking between donors and grantees. Reflect on how these examples might apply to your own nonprofit. Consider your nonprofit's unique niche, distinct capabilities, and the preferences of current donors along with prospective donors you haven't reached yet. The examples might spur your own exploratory conversations with donors or foundations. And if the funding model you need does not exist, you just might invent an altogether new one.

How Do Nonprofits Navigate Donor Partnerships—Both Opportunities and Pitfalls—So That Teams Are Empowered to Innovate?

Much goes on behind the scenes with any donor-grantee relationship. As we know from experience, all interpersonal relationships are complex, and this is no less true for organizational relationships. How do donors and grantees build relationships that make innovation more likely? Take a moment to reflect if any of these relationship pitfalls sounds familiar.

A little relationship introspection never hurts. While a donor and a nonprofit each brings strengths into the relationship, we can bring ego and blind spots into the relationship as well. Both parties are wise to keep

Table 10.1 Possible pitfalls of donor-nonprofit relationships

Donors and foundation staff might be:	Nonprofit staff might:
• Unrealistic—even the wealthiest donors and foundations have limited resources relative to their ambitions	• Treat donors like ATMs
	• Fail to honor donor intentions
• Paternalistic, elite, arrogant	• Overpromise and underdeliver
• Amateurish	• Fail to express appropriate gratitude
• Limited by a short attention span	• Fail to engage in active listening
• Unaccountable	• Fail to follow up on a complaint, or handle it poorly
• Pushy[23]	
• Demanding costly impact data without providing funding	• Engage in a manipulative fundraising approach such as pressure sales
• Neglectful of the chronic need for sustained operational support[24]	• Fail to create an emotional connection between the donor and the nonprofit's vision

Both parties (donors and nonprofits) might engage in:

• Misalignment of interests

• Talking past each other

• Failure to align expectations

their eyes wide open. We can be self-aware of how we might contribute to problems. We can proactively do our best to avoid causing them. We can be cognizant of how our partners might contribute to problems, and proactively establish boundaries or a plan to mitigate those risks. If we don't, the relationship might veer off into stagnation and disappointment.

The good news is that plenty of nonprofits and funders have flourishing, mutually beneficial partnerships. Many of those relationships are mentioned in this book, such as the Mandel Foundation's long-term partnership with Cleveland State University and Case Western Reserve, the Robert Woods Johnson Foundation's commitment to working with partners in the decades-long fight for tobacco reform, and many others.

Attract Donor-Partners Who Fuel Social Change Breakthroughs

The following examples can help us mindfully steer clear of these relationship pitfalls to build a flourishing, healthy partnership that supports innovation.

Building a Common Vision and Shared Expectations

Congrats! You made it past the initial meet and greet or proposal—they like you; you like them. Now you are moving beyond agreement on a shared vision into specifics. But giving money away effectively is harder than it seems. Certain donors, perhaps foundations or those offering major gifts, may need guidance as they create the philosophical vision for their giving strategy. For example, do they want to donate modestly to many organizations or provide targeted, transformational giving to one nonprofit?

There are many ways to frame a social problem and just as many program design options for solving the problem. Following are some examples of donors weighing different options for giving, where clarity is needed:

- Prospective donor Matthew is considering donating to a rehab center that helped his niece in her struggle with opioid addiction. Then he learns of another nonprofit that advocates for legislative changes with the goal of preventing addiction in the first place. How should he compare the two options?

- Jackie is considering donating to a local program that supports at-risk youth. But she isn't sure if her investment should support workforce training, stress management counseling, after-school programs, or housing. Which approach would be the most effective use of her financial gift?

Notice how each donor's giving philosophy may not be fully formed. Drawing out a donor's ideas should be part of your conversation as, together, you think creatively and align expectations. Donors want their generosity to drive real change. They know that good intentions by themselves will not change the world. At this stage of relationship-building, conversations with major donors and foundations are moving from a general agreement on a shared vision toward specifics. This is where you come in. Your expertise as a nonprofit professional is especially helpful in navigating their questions and helping them find clarity of thought on what success might look like.

Some donors find choosing from many possible programming approaches overwhelming, while other donors feel energized by being a part of the search for what works. Still other donors already have a clear and well-thought-out framework.

In either case, muddled expectations will lead to tensions down the road. In one year's time, when the nonprofit shares results, they might not be what the donor had in mind at all.

As the relationship develops, you will be preparing a more specific proposal. You might ask the donor to contribute a specific amount for general operating support, or perhaps to provide restricted funding for specific programming. As those conversations unfold, you should develop shared expectations on:

1. What are the measurable objectives and timeline for achieving them? (Decades? Years?)

2. Who are the beneficiaries?

3. What are the nonprofit's current approaches for achieving the objectives? (If we do X, we believe Y will be the result.)

4. What might cause the effort to fail? What are the risks that will be monitored?

5. What will serve as credible evidence that efforts are succeeding, failing, or lukewarm?

Each donor will bring unique perspectives to bear on these questions. And not every donor will want to discuss their gift at this level of detail. So take their pulse to find out: Do they want to discuss these details? Do they already have clear thinking about their gift, or do they need guidance? Seek to understand a donor's giving philosophy, motivation, understanding of the problem, and any ideas they may have about programmatic solutions. Then plan and communicate accordingly. Building shared expectations strengthens trust so that within the

167

guardrails of the agreed-upon vision, there is room for experimentation, learning, and innovation.

Negotiating Room to Maneuver and Innovate

As any relationship deepens, situations will arise that call for saying no. In any healthy relationship, each person needs room to breathe. Without proper boundaries, or when one party doesn't respect their partner's autonomy, relationships won't flourish. People feel stifled, perhaps resentful. They can't be their creative and innovative best selves.

As we work with donors to align expectations, it is important to recognize that sometimes the right decision is to turn away funding—though this might be excruciatingly hard to do.

A nonprofit might turn down a donation if the amount is not enough for the program to be effective. Leaders have the unenviable responsibility of sometimes turning away funding if the proposed project does not align with the organization's mission and scope. A nonprofit can be in danger of being spread too thin and becoming ineffective.

A nonprofit executive described a situation in which her nonprofit was partway through a funded project when the leadership team realized the project was not right for them, and they could not meet the donor's intent. They ended the project and apologetically returned the grant money they had not yet spent and explained why. The grantmaker was so pleased with the nonprofit's integrity that they continued supporting the nonprofit at a higher level.[25]

Nonprofit leadership and fundraising professionals have to be on guard to preserve mission integrity. Experts in conflict resolution recommend that when you set boundaries, be prepared to back them up. That could mean that the other party decides to walk. It helps to have a backup plan, diversity of supporters and a fundraising pipeline.

How should a donor-nonprofit relationship balance accountability while leaving room for experimentation, learning, and adjusting? This question might cause a donor's alarm bells go off. He or she might ask, What exactly do we mean by "leaving room?" How much room? What then prevents a nonprofit's staff from simply moving the goalpost whenever they are failing to meet objectives? The donor might be concerned about how a nonprofit can be accountable if baselines are constantly changing. Questions like these provide an opportunity to talk about innovation.

There is no better example of quickly pivoting services than World Central Kitchen. The nonprofit, created by Chef José Andrés and his wife, Patricia, has a mission of using the power of food to nourish communities and strengthen local economies through times of crisis and beyond. World Central Kitchen mobilizes quickly to provide food and volunteers in the aftermath of natural disasters, both in overseas locales like Puerto Rico and Haiti, and in communities in the United States when people are, for instance, struggling during the COVID-19 pandemic. They quickly mobilized to set up food distribution at Poland's border to feed Ukrainians fleeing from war.

Similarly, food banks like Loaves & Fishes had to rapidly reinvent themselves in 2020 during the COVID-19 pandemic from a model that had worked well for over 40 years; they closed 41 brick-and-mortar food bank locations and invested their resources in mobile food banks and doorstep delivery.

Though the big-picture visions of World Central Kitchen and Loaves & Fishes never changed, the staff kept finding new and better ways to advance their visions. If their donors had held them to a fixed road map, they may not have had the leeway to innovate so boldly. The point is that treating nonprofit strategy as a fixed detailed road map with no room for learning and iteration would have the opposite effect of its intention, holding both the nonprofit and donor back from discovering better ways to achieve the shared vision. A compass is a better way of imagining a nonprofit's vision, an agreed-upon destination and direction, leaving flexibility to maneuver.

It can be helpful to have conversations with donors about ensuring room for experimentation. Agree together that while a donor's and nonprofit's shared *vision* serves as a North Star, *strategies* represent a nonprofit's best guess at how to solve a social problem *at a particular moment in time*. Strategies, programming, and approaches should change when there is new information or when they aren't working. There must be room for experimentation, learning, and adjusting to find what works. This is the heart of innovation.

Even with leaving room for the nonprofit to shift gears, donors should hold nonprofits accountable. Whenever a nonprofit adjusts its strategies, a donor should expect the nonprofit to provide clear explanations for any major changes, along with sound logic and evidence that hold up to a donor's scrutiny and questions. On a positive note, the better the nonprofit's track record in delivering on outcomes over time, the more it will earn the donor's trust and confidence. The donor will likely grant more leeway to experiment.

Mario Morino spent years donating to nonprofits while also helping them design evaluation systems. Because Morino has been on both sides of the fence, he candidly admits, "We funders, in the name of 'measurement' and 'accountability,' are foisting unfunded, often simplistic, self-serving mandates on our grantees—rather than helping them define, create, and use the information they need to be disciplined managers."[26] Instead, he recommends, "The nonprofit needs to own the process and be the primary beneficiary of it."[27]

Donors should respect the autonomy, strategic insights, and expertise of the nonprofit's staff. They should expect that nonprofit teams doing the work are designing metrics that make sense for them to assess whether they are making progress toward their objective.

Get on the same page with donors about standards of proof. Designing an ideal evaluation system that captures everything we would like to know is probably too expensive. Most nonprofits don't have the budget to conduct double-blind control groups or attain scientific certainty of proof. Often many nonprofits are working on the same issue, and parsing out who gets the credit for achieving success can be impossible. Social change is complex, and causality can be very hard to prove.

Metrics should be practical given the size and resources of the nonprofit. In the absence of perfect information, our best approach is to gather evidence with the resources available to us, balancing accountability and pragmatism. In the absence of hard evidence, ask whether you can instead explain the logic of your decision to your stakeholders. Can you provide cues, indicators, or your assumptions underlying your programmatic investments and the bets you are making? Is your logic transparent and does it hold up to scrutiny? For more on how to do this, see Chapter 7.

If, through conversations with a foundation or donor, you believe they are steering your nonprofit in the wrong direction, be prepared to impress them with your nonprofit's highly thoughtful approach to metrics and evidence. Stick to your guns on this.

Donors don't want to invest in flops. They are looking for evidence of effectiveness, and so are you. Show them that the system you have designed is meaningful for informing your strategies and resource decisions. Metrics and evaluation, when done right, hold us accountable, help us identify flops, and help us make those hard calls to either significantly adjust strategies or wind down programs. Failure shouldn't be a dirty word; it should be seen as an opportunity. Failure should drive action and learning.

Donors are a key part of our ecosystem. We wouldn't get far without them. We can't build an innovative nonprofit without the generous support of donor-partners who share our passion for our vision and mission. In the words of Helen Keller, "Alone we can do so little; together we can do so much." As we can see from these stories, our donor-partners greatly expand the realm of what's possible. By building a clear common vision, negotiating and boundary setting, and by thinking innovatively together, we can solve some of society's most challenging problems.

Bring Your Innovation A Game

As we take a closer look at the traits shared by innovators for social change, we find passion, empathy, curiosity, tenacity, and courage. They have backbone. We find people who know their superpowers and their limitations. We find people who embrace creative collaborations.

Social entrepreneurs are driven and passionate. They are a bit obsessed. Social entrepreneurs don't have to be flashy or seek the limelight, but they feel strongly about the needs in the world around them and the potential consequences if they don't act. They step up because they love what they do, they feel compelled—and that feeling is contagious.

Are there traits we can learn from, and emulate? Anyone can easily sharpen these skills with awareness and practice. It is well established that there is no real psychological difference between innovative entrepreneurs and ordinary executives.[1] These traits can be learned. As you read about these traits in the following chapters, you may find that you are already modeling them. Or you might recognize a trait that you would like to strengthen. These stories may help you in coaching and encouraging fellow team members on their own entrepreneurial journey.

Chapter 11

Discover Your Superpower

I find that social entrepreneurs know their own "superpower," meaning that they know their comparative advantage and when to say no.

I once heard a nonprofit CEO give the following advice to a group of new employees: "Be ruthlessly attuned to your comparative advantage." Later, I kept wondering, what exactly did he mean by that?

It turns out that comparative advantage is not just putting into practice what you are especially good at; you have to make the *best* use of your time, talents, and limited resources.

If someone asked you to describe your secret superpower, what would you say? What are your gifts? Your skills? Your strengths? What fulfills you and puts the fire in your belly? Think about the unique skills and experience that you contribute to your work, your family, and your community. Taking a cue from organizing guru Marie Kondo: What sparks joy?

An executive of a family foundation encourages grantees to "choose the best from the good opportunities" because, of course, we can't do everything. What makes you feel dissatisfied or spread too thin? Are you a guardian of your time and talents in the same way you protect your bank account? Every day we all think through trade-offs: if I spend time/money on X, then I will not have time/money for Y. Achieving clarity about our talents and the best use of our time helps us think through our options and helps us confidently say no—freeing up our resources for better pursuits.

For example, Fred Rogers had a unique combination of (1) expertise in childhood development, (2) a strong desire to be a "healer of creation" rooted in his Presbyterian seminary training, and (3) a deep interest in the burgeoning new field of children's television. When Rogers created *Mister Rogers' Neighborhood*, he had no idea that the program would eventually scale and become a hit with a national audience, but he believed in himself and knew his strengths and comparative advantage.

He was far too humble to call it his "superpower," but Rogers had such a clear understanding of his comparative advantage and such a driving passion for his vision that it helped him to focus and say no to things. He turned down lucrative offers from television studios. He turned down offers to mass-produce his puppets and sell them to children—he felt building trust with children was more important. Knowing his comparative advantage helped him to stay on course and eventually create a wildly successful nonprofit production company.

The nonprofit CEO talking earlier about comparative advantage also said that we all tend to have a built-in bias toward the status quo, and we get comfortable in our routines. He described a mental exercise that helps overcome this, saying, "Always assume you aren't in the right job. Then ask, am I in the right role? What would I be doing if I were not in this current role? How would I design my dream role and market myself if I were an independent consultant?" He said that asking himself these questions kept him from falling into a career rut. He productively changed roles at his nonprofit three times in five years, steadily gaining responsibilities and changing teams. At one point he even left his nonprofit and then, a few years later, he was hired back as the CEO.

Most of us have diverse skills and professional backgrounds. For example, in addition to helping nonprofits to be more effective, I am also experienced in helping organizations vet and implement new software application systems. I spent my early career in the for-profit world in the field of quality systems. I'm also skilled with spreadsheet pivot tables and data analysis. I enjoyed doing all of those projects. But were these projects the *best* use of my time?

It took some years to find the answer for myself. As my career progressed and I gained more nonprofit experience, I found that when I came across a team that didn't have a clear vision or strategy, where they weren't rowing in the same direction, I could help them transform into an effective and innovative team. If in some small way, my help leads to the team firing on all cylinders, empowered and proud of their work, and achieving better outcomes for their beneficiaries, I'm beyond happy. I have learned that this is what I do best, it's what brings me the most fulfillment, and it brings about powerful results. I have learned that this is the best use of my time—my comparative advantage.

In the parlance of economics, the concept of comparative advantage is more nuanced than simply being good at something. For the sake of example, let's say that celebrity Chef José Andrés and I are roommates. He would be far more skilled at cooking a fabulous dinner than me, but hold up—consider the value of his time. Chef Andrés is busy managing Michelin-rated restaurants, running an international nonprofit, writing best-selling cookbooks, and starring in cooking shows. So, his costs (what he would give up) for cooking dinner are much higher than mine. I would have more of a comparative advantage to cook dinner than Chef José Andrés, because I would be giving up less.

If you are reading this book, most likely you are working for a non-profit. I suspect that passion and altruism are values that distinguish you from others. You are mission-oriented and deeply committed to solving a social problem. You might consider yourself an idealist. You might value principles, meaning, and the psychic benefit of advancing a mission over your other career options, where you might make more money. Altruism might be one of your superpowers. What are the others?

For years, I have held mistaken assumptions about letting others know about my own talents. Being a quiet introvert from the Midwest who is content working behind the scenes, the idea of building a personal brand struck me as superficial, I thought of it as shameless self-promotion. But in recent years I have come to realize how mistaken this was. We don't want our talents to be invisible; rather, we need to be visible experts, for others to recognize what we are good at, so we can make the best use of those talents. As we know, we often must break through biases, assumptions, and prejudice to use our talents to do good in the world. Being a visible expert, having credibility, and being top of mind for what you are good at can help you break through those obstacles. Our brand ensures we aren't passed over for an opportunity for which we excel. We don't have to think of building a personal brand as something one does for oneself—rather, the people our nonprofits serve won't get the benefit of our talents if we don't make our talents visible.

Discover Your Superpower

Neither will our colleagues, our boss, or our donors. Build a strong personal brand to help others.

The world is changing rapidly; being clear about our talents can help us find our place in it. Employers are spending massive resources searching for talent. There is a reshuffling of talent as people are reevaluating their roles and expectations in the wake of COVID. Physical location may be less of a constraint—in fact, your dream role might be virtual.

In *Talent: How to Identify Energizers, Creatives, and Winners Around the World*, authors Tyler Cowen and Daniel Gross write that people tend to underestimate themselves and sometimes need some nudging.[1] I have observed this firsthand as a volunteer at a halfway house for men who had been recently released from drug rehabilitation programs or from prison. I would visit with one or two of the residents for a few hours on Saturday mornings, offering résumé coaching and helping with online job applications. These are people who have been through some hard knocks, but even within that context, I still found myself astounded at how little they believed in themselves, and how the small act of paying attention or pointing out their skills brought a light of self-esteem into their eyes. I might look at a résumé and say, "Wow, you have worked at some very posh restaurants," and they would sit up straighter and light up. I'm not sure others have talked to them like this before. In fact, some of the men impressed me with better people skills, emotional maturity, and with deft ways of dealing with trauma and obstacles, as compared to some people I know with graduate degrees and six-figure incomes. Cowen and Gross are right that we often sell ourselves short, lack imagination for ourselves, or don't have enough self-esteem. There might be good reason for that given one's life circumstances and obstacles, but it doesn't have to stay that way. Taking the time to think about your talents and skills can benefit the rest of us. In each generation, I wonder how many people with talents like Mozart or Einstein remain undiscovered because they underestimate themselves? I love reading biographies precisely for this reason, especially stories of people who, despite obstacles, found their superpower, whether Fred Rogers, comedian Mindy Kaling, the great poet Maya Angelou, or the story of the first president of our country, George Washington.

Once you have a good sense of your strengths, ask yourself, Are you making the best use of them? Or do you keep performing lower-value tasks or busywork out of habit, pursuits that are not really the highest-value use of your limited time? What should you be refusing to do? What would free up your time for more entrepreneurial and creative endeavors?

When work piles up and I notice that I'm feeling unfocused and spread too thin, I keep a journal to track my time usage for a few weeks. I list the tasks I complete each day and approximately how much time each took. At the end of the week, I rank which of the tasks were the highest-value use of my time and which were the least valuable. I notice what I could say no to and which meetings I did not really need to attend. It helps me recognize which activities represent the best use of my time so I can make better trade-offs.

You too have a diversity of skills and talents. What do you consider the best use of your time? This question may take time and experimentation to answer. We tend to get caught up in the busyness of our lives and may not realize our own gifts. You may want to take a skills inventory. There are many good online strengths finder assessments, such as the CliftonStrengths self-assessment offered by Gallup or the High5 Test. As you consider your skills, ask yourself: Of your various talents and skills, which of them brings you the most personal satisfaction? Which of them puts fire in your belly?

Ask some of your colleagues to give you feedback on your strengths. They won't mind. They might point out that you are great at coaching, thinking about the big picture, or sorting through details. They might say you are a creative problem solver. They might observe that you have high empathy, fortitude, or patience.

A superpower might come from a completely unexpected mix of interests from distinct fields (economics and chess, hip hop and engineering, puppetry and seminary). Consider the cross-section of skills and values that led Fred Rogers on his career path. How might your diverse interests come together in a completely unique way?

Asking yourself whom you admire and why can also help identify your passions or patterns in your thinking. I have had great admiration for the writing and thinking of Edward Deming, Peter Drucker, and the

1,500-year-old rule of Saint Benedict which is remarkably still in use for the daily management of monasteries today. Each of these is related to healthy, optimal workplaces so that people can be their best. This is a driving motivation for me. Who are thinkers or doers that you admire, and why? How might that inform your career path?

Many of the nonprofit founders we have read about in this book found their calling as a result of a major life challenge such as addiction or racial injustice. For example, Fred Rogers suffered from severe childhood asthma and was often on his own; as a young man he became quite skilled at creating puppets and skits. Our biggest life trials might tell us something about what shaped us and formed our inner motivations. In the last months of his life, during a congressional hearing, civil rights activist and Maryland Rep. Elijah Cummings shared advice he gave his own children, "When bad things happen to you, do not ask the question 'Why did it happen to me?' Ask the question, 'Why did it happen for me?'"[2] This strikes me as good advice, to recognize that our struggles contribute to our personal formation and who we are.

Know thyself, as the great philosophers say. Seek out great interview questions and then ask yourself some of these questions. The Cowen and Gross book shares excellent interview questions designed to draw out hidden talents and find contrarian thinkers. For example, "What is it you do to practice that is analogous to how a pianist practices scales?"[3] Or, "What are ten words your spouse or partner or friend would use to describe you?"[4] You might ask yourself these questions prior to your annual performance review, or if you are considering a new job or organization.

If you have been in the position to interview and hire others, you might ask, Who have been your proudest hires and why? This might tell you something about your own values. For example, the two best hires I ever made, though decades apart, had these traits in common: emotional intelligence (empathy, ethics, a sense of humor), and entrepreneurship (curiosity, can-do attitude, a love of problem solving). I learned daily from both of these hires and knew enough to get out of the way. They both continue to be superstars in their careers. What I admire about them tells me something about my own values.

To stretch your imagination, you might write out your dream job description, a business plan for your dream nonprofit, a strategy for your dream nonprofit program, your dream syllabus for a topic you would love to teach, or a personal strategic plan.

Being clear about your unique talents can help you say no to things, freeing you up to do what you do best. It can give you the confidence to be innovative. Making the time to better understand your unique skills may take you in incredible new directions.

Chapter 12

Challenging the Status Quo

During my Peace Corps service some years ago, I was teaching computer literacy at a teachers college in a dangerous part of Kingston, the capital city of Jamaica. The school was administered by a small, determined band of Franciscan nuns.[1] They were hardworking and often had a twinkle in their eye. In addition to the college, they ran several other schools in the area. I noticed right away the respect the students had for the sisters. They were kind, generous, savvy, and strong. They ran a tight ship. They made sure the grounds were beautiful. They raised money for scholarships. They raised money for the sparkling new computer lab where I would be teaching. They did a lot of good, not just for the school but in the community.

When one of the elderly sisters had to run an errand one day, she took me along. I don't recall the errand, but that day will forever be etched in my mind. We drove into a dangerous Kingston community, Trench Town, where Bob Marley was from. Trench Town was run by drug dons, and gunmen were posted every few blocks to keep rival gangs out. It was so dangerous that US marines posted at the embassy nearby received hazard pay.

As our van rounded a street corner, suddenly a gang member with a gun walked into the middle of the road and stopped us, I tried to stay calm. He was a large man with a fierce expression. The sister seemed to know him, and she gave him a lecture about how drugs were destroying the community and urged him to get out of the business. Not making me feel any calmer, the petite sister shook her finger in his face as she scolded him. Yet he listened attentively, looked at his shoes and nodded, then waved us through. I realized he *respected* her.

Not only did this little band of nuns manage to help the college survive—they helped it thrive—in the midst of a poverty-ridden and dangerous community. They did not accept the status quo of poorly run educational institutions. They were always making things better for the students, whether landing a grant for a brand-new computer lab, applying for and getting a peace corps volunteer (me) as a computer literacy instructor, or making the grounds more beautiful. They were restless and constantly innovating.

Thanks to the generosity of sisters like these, generations of students have gained a quality education. Those trained by the teachers college have graduated to teach classrooms of their own across Jamaica, paying it forward. How many lives, I wondered, have they impacted? Speaking for myself, the opportunity to work closely with them and learn from them had an impact on my life and career choices. Though seemingly small, these sisters were a force. They challenged the status quo. I will never forget them.

How did they achieve this? Three traits in particular stood out to me during my time with these remarkable women: they were **curious**, they were **contrarian**, and they were **diplomatic**. Being curious and contrarian is what motivated them to challenge the status quo and seek ways to make things better. But equally important, diplomacy ensured that they were listened to, respectfully, even by someone as unlikely as a gang member. Being curious or contrarian without the aid of diplomacy would surely be counterproductive. These skills helped them to be effective in incredibly difficult circumstances.

Let's further explore these skills and what they look like in practice.

Paving the Way for Collaborative Ideation

In *How Innovation Works*, author Matt Ridley describes the collaborative creative cultures that led to the inventions of the jet engine, Google's search engine, and Twitter—all made possible by workplaces that unlocked people's potential for bottom-up innovation.

Ridley's book makes the case that the widespread myth of the lone inventor or the solitary genius is misleading. It exists because journalists, biographers, and inventors themselves like to romanticize the idea of the rugged individualist struggling against all odds. But in reality, he writes, "Innovation is a team sport, a collective enterprise, far more than is generally recognized."[2] For example, we have all heard the story of Thomas Edison's invention of the lightbulb, but how many know that Edison's New Jersey company employed 200 skilled craftsmen and scientists who collaborated on tens of thousands of experiments resulting in hundreds of patents?

Does collaborative innovation only apply to for-profit firms? To the contrary, Ridley's observation is true of nonprofits as well. Collaborative work cultures lead to far more innovation than what can be accomplished by a solitary genius.

Discoveries are more likely to happen when we are open to the insights of others and what skeptical colleagues have to say. The problem is that having others stress-test our ideas means we may need to set our egos aside. We will need to employ diplomacy at the same time that we are being curious and contrarian. This might mean we have to collaborate with difficult personalities. At times, others may not be automatically swept away by our staggering genius. And we all know from experience that at times, collaboration can be bumpy, if not downright infuriating, because of, well, people.

Diplomacy can smooth over the bumps in the road as we engage in uncomfortable conversations. And this will have big payoffs. This can lead to learning, discoveries, and breakthroughs. Collaborating to stress-test ideas is an essential ingredient for helping good ideas become great ideas. This prompts some obvious questions:

- If uncomfortable conversations are so great, why don't we have them more often? What gets in the way?

- How do uncomfortable conversations and collaborations affect our ability to ideate and innovate? What do they look like in practice?

- How can we get the most out of uncomfortable conversations? How do we ensure ideas get a fair listen and that we aren't tuning each other out?

This chapter won't shy away from what makes these practices difficult. People with different backgrounds and experiences have different ideas of what the best way is to get work done. No one person has the best answer every time. While viewpoint diversity adds richness to our efforts, how do we bring out the best from each other without devolving into hurt feelings and unproductive efforts? What gets in the way of entrepreneurial collaborations?

Why We Sometimes Hesitate to Be Contrarian

On the one hand, human beings are imbued with logic and the ability to communicate complex ideas, yet we also come packaged with cognitive bias. We often make decisions based on emotion rather than objective data, or we give too much credence to data that confirms what we already believe. It might be more comfortable to not raise questions.

Recently, I was developing a facilitation exercise for a leadership team and thought my approach was dazzling, the stuff of genius. But in the process of getting feedback from a few colleagues, I soon realized it had some weaknesses and could be much stronger. Thanks to someone else's input, I learned I was not seeing the whole picture, just a piece of it.

We often dig in with our own position and become emotionally vested in our ideas. Our pride may be involved, because we really put ourselves out there with the idea. No one wants to be embarrassed in front of colleagues or our boss. We are only human. But if we can't productively engage with others to explore ideas, if we can't risk admitting that sometimes we are wrong, we are stifling innovation.

Call to mind a recent disagreement. Whether it was in the workplace, with a family member, or perhaps when you were making a purchase. How did you feel in that moment? Did you feel some stress or frustration, or maybe your blood pressure went up? Believe me, you aren't alone.

A common misconception is that disagreement requires becoming a pushy, disagreeable, confrontational winner-take-all type. If this makes you nervous, your instincts are right on. Aggressive confrontation is not part of a healthy challenge culture.

Here is how we should think about healthy disagreement in the workplace. When done right, it can enhance mutual learning.

For example, a nonprofit that works in advocacy encourages and rewards team members when they are diplomatic, contrarian, and curious. Team members are empowered to respectfully challenge the status quo, even if the culprit is management. They are evaluated in their annual performance reviews on these skills. The nonprofit has a reputation among its peers as having a healthy culture of entrepreneurial collaborations. And, to ensure they were walking the talk, the leadership team issued a survey to the staff, asking about their experience of disagreement in the workplace, which they call "challenge culture." One question on the survey was: What is the purpose of healthy workplace disagreement? Take a look at their nuanced responses:

- "With more communication and the willingness to listen and be receptive, we can understand what another team's obstacles are or what their day-to-day is like and why certain things are done in a certain way or how they can be improved."

- "Challenge can be seen to imply a zero-sum game. So, it is important for people to think about what the goal is and what success looks like. In many cases, the result from a challenge will be to learn something, not necessarily to change existing strategies or practices."

- "The challenge is getting at—why do we do this? Why do we do it this way?"

- "There is a difference between a positive suggestion to improve versus just finding fault or venting dissatisfaction."[3]

Notice the sensitivity, respect, and diplomacy underlying their answers. Obviously, they aren't trying to dunk on each other or be right at someone else's expense. The survey respondents seemed to recognize that a healthy workplace culture involves openness and asking questions. Their responses demonstrate a level of humility and an understanding that healthy challenge can spark learning.

Challenging the Status Quo

Curiosity motivates us to face uncomfortable truths. If we aren't curious, if we aren't raising contrarian questions, then we are not learning or even doing our jobs. While the process is not always comfortable, we are showing respect to the organization, our team, our customer, and to each other.

Sometimes experts or people in leadership positions are dead wrong. Remember when Apple fired Steve Jobs and then eventually realized their mistake and brought him back? Remember when economist and *New York Times* columnist Paul Krugman famously predicted that the internet would be a flop? Consider some of the nonprofits we have read about in this book that were struggling with preventable issues, like Hull House or the Newseum. At work, if we believe someone is taking our nonprofit down the wrong path, we have a duty to speak up. Our beneficiaries and donors are counting on us to be contrarian and curious.

Nonprofit CEO Emily Chamlee-Wright describes challenge as a way of honoring learning and honoring each person's dignity. "We should always assume everyone in the conversation is our dignified equal. And that there are times, especially when there is injustice, that require us to step outside of politeness as you speak truth to power. You have a duty to speak up; you are actually embodying the height of civility with courage, when doing so."[4]

This is a two-way street. We should have the courage to speak up, and we should also have the courage and inner strength to be open-minded when people disagree with us.

With a humorous touch, Pulitzer Prize–winning journalist Kathryn Shulz warns of our human tendency toward what she calls "error blindness." In her book, *Being Wrong: Adventures in the Margin of Error*, she writes about how we don't like to admit we are wrong, but that it is far better to know we are wrong and make a change than to continue along blindly in the error of our ways.[5]

Think about the times when we have been wrong, or missing key information, and a colleague's contribution helped set us on the right path. For example, a few years ago, I was convinced my nonprofit needed to do monthly results reporting, based on what I heard from stakeholders. But teams kept saying, this is too much work! I disregarded this feedback for a time, but after they persisted, I finally agreed to a one-time experiment to try quarterly instead of monthly reporting. Lo and behold, stakeholders still got the information they needed, and reporting became a lighter lift for all the teams. We made the change permanent. My colleagues' challenge saved all of us, me included, from wasted effort.

Think about your own experience of suspending your own views. Do you have similar stories?

A team of researchers designed a survey to better understand what holds people back from workplace disagreement. For example, they found that 50% of people hesitated due to political factors, 32% didn't want to stir up tension, and 18% didn't want to hurt people's feelings or discourage them.[6] These findings may resonate with your experience.

We might shy away from being curious and contrarian because we fear repercussions. We might fear crossing someone in executive leadership. We might fear shaking things up. Subtle peer pressure might lead us into groupthink. And in a dysfunctional workplace culture, or one where we fear being embarrassed or losing our livelihood, we are that much more likely to shy away from challenging the status quo. Depending on the culture of the organization, fear may be the appropriate response. But if we are curious and contrarian, we might just overcome our tendency toward error blindness and be willing to raise questions that need to be asked.

No doubt about it, disagreement can be awkward and unpleasant, but challenging the status quo is when the best learning and innovation occurs. Big and little conflicts, problems, and tensions are bubbling up all day long in the workplace. This is simply the nature of work. We are always problem solving, troubleshooting, and disagreeing with each other as we wrestle with budgets, priorities, staffing, resources, approaches, roles, responsibilities, and well, pretty much everything. Sometimes we are balancing competing principles. Yet a groundbreaking innovation might be just around the next corner if team members hear each other out and seek creative solutions. Here are some more practical ways to do that.

Methods for Coaxing Curious Contrarians Out of the Closet

Though this may take some courage on our part, **feedback from skeptical colleagues** can go a long way toward improving a proposal. When we are making proposals for new ideas, we can run an early draft by others to get feedback and incorporate their perspectives. We can ask colleagues: What is my weakest argument? We shouldn't ask our mom or best friend, but seek out feedback from those who might be skeptical, or from whom we'll later need buy-in.

A neutral third party with fresh eyes might help ensure the team is **asking the right questions in the first place**. Using an example whose story we are already familiar with, let's imagine that a team at Habitat for Humanity has two ways of defining a problem:

1. How can we build the maximum number of shelters efficiently and cheaply to reduce the number of homeless people? Or . . .

2. How can we eradicate substandard poverty housing worldwide, in a way that honors people's dignity and empowers them to put skin in the game, build equity and credit, and contribute to community life?

Imagine yourself participating in this discussion. Which of these is the better question? If the Habitat team addressed question #1, they would likely focus on finding the best way to get donations and hire construction companies to build high-rise apartment buildings for low-income residents. But if the Habitat team is solving question #2, they might design programming that looks more like Habitat's unique "sweat equity" model, where homeowners and their friends and family help build the home.

But what if no Habitat team members ever asked the second, far better question? The team might miss an opportunity to design solutions that powerfully advance its mission. Sometimes we are so immersed in the details of our work that we fail to ask the right questions. This happens all the time. People who are curious and contrarian are more likely to ask good questions. We can sharpen our skills at drawing the "why" out into the open. Do not hesitate to interrupt a conversation or a meeting with:

- Are we solving the right problem?
- Are we all on the same page about the problem we are trying to solve?
- Before we get too far down the road, is the problem well defined? Is the scope clear?
- Do we share the same assumptions? What are our hidden assumptions?

Questions like these represent entrepreneurial thinking at its best, laying the groundwork for creative thinking and innovative problem solving. They will help uncover any weak thinking or problematic assumptions in a proposal. We might preemptively ask and answer these questions of ourselves before seeking out help from our colleagues.

A neutral colleague might help surface faulty **mental models**, which are beliefs or assumptions that we may not realize we hold. A telling example is how Japanese automakers gained significant market share in America during the 1970s. Detroit automakers held fast to the mental model that all consumers cared about is styling. This was a flawed assumption that no one questioned. Japanese automakers had a more accurate model of what customers wanted: smaller, more affordable cars. Because of this insight they unexpectedly outperformed American automakers.[7]

Likewise, some of the best examples of innovation occur in nonprofits when social entrepreneurs challenge deeply entrenched, long-held mental models. By being contrarian and curious. These new ideas might seem counterintuitive. Take the Good Food Institute, an international nonprofit researching and advocating for healthier, more sustainable alternatives to the current meat industry. They are challenging how people think about the food they eat. In fact, they are currently experimenting in Singapore, where consumers have been enjoying chicken nuggets from lab-grown meat, cultivated from cells rather than from the slaughter of an animal.[8] Or consider the Working Group for Women and Land Ownership

(WGWLO). In developing countries, women's agricultural work is often invisible. Through pro bono legal clinics, WGWLO is directly challenging mental models and discrimination toward women and has helped 9,000 women secure land rights to the land on which they toil.[9]

What if educators in Kenya asked the question, What might have the greater impact on learning outcomes in K–12 schools—smaller class sizes, more textbooks, or, what about treating intestinal worms in children? Though this was not an expected idea for improving school outcomes, random controlled trials demonstrated that deworming reduced absenteeism by one quarter.[10]

Challenging assumptions can help us discover breakthroughs.

Another technique for inviting help from outsiders is a **red team**. This is a technique where a group is assigned to play a role of an adversary and provide feedback from that perspective. For example, in cybersecurity, a red team might play the role of hackers and test system vulnerabilities. In airports, a red team member might hide a weapon in luggage to see if they can pass through airport security undetected. The military and intelligence communities make use of red teams for assessing enemy reactions to their strategies. What might this look like in nonprofits?

A nonprofit might assign a few members to a red team to stress-test a proposal. Or, the team getting the assessment may not know who is on the red team or when or how the red team will make its assessment. A red team member may pretend to be a consumer of the nonprofit's services, like a management consultant who fakes an injury to assess the customer service experience at a hospital. The red team's role is to look at the proposal with fresh eyes, not take anything for granted, and challenge any potential vulnerabilities.

Similarly, a **premortem** is a technique where team members pretend, imagine, and anticipate what might cause a project to fail. This is an exercise designed by psychologist Gary Klein.[11] Gather a team and ask them to pretend that their project has crashed and burned. Ask them to write down all possible reasons for the failure. This is an exercise requiring imagination. This exercise can be helpful in anticipating risks while there is time to adjust. It sets a norm within the team to look for early warning signs.

The facilitator briefs a team about a program or project, then tells them that the project failed. The facilitator asks participants to conjecture and write down every reason they can think of for what caused the failure. Team members might surface vulnerabilities such as:

- Our beneficiaries prefer the new online education offered by our competitors, so they stopped coming to our in-person training sessions.
- By shifting our funding primarily to government grants, we changed the nature of our core business, programming and organizational identity, and lost our base of local committed donors
- For our drug abstinence programming for teens, our presenters (police officers) came across as more adversarial than educational.[12]

A premortem can help address overconfidence. It empowers people to speak up who might otherwise be hesitant. It can help identify gaps in thinking that can then be followed with brainstorming for solutions.

A variation of the premortem is a facilitated exercise I've affectionately dubbed **the "Miranda Priestly" exercise**. Team members find it fun and months later have mentioned how helpful they found it. It is my favorite too.

Inspired by an unforgettable character in the movie *The Devil Wears Prada*, I tape a picture on the wall of Miranda Priestly, the tough-as-nails editor of *Runway* magazine played by Meryl Streep. Ms. Priestly is peering over her eyeglasses in the photo, looking skeptical and intimidating. I ask participants to imagine that she is a key financial supporter on our board of directors. I ask them to imagine that our team leader, Kevin (who is also present for this exercise), is preparing to visit Ms. Priestly next week to ask for a donation of $3 million. Our job is to help Kevin prepare for this visit and make a compelling pitch.

The participants' job is to brainstorm the tough questions Ms. Priestly might ask so Kevin will be well prepared. Examples of questions teams have surfaced include:

- Ms. Priestly might hear our proposal and then ask, "So what? Aren't there more pressing problems in the world?"
- What makes you the right group to address this opportunity? Why not someone else?

- Who else is operating in this space? Do you see them as friends, foes, or neutral? Is there coalition-building or partnership potential?

- Are entrenched interests likely to oppose your efforts? What will you do about them?

- What are your risks versus the likelihood of success?

- Given your small team and limited resources, is your plan realistic?

This is an exercise that helps us have the courage to be contrarian and curious. Relying on Ms. Priestly as a foil provides a safe space for participants to ask questions they may have been afraid to ask. "Ms. Priestly is asking the tough question—not me." When you facilitate this type of pre-mortem, you might be surprised by the team's creative and tough-minded thinking. The team can then work on building stronger arguments into the proposal that address the questions they brought to light. Well done.

Embrace humility. A workplace culture that encourages healthy disagreement does not mean tolerating arrogance and bluster. At my nonprofit, an intern fresh out of college would barrel into meetings to share ideas without asking any questions about context or what had been tried before. His supervisor took him aside and reminded him that he was new to the organization. He was making incorrect assumptions, and he would be more successful by first asking questions. Unfortunately, he continued with the behavior, burned his relationships, and did not finish his internship.

While boldness is a key part of challenge, so is humility. Advancing an idea is not an opportunity to dunk on people or prove that we are the smartest person in the room. Far from it. Asking and learning are fundamental for a healthy, thriving challenge culture. Someone may have an incredible idea, but first, they have to investigate if it has already been considered and find out what was learned from those efforts. Find out who has the expertise on this question, seek them out, and learn from them. An entrepreneur cannot assume she knows everything. Be prepared to discover that we might not be right, or we may not be aware of a complication. Be prepared that we may not persuade others of our position. That is all right. We can learn from this, and the next time we are more likely to have a more informed idea.

Build trust. The ability to laugh at ourselves earns enormous credibility with colleagues. Research shows that self-deprecating humor goes a long way toward putting people at ease, whether in public speaking or in one-on-one relationships.

The Joy of Painting television host Bob Ross would sometimes make a mistake in the middle of demonstrating a landscape painting. Rather than edit it out of the segment, he would point it out to his viewers, laugh, and call it a happy accident. He would proceed to work the happy accident into the painting. He had a way of putting the viewer at ease. We can learn from his example.

A project management expert agrees that regularly admitting mistakes has a positive effect on team collaboration. "Offering an example of something you'd like to do differently in the future creates an open atmosphere for others to evaluate their own behavior. The more often you do so, the stronger this aspect of your team's culture becomes."[13]

It takes courage to admit to others that we made a mistake, or that we may not know something. But that opens the door for trust building and breakthroughs.

In his classic book *The Seven Habits of Highly Effective People*, management guru Stephen Covey likens relationships to a bank account. Only after we have built deposits of trust can we have difficult conversations that are productive. When we have built a relationship with a person so that they feel confident about our intentions, and our respect for them, they will be far more likely to hear us out. But without a track record of trust, the ground is much shakier when we need to constructively disagree. They may feel defensive and tune us out.

One nonprofit has been putting this idea to the test since 1993. Seeds of Peace is one of the largest conflict-resolution programs in the world. They provide immersive experiences that foster personal and interpersonal transformation to equip participants with skills to navigate relationships across lines of conflict. For example, they run a three-week summer camp in Maine that brings Israeli and Palestinian teenagers together. They "sleep, eat and play games together, and engage in daily sessions to talk about the conflict between their groups and their own experiences with it."[14] A team of scholars reviewed seven years of Seeds of Peace program data and interviewed alumni, and found that structured, meaningful engagement and in-person proximity lead to a positive correlation with trust.[15]

Think of someone in your life who gives you constructive feedback that makes your work stronger. What has brought about that level of productive collaboration?

If you engage with a colleague or another team and you find that you are not making inroads, think about what you might do to build trust. If the relationship feels stiff, perhaps have a few informal coffees. Ask your colleague about their challenges, ask how you can be helpful. Perhaps try embedding on each other's teams for a few hours per week for cross-training. This process does take time. But by walking around in each other's shoes, you are building trust. The more we build strong personal relationships, the easier joint problem solving becomes.

Whether you are a manager, supervisor, or someone who leads team brainstorming sessions, creating an atmosphere where team members feel comfortable sharing ideas or disagreeing with each other is critical.

If a person doesn't feel respected or sense kindness, they will feel defensive. We can be thoughtful in how we phrase a challenge, usually as a question. That signals our openness to hearing opposing views and encouraging colleagues to share information we may be missing. For example:

Focus on the system, not the person. Not "Jill let the servers go down." Better to say, "Our server downtime is 5%, and the industry average is 3%. This costs us $20,000 per year. Let's explore ideas together for improving this."

"Kate, I am sensing XYZ as a problem, but I don't necessarily know what the solution might be. Can we discuss ideas together?"

"Sam, I understand your point, but let me respectfully challenge that, and you can let me know if you disagree. Let me share my reasons with you [describe]. I'd like to hear your reaction and you can tell me what I'm missing."

"Would you mind if I challenge that? I'll share what I'm concerned about, but push back if you disagree. I might be overthinking this."

The Intellectual Turing Test. Another way to ensure colleagues give you candid feedback is to fairly characterize their best arguments.

This doesn't mean you have to agree. Showing that you heard them and respect them builds trust and provides opportunities for learning.

Considered the father of theoretical computer science and artificial intelligence (AI), Alan Turing led a team responsible for breaking German codes during World War II. Turing was known in the AI field for creating what became known as the Turing Test. Simply put, if an evaluator can't tell the difference between the responses of a machine and a human, the machine passed the test. Think of times when you thought you were interacting with an online "customer service representative" who has an on-screen photo of a smiling person with a name like Beth. But in fact, "Beth" is an automated chatbot. Beth might have passed the Turing Test.

George Mason University economist Bryan Caplan takes the idea a step further, applying the Turing Test idea to the art of uncomfortable conversations and mutual learning. Can you argue your opponent's side so convincingly that an observer would not realize you are actually an opponent? Writing about Caplan's test, technology journalist Nathan Taylor wrote, "An Ideological Turing Test is not just a test. It's about taking a mental stretch to empathize with your opponent's position." He cites neuroscientist Tom Stafford who expands on this idea, "In many instances people believe they understand how something works when in fact their understanding is superficial at best."[16] Author and philosopher Daniel Dennet builds on this concept, suggesting, "Attempt to re-express your target's position so clearly, vividly, and fairly that your target says: "Thanks, I wish I'd thought of putting it that way." Only then are you permitted to say so much as a word of rebuttal or criticism."[17] Caplan applies this technique in his classroom, creating role-playing drills for his students. Many nonprofits working in the space of polarization are experimenting with similar techniques.

As the conversation unfolds, active listening is an essential part of openness. It involves repeating back to the person what you heard them say in your own words: "I'm going to repeat what I think I heard you say . . . [insert] . . . did I get that right?" Active listening validates the other person and signals that you are really trying to hear them out. Active listening is a way of putting yourself in their shoes. "I can see from your perspective why you say X . . ."

This requires stretching ourselves. As we prepare for this kind of a conversation, think about:

- What would success look like for me, and for her? What do I want? What does she want? And is there a range in which we can compromise?

- What does she value? Perhaps this person needs to be seen as a manager, as a coach who offers useful advice. So, make sure she feels heard.

- Toward the end, you might ask her, how did you feel this conversation went? Did you feel like I heard you?

By modeling active listening, creating a safe environment, and showing a colleague respect, you will make team members more comfortable with asking tough questions. We in turn will be less likely to be tuned out as we stress-test ideas to find the best way forward, for discoveries and innovation.

Have Courage

We all want the best for our organization, and we are not always going to agree. Let's acknowledge that being curious and contrarian can feel awkward and that is OK. As my yoga instructor loves to say, being comfortable is not always the right thing. We should be sure to give ourselves credit— being innovative requires a lot from us, and we are doing the hard work of breaking out of complacency. Sometimes when we disagree with each other, the discussion may heat up or get emotional. It happens. Nonetheless, you have a good idea worth going to the mat for. Your nonprofit's beneficiaries might be better off thanks to your idea and your courage. So, raise your challenge. Disagree when it is appropriate. Be sure to bring along your diplomacy A game. You can say it tactfully but also forthrightly.

Don't give up on great ideas. Life is too short, needs are too great, and too much is at stake not to explore ways to make the world a better place. Successful social entrepreneurs believe that their ideas are worth fighting for. Challenging the status quo will always involve facing hurdles. And as I learned in a dangerous neighborhood one day in Trench Town, being contrarian, curious, and diplomatic will be among your best assets.

Chapter 13

Win Others Over to Your Cause

No matter what our nonprofit's mission, we need resources to implement our ideas. We often find ourselves persuading others. Innovation requires resources, a budget, talented team members, and buy-in. Two stories of persuasive and tenacious social entrepreneurs are illustrative.

Dr. Nancy Harris, founder of the Terma Foundation, exemplifies tenacity. The mission of the Terma Foundation is to develop integrated health programs to educate, research, treat, and prevent illness in vulnerable communities around the world. The path to launching the nonprofit and saving lives was fraught with obstacles.

In 1990, Harris was a young American doctor studying medicine in China. When traveling in Tibet, she noticed something very wrong in many of the children: stunted size. The current theory of the medical community was that this was caused by high altitudes, but she knew this couldn't be the case. She had observed healthy children living in high altitudes in Chile. After she returned to the United States, she couldn't get the problem out of her mind. She kept asking questions and talking with doctors, but it would take three years for her visa to be granted so she could return and further investigate.[1]

When she finally got permission from the Chinese government to return, she was prepared. She and her team examined 50–100 children a day. They found that 71% of the children had intestinal parasites, 41% had chronic malnutrition, and 67% had rickets. Her hunch had been right. Harris published her findings in a medical journal, drawing attention to the issue.

Up to that point, she had funded her research with her own savings, but in order to design treatments for the Tibetan children, fundraising would be required. She taught herself to write grant proposals. Though she was often turned down, eventually an individual wrote a check for $30,000 which established the beginnings of the Terma Foundation. Terma is a Buddhist word meaning "hidden treasure."

Harris and a few colleagues launched their efforts by building a network of medical workers, creating education programs about nutrition and hygiene, and distributing vitamins.

The approach of the Terma Foundation is bottom-up. In Harris's words, it involves "listening and observing for a long time. Before proposing things, you have to understand what people within that culture perceive their needs to be . . ."[2] and, "Often, the best solutions are not the ones that worked somewhere else in the world and are then imposed upon a situation from the top down. Rather the most sustainable approaches are ones that come from understanding the culture and then creating health solutions within that culture."[3]

None of this would be easy. Travel was difficult. Treacherous roads and mudslides caused delays. The local bureaucracy demanded bribes. It took months of negotiation to gain permission to enter an area to treat patients. People working in the Health Department were untrained. Medicines sold locally were fake or sub-quality. Customs officials often confiscated medicine that Terma imported.

Pushing through many obstacles, they persisted. In the years to come, the work of Terma uncovered tuberculosis as an epidemic. They quickly designed programs to address it. And in the last 25 years, the efforts of Dr. Harris and her colleagues at the Terma Foundation have saved lives and improved the health of over 1.5 million people in vulnerable communities in Tibet (Tibet Autonomous Region, China), Mexico, Myanmar, and Brazil.[4]

Social entrepreneurs must not only be persuasive, but they must also be tenacious. They are fighters. They are willing and ready to face unexpected obstacles, setbacks, and bureaucracies, fueled by empathy and commitment to the people they serve.

Likewise, when Mother Teresa proposed founding the Missionaries of Charity to serve the poorest of the poor, her archbishop's answer was no.

Despite her stellar reputation as a nun, the strength of her proposal, and the support of allies, the archbishop had concerns. He wasn't yet confident that her calling was real. He suspected other groups were already doing similar work. He feared public criticism for assigning a woman to work alone in the dangerous slums of Calcutta. While his answer was no, she was told she could reapply in a year. At that time Mother Teresa brought her proposal again, and this time she got a yes. Before long, the Missionaries of Charity grew to 4,500 nuns in 133 countries managing homes for the sick and dying, soup kitchens, mobile clinics, orphanages, and schools. She would win the Nobel Prize. The same archbishop would become an involved supporter and one of her biggest fans.[5]

Even the most successful social entrepreneurs have to knock on closed doors, field tough questions from skeptics, and brace themselves for the answer.

These are essential skills for anyone working in nonprofits. At times we have to convince our colleagues down the hall to lend their time or resources to our project. They must make their best decisions for their time and a variety of requests from other teams. At other times we are persuading executive leadership to increase our team's budget in order to hire a new team member or expand our programming. If our nonprofit works in issue awareness or advocacy, we must persuade journalists, policymakers, and the public to agree with our cause. Sometimes we are making the case to donors about why our unique services are deserving of a grant.

Simply persuading members of our own team might not be easy. We may have great ideas about how best to implement a program—but so do our colleagues. We may not always be on the same page with each other. As we make our most persuasive case, though, we will learn from each other and perhaps innovate together.

The reality is that far more innovative ideas exist than resources. We may hear no quite often. Nonprofit budgets are finite. Managers can't say yes to everything. Ideas, projects, programs, and organizations compete for resources. How can we stand out from the crowd, secure resources, and win buy-in for our ideas? Consider these four practical steps:

1. Identify what decision makers are looking for.

2. Bring your A game and your best tough-minded logic.

Win Others Over to Your Cause

3. Create a compelling elevator speech.

4. Be scrappy, flexible, and have a thick hide.

These steps will help an idea stand out from the crowd of *good* ideas and make a compelling case that yours is a *great* idea.

Identify What Decision Makers Are Looking For

Whether we are applying for a scholarship, a grant, a raise, a budget increase, or approval to hire staff, we need to know: What are the standards? What are decision makers looking for?

Are they looking for an emotional appeal and stories? Data and hard evidence? Or perhaps both? What kind of trade-offs are they making? What information would help them feel confident in your proposal? How stiff is the competition? Is the acceptance rate 2% or 40%? What are their inner motivations? Perhaps they fear making a bad investment or fear missing an opportunity.

Put yourself in the shoes of the decision maker. Imagine multiple requesters coming to you with myriad ideas and requests for budgets and resources. You can't say yes to everyone. Why would that be frustrating? Would you feel pressure? Who actually enjoys rejecting great proposals? What information would you need? What would help you sift through the proposals more quickly and throw out the ones that are out of scope? What clarifying questions would you ask?

Speculate and write the answers down. This can help you know your audience and shape your pitch accordingly.

Below are some examples of criteria that decision makers might use to sift through opportunities.

At my nonprofit, when executive leaders are considering annual budget allocations for many teams, they consider questions such as:

- What are the team's measurable objectives and the timeline for achieving them? (Decades? Years?)

- What does the team's past performance tell us about how they might do on this project? (This question is weighted heavily.)

- Who are the intended beneficiaries?

- What is the team's thinking and approach for achieving the objectives? (If we do X, we believe Y will be the results.)

- What might cause the effort to fail? What risks need to be monitored?

- What will serve as credible evidence that efforts are succeeding, failing, or lukewarm?

A consortium of NGOs recommends the following criteria for evaluating grants:

- Does the applicant have the necessary skills, reputation, experience, and potential to achieve program goals?

- Is the proposed approach clear, logical, and well-conceived?

- Are the activities and results realistic?

- How significant is the expected project impact?

- Will the project establish a model or approach that can be replicated?[6]

On the other hand, some individual donors who give from the heart may not have a list of premeditated questions and criteria like these. Rather, they may value stories.

Stories can convey need and urgency. MercyShips, a Canadian nonprofit, sends two surgical ships, *Global Mercy* and *Africa Mercy*, around the world. Their website displays personal stories and videos of the people whose lives they have saved, such as the story of Mabouba, a young woman in Togo who had a life-threatening tumor that began to block her esophagus and windpipe. Her family described how she struggled to breathe and eat. In 2016, she arrived at a MercyShip, and a nine-hour surgery saved her life. In the video, we learn that Mabouba is now healthy, married with a daughter, and runs her own tailor shop.[7]

Likewise, DonorSee's website landing page runs brief video stories of real people who are requesting help in overcoming specific challenges. One video showed a six-year-old girl who needed a prosthetic leg. Another video had an undernourished baby who needed nutrient-rich formula milk. People visiting the website can choose a beneficiary and how much to contribute. Later, a donor will receive a series of short video updates demonstrating visible progress. For example, you might receive video clips of the baby gaining strength and weight over time, or you might receive video clips of the young girl participating in school and playing with friends thanks to her new prosthetic leg. A donor can actually see how a life is transformed. The videos are intended to provide evidence that a donation makes a difference. As DonorSee's website states, "We take you to the scene of your giving."[8]

DonorSee and MercyShips excel at making a persuasive case to a large number of donors and prospective donors. Know your audience and then shape your pitch accordingly.

We also find ourselves persuading members of our own organization to lend support to our projects. Consider a nonprofit's marketing team with a small team and budget. Because they support 12 program efforts across the organization, they must choose where best to spend their time and where they can make the biggest impact. When programs approach them for help with marketing, they rely on criteria to help them prioritize, such as:

- Has the program clearly defined what a win looks like?
- Does the program define specifically, in detail, who the target audiences are?
- Has the program defined what specific actions they want the audiences to take (for example, register for our events, visit our website, read our publications, write a letter to the editor in support of our cause, donate)?

A marketing team's motivation is that they want their work to matter. If a program team provides clear answers to these questions, then marketing team members have a clear sense of how they might help. They can better plan and make trade-offs with their limited time and resources.

Thinking of any recent requests you have presented to decision makers, what criteria might be important to the people you need to persuade?

Outcomes Please, Not Outputs

In the nonprofit world, most funding proposals require us to show our thinking about outcomes. But often teams either confuse outputs with outcomes, or neglect outcomes altogether. This is a death knell for any proposal.

For the sake of jogging our memories, which of these is an outcome?

1. Produce research on affordable housing.

2. By YYYY, at least two city administrations considering affordable housing initiatives meaningfully cite or rely on our research in their efforts.

If you recognized the second option as an outcome, good work. Yet many nonprofit teams will focus on outputs and neglect outcomes. Why is this such a common problem?

An outcome is a meaningful external change in the world. Outcomes might be a change in conditions or behavior, or a measurable change in people's lives. An outcome might be evidence of learning or behavior change in program participants, or a policy change from advocacy efforts. An outcome is what we want to achieve, a result, whereas outputs are the activities necessary to achieve the outcome.

Outcomes are daunting because they are not fully within our control. They might take years or decades to come to fruition. Fear of committing to an outcome is understandable—what happens if we don't achieve it? We might feel frustrated because we are already working very hard on our outputs. Isn't that enough?

Consider how the world of sports approaches outcomes. Let's say your favorite NFL team has a three-year plan to build a strong team, beat their rivals, and win the Super Bowl. Are these long shots? Perhaps. Can the team or coach guarantee this? Of course not. But they aren't shy about articulating their goals, which is what gets fans excited. Similarly,

205

for us in nonprofits, we shouldn't shy away from articulating outcomes. We are simply stating our intent. This is what inspires others to support our project.

Grantmakers and executive leaders are interested in the big picture; they expect to see outcomes in a proposal. Proposals that include a laundry list of activities and tactics will go to the bottom of the pile. Don't be shy about verbalizing your long shots, as long as they are realistic. If it helps, remember that outcomes are about aspirational direction, not perfection.

Weak proposals tend to focus on tactics (first WE will do this, then WE will do that), which gives the impression that the focus is internal rather than external. A proposal that emphasizes the beneficiaries and meaningful external change is stronger. Another tendency of weak proposals involves leaping from a big-picture vision (the why) directly into tactics and activities (the weeds) without providing the very important in-between strategy (the how). The strategy provides your rationale or step change for how you'll accomplish the vision.

What Is Your Value Proposition?

To stand out from the crowd and attract funding partners, you may want to consider developing a value proposition.

A value proposition is a belief from the (customer's, beneficiary's, or donor's) point of view about how value or benefits will be delivered, experienced, and acquired. What is the promise of value that our team or nonprofit will deliver and communicate? Developing a value proposition is based on a review and analysis of the benefits, costs, and value that we can deliver to customers, prospective customers, and other constituent groups within and outside our organization.

Describing our value proposition can also counter our natural tendencies to be absorbed and distracted by tasks and processes occurring within our four walls. The more we shift our attention to our clients and the value we offer them, the better we are able to achieve our mission. For example, take a look at the value proposition for the American Cancer Society:

> Together with our millions of supporters, the American Cancer Society saves lives by:
>> Helping you stay well: We help you take steps to prevent cancer or detect it early.
>>
>> Helping you get well: We're in your corner to guide you through every step of a cancer experience.
>>
>> Finding cures: We fund groundbreaking research into cancer's causes and cures.
>>
>> Fighting back: We work with lawmakers to pass laws that defeat cancer and rally communities to join the fight.[9]
>
> You might ask your team to do some thinking about your program's or your nonprofit's value proposition. Who are the beneficiaries of what we do, and what do they gain?

Whomever you are trying to persuade, whether downstream teams, your colleagues, your manager, or a grantmaker, the strongest cases are made when teams have a solid understanding of the decision maker's criteria and anticipate those criteria when making their pitch.

Bring Your Best Tough-Minded Logic

Archbishop Desmond Tutu of South Africa did not let threats, jail, harassment, or racism get in the way of speaking truth to power. He spent his career making unpopular arguments. He played a key role, among others, as a highly influential social entrepreneur, transforming the rights of black South Africans and democracy in his country, winning the Nobel Peace Prize. He once said: "Don't raise your voice, improve your argument."

We would be wise to heed his advice. We improve our arguments not by being loud or pushy, but by truly hearing out our opponents, anticipating weaknesses in our own arguments, and recognizing risks that could cause our effort to fail. We can show we've done our home-work and how we have thought about feasibility. We can make sure our arguments hold up under tough scrutiny. Let's look at some examples.

Crafting a Persuasive Justification

Let's imagine that two teams are trying to persuade their nonprofit's IT director that the organization needs a new online donation system. But the IT team is overloaded. Like most IT departments, they have 50 requests but only have time to work on 10 projects this year. Each team is hoping that their IT request doesn't end up at the back of the line. Following are two justifications; let's see which team you find more persuasive.

Team A's justification:

Dear IT team, we need to upgrade how we process online credit card donations. Our current system is eight years old, clunky and outdated. We believe the newer system will increase donations, that our donors will prefer the new system to the old way, and it may save us time. Thanks for your time, Team A

Team B's justification:

To comply with new federal privacy and security regulations, we must replace our online donation credit card system by next August or we will no longer be able to process online donations. This would put 13% of our total annual donations at risk; online donations average $10,000 per year.

Our current donation system does not have defenses against increasingly sophisticated forms of cyberattack. Credit card processing is the #1 target of cybercriminals, according to the Department of Homeland Security. Stolen data will lead to lost donations, damage trust, and irreparably harm our brand with supporters.

The good news is that by increasing donor confidence in our security and making a smoother process with fewer clicks, we believe we would increase online donations from $10,000 to $15,000 per year, a 50% increase. This estimate is based on similarly sized organizations that made the switch. We estimate that the new system will save 40 hours or $1,000 in internal labor per year, as we currently do manual workarounds that will no longer be necessary.

The cost of implementation and one-time customizations is $2,000, and three user licenses cost a total of $200 per year. We will treat this as a one-year experiment. Given the increased donations, the new system will pay for itself within the first year. We would like IT's help in vetting our analysis and whether QuickDonate is the right tool and meets our internal security policies.

We identified two key risks and would like your advice about other risks and the best approaches for mitigation:

- Frequent changes in security and privacy laws are hard to keep up with. Mitigation: QuickDonate, our top choice for a software vendor, makes a contractual commitment to stay abreast of these changes and makes updates to their software for compliance. We believe we can switch to another vendor with no penalties if they do not honor this commitment.

- Better or less expensive systems may be offered by competitors after we commit to a contract. Mitigation: we reviewed ten software vendors and participated in demos for five different systems, we based our questions to the vendors on our research of user reviews, and we believe QuickDonate met all of our needs within our price range. If we later identify a better vendor, our contract allows us to switch to a competitor vendor annually with no penalties, though there will be internal costs to adjust our processes and learn a new system.

Given team A's and team B's justifications, which do you think the IT director would be more likely to support? Which team asked the hard questions and explored the risks so that the IT director doesn't need to? Clearly, Team B provided better analysis, evidence, and persuasiveness.

Win Others Over to Your Cause

When you need to be persuasive at your nonprofit, it may not require a formal written justification like that of Team B. You might make your pitch in an informal conversation. Either way, you will want to be sure you provide evidence, show that you have considered risks, and have done your homework on the cost-benefit. It may be helpful to ask someone at your nonprofit for examples of project justifications.

Create a Compelling Elevator Pitch

When you look over a restaurant menu, what information do you need to make your decision? A 10-page description of the steps for how each dish will be prepared, or a phrase describing the meal?

Like you, decision makers are busy people. They want to reach a decision quickly. They may have to sift through many proposals, and you want to get their attention and hold it. You want to make the first cut. A short, powerful, and compelling argument will help you get the decision makers' attention.

If decision makers must hunt through a 40-page proposal where your best arguments are buried in footnotes, they may shelve your proposal by the time they get to page 3. To avoid wasting their time, can you boil your proposal down to a two-minute verbal pitch, or a one- or two-page executive summary? The Upward Bound proposal mentioned in Chapter 4 is a great example.

Many teams succumb to the temptation to write lengthy, detailed proposals. There might be seemingly sound reasons. Maybe we mistakenly think that the decision makers need to know how we make the sausage. But that isn't necessarily the case.

Decision makers are our customers, and as we'd do with any customer, we should respect their time and get right to the point. Make it easier for stakeholders to quickly grasp our goal and rally to our cause. Boiling down all of your reasons is hard work but worth it. Sharper arguments will reward you with grateful reviewers.

When boiling down your best arguments for a short verbal pitch or executive summary, the essentials are: the problem and stakes if we don't act, why now, our vision, why us, and what we can do about it—a concise rationale. That said, however, always follow your funding opportunity's instructions for the application format, which will vary widely.

In addition, you or your team have probably conducted additional analyses that might be of interest to the decision makers. These can optionally be attached as supporting documents, in an appendix, or listed as "available upon request." This way you aren't drowning busy decision makers in details. Those additional supporting documents might include your SWOT analysis, theory of change, assumptions and program strategy, planned activities, a plan for evaluating the program, staff bios, partnering organizations, a marketing plan, a line-item budget, and so on.

Concise, clear proposals are not only useful for grantmakers and executives. They can also help communicate your project vision to downstream teams at your nonprofit. If a marketing team or a fundraising team is providing support across 12 programs, they don't have the time to sift through twelve 40-page project plans. Your concise, clear one- to two-page synopsis of what your team is trying to achieve will help them quickly understand the essentials of your program so they can jump in to support your team.

The last step is to mentally prepare for a number of ways the pitch might unfold.

Be Scrappy, Flexible, and Have a Thick Hide

Making your best pitch takes courage. You are putting yourself out there. As they say, "No guts, no glory." When you make your pitch, be confident, but also recall Mother Teresa's experience from the beginning of this chapter—we should be mentally prepared for a no, for delays, roadblocks, or getting less than what you had in mind.

Sometimes a rejection has nothing to do with the quality of your proposal. It might stem from a lack of funding or bad timing, changing circumstances like a pandemic or financial crisis, or the decision maker may have a new set of priorities.

Sometimes when we are turned down, we need to rethink our proposal. A first step in that process is asking the decision maker to share their reasoning so we can learn and adjust. Rejections are tough, but like Mother Teresa, social entrepreneurs are good at dusting themselves off, learning, adapting, and going back to the mat.

You can have a plan B. Spread your bets. If you are working on a grant proposal, you will probably have a number of foundations you plan to solicit. For any kind of proposal, you can offer a phased-in approach. This is appealing and persuasive. That is, in phase 1 we will keep to small experiments, and if we can prove we can accomplish X results by YYYY, then we will ask for an increase in funding of $$$. But if results show X, then we will adjust or sunset the effort.

Or propose a range of options and alternatives. With $3,000 I can do X; with $10,000 I can do XX. Decision makers appreciate having a range of choices, which empowers them to make a better decision and consider their own trade-offs.

For example, a few years ago one of the teams I supervised was constantly underwater. They were short-staffed and couldn't keep up with the many requests they received from other teams. I felt they were understaffed by two team members. Since it was a medium-size non-profit with a tight budget, I knew asking for more would be a tough sell.

In my proposal to my manager and her boss, I provided a range of options and made clear which one I thought was best. At the same time, I stated that the team would be ready to accept any decision from leadership and shared what the trade-offs would be depending on the choice. For each option, I explained what the results would be and how each approach would impact the team's deliverables to the organization, including expensive workarounds, complaints, morale, and burnout.

In this case, they approved my proposal. But I've also experienced many nos. Let's not pretend this process is easy or comfortable. If the answer to your proposal is negative, be ready to revise or take your proposal elsewhere.

Don't give up on great ideas. Needs are too great not to explore ways to make the world a better place. Challenging the status quo always involves facing hurdles. Successful social entrepreneurs believe their ideas are worth fighting for. Be scrappy.

In the words of Pat Riley, one of the greatest NBA coaches of all time, "You have no choices about how you lose, but you do have a choice about how you come back and prepare to win again."

I hope that, like me, you find inspiration from these social entrepreneurs who recognize the importance of persuasion and who excel at making their best case, learning and strengthening their arguments in the process. We must stand out from the crowd of *good* ideas and make a compelling case that ours is a *great* idea.

Epilogue

What's at Stake

*Never doubt that a small group of thoughtful, committed people
can change the world. Indeed, it is the only thing that ever has.*
—*Margaret Mead*

We dedicate our time, energy, and careers to a particular nonprofit mission because of our discomfort with "the way things are," socially as well as personally.

There is nothing in the world like making a difference, to see the flash of newfound self-esteem and hope in a person's eyes. This is what kindles our passion and commitment to our work.

Perhaps we are working in a local food bank or animal shelter. Perhaps we donate to nonprofits working on land conservation or cleaning up the environment. Perhaps we are working in our community or church to address addiction, job skills training, or to help our neighbors who are suffering from a global pandemic.

Perhaps our work in some way alleviates the suffering of the more than 736 million people who live below the international poverty line, or the 10% of the world population living in extreme poverty and struggling to fulfill the most basic needs like health, education, and access to water and sanitation. Perhaps our efforts are aimed at freeing the approximately 24.9 million people in forced labor, 4.8 million of whom are in forced sexual exploitation. We know that the stakes are high.

Passion and commitment aren't enough to change the world. As Margaret Mead points out in the epigraph, we must also be *thoughtful*. The stakeholders we care deeply about are counting on us to be our innovative best selves. We need well-run organizations and an infrastructure that equips us to meet these challenges, so we can discover what works.

Yet we know from experience that this is not always the case. In the same way that customers will go elsewhere when a for-profit business fails to keep innovating, if a nonprofit fails to make a meaningful difference for those we serve, our stakeholders (donors, beneficiaries, volunteers, and talented team members) will also take their time, money, and talents elsewhere.

Even if our nonprofit is wildly successful, we can't rest on our laurels. We must constantly evolve and discover better approaches. We saw this in some of the examples, such as Hull House, which succumbed to mission creep and closed its doors despite 100 years of success. Even with the best intentions, nonprofit managers and staff can get tangled up in the tyranny of the urgent and in misguided approaches to program planning and evaluation. This leads to missed opportunities, lack of buy-in, wasted time, and uninspired—uncommitted—donors. We can learn from these examples and not make the same mistakes.

There is also no shortage of inspirational examples. We learned about nonprofits with outsize impact—"Davids" facing Goliath problems—which started small and thoughtfully discovered ways to punch above their weight, such as St. Benedict's Prep School and the Southern Christian Leadership Conference.

Human ingenuity and creativity are limitless. There are many ways to innovate, big or small. We learned about the daily workplace practices that enable nonprofit Mayo Clinic to win patents for new discoveries that save lives and cure diseases. Collaborative innovation is part of their organizational DNA, and nonprofits of any size or mission can replicate it. We can thank philanthropy for breakthroughs like hospice care, public libraries, and the discovery of insulin to treat diabetes.[1]

Innovation is, in short, about finding new, surprising ways to get results and value. It involves creativity, originality, and some risk taking. An innovative manager or frontline worker is one who asks, "What could be better?" and then tinkers and experiments. Innovation is the opposite of business as usual. While it can be big and disruptive, more often than not innovation happens on the margins—such as reducing program costs by 5%.

We also find ourselves in a reality where there are far more needs, opportunities, and ideas than there are resources. Managers can't say yes to everything. Ideas, projects, programs, and organizations compete for resources. When a social entrepreneur like Mother Teresa faces setbacks and rejection, we can safely assume that we will too. We must stand out from the crowd of *good* ideas and make a compelling case that this is a *great* idea. We learned from examples of social change innovators who mastered the art of persuasion and making a strong pitch.

These practices might require a change in thinking. In the words of astronaut Buzz Aldrin, you may have to "get out of your comfort zone and be willing to take some risks."

Nonprofit innovation is at the center of making our world a better place. What kind of human endeavors and social good will come about 50 years from now that we can't even imagine now? My hope is that the case studies and practices in this book will inspire current and future social entrepreneurs and those with generous spirits to continue to dream big, ask the right questions, experiment, and innovate boldly.

Are you ready to make transformational change? I wish you happy innovating!

Notes

Acknowledgments

1. F. A. Hayek, "The Dilemma of Specialization," in *The State of the Social Sciences*, edited by Leonard D. White (University of Chicago Press, 1956): 463.

Introduction

1. Nick Skillicorn, "What Is Innovation? 26 Experts Share Their Innovation Definition." Idea to Value—Creativity and Innovation with Nick Skillicorn. Retrieved from: https://www.ideatovalue.com/inno/nickskillicorn/2016/03/innovation-15-experts-share-innovation-definition/
2. Tony Wagner, *Creating Innovators: The Making of Young People Who Will Change the World* (Scribner, 2012): 8.
3. Chuck Frey quoting Norman Bodek in "How Do You Define Innovation and Make It Practical and Saleable to Senior Management?" *Innovation Management* (January 7, 2008). Retrieved from https://innovationmanagement.se/imtool-articles/how-do-you-define-innovation-and-make-it-practical-and-saleable-to-senior-management/
4. Tony Wagner, *Creating Innovators*: 9.
5. Frank Langfitt, "Wal-Mart Aid Outpaced Some Federal Efforts" *NPR, All Things Considered* (September 9, 2005. Retrieved from: https://www.npr.org/templates/story/story.php?storyId=4839696
6. Brice McKeever, "The Nonprofit Sector in Brief 2015: Public Charities, Giving and Volunteering," The Urban Institute, 2015. Retrieved from: https://www.urban.org/sites/default/files/publication/72536/2000497-The-Nonprofit-Sector-in-Brief-2015-Public-Charities-Giving-and-Volunteering.pdf
7. Leslie Crutchfield and Heather McCleod Grant, *Forces for Good: The Six Practices of High-Impact Nonprofits* (Jossey-Bass, 2012): 14.

8. Brice McKeever and Marcus Gaddy, "The Nonprofit Workforce: By the Numbers," *Nonprofit Quarterly* (October 24, 2016). Retrieved from: https://nonprofitquarterly.org/nonprofit-workforce-numbers/

Chapter 1

1. Scott Pelley, "The Resurrection of St. Benedict's," 60 Minutes, CBS News, June 26, 2016. Retrieved from: https://www.cbsnews.com/news/60-minutes-newark-school-st-benedicts-scott-pelley-2/
2. Adapted with permission from: Thomas A. McCabe, *Miracle on High Street: The Rise, Fall and Resurrection of St. Benedict's Prep in Newark, N.J.* (Fordham University Press, 2010): 198–240.
3. McCabe, *Miracle on High Street*: 214.
4. McCabe, *Miracle on High Street*: 208.
5. McCabe, *Miracle on High Street*: 198.
6. McCabe, *Miracle on High Street*: 212.
7. McCabe, *Miracle on High Street*: 233.
8. McCabe, *Miracle on High Street*: 239.
9. McCabe, *Miracle on High Street*: 222.
10. McCabe, *Miracle on High Street*: 208.
11. McCabe, *Miracle on High Street*: 230.
12. McCabe, *Miracle on High Street*: 233.
13. McCabe, *Miracle on High Street*: 240.
14. Peter M. Senge, *The Fifth Discipline: The Art & Practice of the Learning Organization* (Currency, 2010): 172.
15. Julie Straw, Barry Davis, Mark Scullard, and Susie Kukkonen, *The Work of Leaders: How Vision, Alignment, and Execution Will Change the Way You Lead* (Pfeiffer, 2013): 80.

Chapter 2

1. Jean Case, *Be Fearless: 5 Principles for a Life of Breakthroughs and Purpose* (Simon & Schuster, 2019): 39.
2. Tim Brown, *Change by Design: How Design Thinking Transforms Organizations and Inspires Innovation* (Harper Business, 2019): 57.
3. Pavithra Mehta and Suchitra Shenoy, *Infinite Vision: How Aravind Became the World's Greatest Business Case for Compassion* (Berrett-Koehler, 2011).

4. Susan Kelley "Rethinking Revenues at Health Care Nonprofits," *Cornell Chronicle* (November 26, 2018). Retrieved from: https://news.cornell.edu/stories/2018/11/rethinking-revenues-health-care-nonprofits

5. "History Timeline: Post-it® Notes," 3M website. Retrieved from: https://www.post-it.com/3M/en_US/post-it/contact-us/about-us/

6. Michaela Haas, "How Richard Gere and Bernie Glassman Offer Solutions for the Homeless," *Huffington Post* (September 17, 2015). Retrieved from: https://www.huffpost.com/entry/how-richard-gere-and-bern_b_8149208

7. Barbara Steward, "In the Hood, Jobs for the Poor," *New York Times* (February 3, 2003). Retrieved from https://www.nytimes.com/2003/02/23/nyregion/in-the-hood-jobs-for-the-poor.html

8. Jeanne Liedtka, "Why Design Thinking Works," *Harvard Business Review* (Sept–Oct 2018). Retrieved from https://hbr.org/2018/09/why-design-thinking-works

9. Olivier D. Serrat, "The Five Whys Technique," Asian Development Bank *Knowledge Solutions* (February 2009). Retrieved from: https://www.adb.org/publications/five-whys-technique

10. "Embrace," Extreme Design for Extreme Affordability, Stanford, 2007. Retrieved from: https://extreme.stanford.edu/projects/embrace/

11. Lyndsey Gilpin, "The Woman Who Turned Her High School Science Project into a Global Solar Nonprofit," *Forbes* (October 28, 2015). Retrieved from: https://www.forbes.com/sites/lyndseygilpin/2015/10/28/the-woman-who-turned-her-high-school-science-project-into-a-global-solar-nonprofit/?sh=4f15d2a64cb8

12. Hal B. Gregersen, *Questions Are the Answer: A Breakthrough Approach to Your Most Vexing Problems at Work and in Life* (Harper Business, 2018): 44; and Rhinos Without Borders website, retrieved from: http://www.rhinoswithoutborders.com/about-the-project/

13. Gregersen, *Questions Are the Answer*: 17–18.

Chapter 3

1. Association for Vision Rehabilitation and Employment, Inc. Website. Retrieved from: https://www.avreus.org/services/career-opportunities-46.html

2. Tim Hains, "Van Jones: Criminal Justice Reform Bill 'A Christmas Miracle,'" *RealClearPolitics* (December 19, 2018). Retrieved from: https://www.realclearpolitics.com/video/2018/12/19/van_jones_prison_reform_bill_a_christmas_miracle.html

3. Ernie Smith, "The Curious History of the 911 Emergency System," *Popular Mechanics* (June 28, 2017). Retrieved from https://www.popularmechanics.com/technology/infrastructure/news/a27114/911-emergency-system/

4. Digby Diehl, *The Emergency Medical Services Program, 2000*, Robert Woods Johnson Foundation.

5. Digby Diehl, "To Improve Health and HealthCare," Chapter 10, *The Emergency Medical Services Program, 2000*, Robert Woods Johnson Foundation.

6. John Kania and Mark Kramer, "Collective Impact," *Stanford Social Innovation Review* (Winter 2011). Retrieved from: https://ssir.org/articles/entry/collective_impact

7. Nona Martin Storr, Emily Chamlee-Wright, and Virgil Henry Storr, *How We Came Back: Voices from Post-Katrina New Orleans* (Arlington, VA: Mercatus Center at George Mason University, 2015).

8. Emily L. Chamlee-Wright and Virgil Henry Storr, "Filling the Civil-Society Vacuum: Post-Disaster Policy and Community Response," *Mercatus Policy Series*, Policy Comment No. 22 (February 20, 2009). Retrieved from: https://papers.ssrn.com/sol3/papers.cfm?abstract_id=1349871

9. John Kania and Mark Kramer, "Collective Impact," *Stanford Social Innovation Review* (Winter 2011). Retrieved from: https://ssir.org/articles/entry/collective_impact

10. Nonprofit Vote, retrieved from: https://www.nonprofitvote.org/our-mission/

11. Leslie R. Crutchfield and Heather McCleod Grant, *Forces for Good: The Six Practices of High-Impact Nonprofits* (Jossey-Bass, 2009): 119.

12. Crutchfield and Grant, *Forces for Good*: 132.

13. Sunny Aggarwal, "The Tipping Point by Malcolm Gladwell – Chapter 1," Book Review of *The Tipping Point* by Malcolm Gladwell, Medium (August 13, 2013). Retrieved from: https://medium.com/sunnya97/the-tipping-point-by-malcolm-gladwell-ch-1-b3271f1e23ed#:~:text=The%20name%20given%20to%20that,threshold%2C%20the%20boiling%20point.%E2%80%9D

14. Anita Tun, "Clementine Jacoby Combats Recidivism Through Nonprofit Recidiviz," *The Stanford Daily* (January 27, 2021). Retrieved from: https://stanforddaily.com/2021/01/27/clementine-jacoby-combats-recidivism-through-nonprofit-recidiviz/

Chapter 4

1. Martin Morse Wooster, The Spectacular Failure of One Laptop Per Child, *Philanthropy Daily* (May 24, 2018), retrieved from: https://www.philanthropydaily.com/the-spectacular-failure-of-one-laptop-per-child/;

see also, Namank Shah, "A Blurry Vision: Reconsidering the Failure of the One Laptop Per Child Initiative," *WR: Journal of the CAS Writing Program,* 3 (2010/11): 88–98, retrieved from: https://www.bu.edu/writingprogram/journal/past-issues/issue-3/shah/#:~:text=However%2C%20it%20is%20important%20to,the%20local%20cultures%20and%20societies; see also, Adi Robertson, "OLPC'S $100 Laptop was Going to Change the World—Then It All Went Wrong," *The Verge* (April 16, 2018), retrieved from: https://www.theverge.com/2018/4/16/17233946/olpcs-100-laptop-education-where-is-it-now

2. "Reflections: Smoke 'em If You Got 'em," Army Historical Foundation website. Retrieved from: https://armyhistory.org/reflections-smoke-em-if-you-got-em/
3. "Timeline of Tobacco Industry Hollywood Involvement," Smoke Free Media. Retrieved from: https://smokefreemedia.ucsf.edu/history/timeline
4. "A Historical Review of Efforts to Reduce Smoking in the United States," *2000 Surgeon General's Report*, Chapter 2, Center for Disease Control, 2000. Retrieved from: https://www.cdc.gov/tobacco/data_statistics/sgr/2000/complete_report/pdfs/chapter2.pdf; see also "Timeline of Tobacco Industry Hollywood Involvement," Smoke Free Media Website.
5. "A Historical Review of Efforts to Reduce Smoking in the United States," *2000 Surgeon General's Report*: 56.
6. Matt Berry, "3 Reasons Why the DARE Program Failed," American Addiction Centers (February 9, 2021). Retrieved from: https://americanaddictioncenters.org/blog/why-the-dare-program-failed
7. Example is loosely based on the nonprofit, ROCA. See "How We Do It," ROCA, Inc. Retrieved from: https://rocainc.org/work/our-intervention-model/
8. Sarah Cascone, "In a Landmark Move, the Metropolitan Museum of Art Has Removed the Sackler Name from Its Walls," *Art.net News* (December 9, 2021). Retrieved from: https://news.artnet.com/art-world/met-museum-removing-sackler-name-2046380
9. Laura Nahmias, Dan Goldberg, and Nidhi Prakash, "The Wrecking of a Blue-chip New York Nonprofit," *Politico* (March 13, 2015). Retrieved from: https://www.politico.com/states/new-york/albany/story/2015/03/the-wrecking-of-a-blue-chip-new-york-nonprofit-087679; see also, Stephen Franciosa, "Voices FEGS: Is the Nonprofit's Collapse a Debacle, or a Cautionary Tale?" *Accounting Today* (May 19, 2017), retrieved from: https://www.accountingtoday.com/opinion/fegs-debacle-or-cautionary-tale
10. James Baldwin, "As Much Truth As One Can Bear," *New York Times,* Book Review (January 14, 1962).

11. Maxwell King, *The Good Neighbor: The Life and Work of Fred Rogers* (Abrams Books, 2018): 184.

12. Katie Canales, "Austin's Homeless Crisis Is So Dire, a Nonprofit Built an $18 Million Tiny-home Village to Get the Chronically Homeless off the Streets. Take a Look Inside Community First Village," *Business Insider* (October 10, 2019). Retrieved from: https://www.businessinsider.com/austin-homeless-tiny-homes-village-community-first-photos-2019-10

13. Matt Coles, "Winning Marriage: What We Need to Do," White paper, 2005. Also described by Leslie Crutchfield, *How Change Happens: Why Some Social Movements Succeed While Others Don't* (Wiley, 2018): 56.

14. Ibid.

Chapter 5

1. Peter Murray and Steve Ma, "The Promise of Lean Experimentation," *Stanford Social Innovation Review* (Summer 2015). Retrieved from: https://ssir.org/articles/entry/the_promise_of_lean_experimentation

2. Joseph Paris, "Fail Fast, Fail Small, Learn, and Move On." *Operational Excellence Society* (November 15, 2016). Retrieved from: https://opexsociety.org/body-of-knowledge/fail-fast-fail-small-learn-move/

3. Alvin Ward, "15 Fantastic Buzz Aldrin Quotes," *Mental Floss* (January 11, 2019). Retrieved from: https://www.mentalfloss.com/article/570233/buzz-aldrin-quotes

Chapter 6

1. Do Good Jamaica, Habitat For Humanity. Retrieved from: https://dogoodjamaica.org/organization-search/item/habitat_for_humanityjamaica_abode/#:~:text=Habitat%20for%20Humanity%20Jamaica%20Ltd,foot%20lot%2C%20costs%20%24250%2C000.00%20Jamaican

2. Millard Fuller, "Chapter Two: How Did It All Begin? The Personal Story Behind Habitat for Humanity." In *A Simple, Decent Place to Live: The Building Realization of Habitat for Humanity* (Thomas Nelson, 1995).

3. Fuller, *A Simple, Decent Place to Live*:10.

4. Fuller, *A Simple, Decent Place to Live*: 123.

5. Fuller, *A Simple, Decent Place to Live*: 3.

6. Fox Butterfield, "From Ben Franklin, a Gift That's Worth Two Fights," *New York Times* (April 21, 1990). Retrieved from: https://www.nytimes.com/1990/04/21/us/from-ben-franklin-a-gift-that-s-worth-two-fights.html

7. Fuller, *A Simple, Decent Place to Live*: 123.
8. Martin Luther King Jr., *The Autobiography of Martin Luther King, Jr.,* ed. Clayborne Carson (Grand Central Publishing, 2001): 272.
9. Charles Marsh, *The Beloved Community: How Faith Shapes Social Justice from the Civil Rights Movement to Today* (Basic Books, 2008): 44.
10. Martin Luther King Jr., *The Autobiography*: 220.
11. Marsh, *The Beloved Community*: 93.
12. Martin Luther King Jr., *The Autobiography*: 88.
13. Martin Luther King Jr., *The Autobiography*: 277.
14. Martin Luther King Jr., *The Autobiography*: 168.

Chapter 7

1. Jerry Z. Muller, *The Tyranny of Metrics* (Princeton University Press, 2019): 2.
2. "Anecdotes Aren't Enough: An Evidence-Based Approach to Accountability for Alternative Charter Schools." National Association of Charter School Authorizers, 2017. Retrieved from: https://www.qualitycharters.org/wp-content/uploads/2017/08/AnnecdotesArentEnoughNACSAReport.pdf
3. *Saving Philanthropy*, a documentary short produced by Failing Forward (2011). Retrieved from: https://www.nonprofitsfailingforward.org/films
4. William F. Meehan and Kim Starkey Jonker, *Engine of Impact: Essentials of Strategic Leadership in the Nonprofit Sector* (Stanford University Press, 2017): 87.
5. The Kellogg Foundation, "Logic Model Guide" (2004): 17. Retrieved from: https://www.wkkf.org/resource-directory-old/resources/2004/01/logic-model-development-guide
6. Mario Morino, *Leap of Reason: Managing to Outcomes In an Era of Scarcity* (Venture Philanthropy Partners, 2011), Chapter 1, "We're Lost But Making Good Time," Kindle location 404.
7. Reprinted with permission from Emily Chamlee-Wright. Emily Chamlee-Wright, "Local Knowledge and the Philanthropic Process: Comment on Boettke & Prychitko." *Conversations in Philanthropy* 1, no. 1 (2004): 49.
8. Robert M. Wachter, describing the Avedis Donabedian model in, "How Measurement Fails Doctors and Teachers," *New York Times* (January 16, 2016). Retrieved from: https://www.nytimes.com/2016/01/17/opinion/sunday/how-measurement-fails-doctors-and-teachers.html
9. R. Abelson, "Managing Outcomes Helps a Children's Hospital Climb in Renown," *New York Times* (September 15, 2007). Retrieved from: https://www.nytimes.com/2007/09/15/business/15child.html

10. Paddy Miller and Thomas Wedell-Wedellsborg, *Innovation as Usual: How to Help Your People Bring Great Ideas to Life* (Harvard Business Review Press, 2013): 19.

11. Michael J. Marquardt, *Building the Learning Organization: Achieving Strategic Advantage through a Commitment to Learning* (Nicholas Brealey, 2001): 47.

12. Martin Luther King Jr., *The Autobiography of Martin Luther King, Jr.,* ed. Clayborne Carson (Grand Central Publishing, 2001): 168 (emphasis added).

13. Peggy McGlone and Manuel Roig-Franzia, "The Newseum Was a Grand Tribute to the Power of Journalism. Here's How It Failed." *Washington Post* (February 1, 2019). Retrieved from: https://www.washingtonpost.com/enter-tainment/museums/the-newseum-was-a-grand-tribute-to-the-power-of-journalism-heres-how-it-failed/2019/02/01/aeeb2482-25a4-11e9-81fd-b7b05d5bed90_story.html

14. Louise C. Wade, "The Heritage from Chicago's Early Settlement Houses," *Journal of the Illinois State Historical Society* (Winter 1967) 60 (4): 411–441.

15. Daniel Flynn and Yunhe (Evelyn) Tian, "Nonprofit Deaths, Near Deaths and Reincarnations: Part 1 of 5, Hull House," *Nonprofit Quarterly* (February 10, 2015). Retrieved from: https://nonprofitquarterly.org/nonprofit-deaths-near-deaths-and-reincarnations-part-1-of-5-hull-house/

16. Leah Kral, "Property Rights as a Precondition to Development: A Case Study of Jamaica." Thesis, Duquesne University, 2006.

17. Céire Kealty, "Our Clothing Donations May Cause More Harm Than Good," *National Catholic Reporter* (November 25, 2021). Retrieved from: https://www.ncronline.org/news/opinion/our-clothing-donations-may-cause-more-harm-good

18. Bill Easterly, *The White Man's Burden: Why the West's Efforts to Aid the Rest Have Done So Much Ill and So Little Good* (Penguin Books, 2006); Christopher Coyne, *Doing Bad by Doing Good: Why Humanitarian Action Fails* (Stanford Economics and Finance, 2013); Gary Haugen, *The Locust Effect: Why the End of Poverty Requires the End of Violence* (Oxford University Press, 2014); Peter Greer, *The Spiritual Danger of Doing Good* (Bethany House Publishers, 2013).

Chapter 8

1. Ben Harder, "America's Best Hospitals: The 2021–22 Honor Roll and Overview," *U.S. News & World Report* (July 27, 2021). Retrieved from: https://health.usnews.com/health-care/best-hospitals/articles/best-hospitals-honor-roll-and-overview

2. Kent D. Seltman and Leonard Berry, *Management Lessons from Mayo Clinic: Inside One of the World's Most Admired Service Organizations* (McGraw Hill, 2008): 251. (Emphasis added.)

3. Seltman and Berry, *Management Lessons from Mayo Clinic*: 53.

4. "Why It Matters," Second Chance Business Coalition website. Retrieved from: https://secondchancebusinesscoalition.org/why-it-matters

5. Mayo Clinic Mission and Values, Retrieved from: https://www.mayoclinic.org/about-mayo-clinic/mission-values

6. "The Mayo Clinic: Faith—Hope—Science." Ken Burns, PBS, 2018. And, "Study Finds High Levels of Hospital Noise," *ABC News* (January 6, 2006). Retrieved from: https://abcnews.go.com/GMA/story?id=127795&page=1

7. Seltman and Berry, *Management Lessons from Mayo Clinic*: 31.

8. Patton McDowell, "Challenging the Nonprofit Status Quo," podcast interview with Tina Postel, episode 42, June 2020, minutes 23–30. Retrieved from: https://www.pattonmcdowell.com/news/2020-06/challenging-nonprofit-status-quo-tina-postel/

9. Nicole Wallace, "Employee Feedback Helps Nonprofits Refine Programs," *The Chronicle of Philanthropy* (March 18, 2012). Retrieved from: https://www.philanthropy.com/article/employee-feedback-helps-nonprofits-refine-programs/

10. Hal B. Gregersen, *Questions Are the Answer: A Breakthrough Approach to Your Most Vexing Problems at Work and in Life* (Harper Business 2018): 77; 95.

11. Paul Roberts, "The Agenda—Total Teamwork," *Fast Company* (March 31, 1999). Retrieved from: https://www.fastcompany.com/36969/agenda-total-teamwork

12. Seltman and Berry, *Management Lessons from Mayo Clinic*: 262.

Chapter 9

1. Friedrich August von Hayek, *The Constitution of Liberty* (University of Chicago Press. 1960): 37.

2. Charlie Sorrell, "Swedish Speed-Camera Pays Drivers to Slow Down," *Wired* (December 6, 2010). Retrieved from: https://www.wired.com/2010/12/swedish-speed-camera-pays-drivers-to-slow-down/

3. Thomas Graham, *Innovation the Cleveland Clinic Way: Transforming Healthcare by Putting Ideas to Work* (McGraw-Hill Companies, 2016): 45.

4. Graham, *Innovation the Cleveland Clinic Way*: 158.

5. "Guide to Performance-Based Contracting for Human Services Contracts, An Agency User Guide" developed by the Nonprofit Resiliency Committee (NRC), August 2019. Retrieved from: https://www1.nyc.gov/assets/nonprofits/downloads/pdf/Guide%20to%20Performance_Based%20Contracting%20PDF.pdf

6. Jaclyn Kelly and Margaret Ross-Martin, "Performance-Based Contracting Can Provide Flexibility, Drive Efficiency, and Focus Resources on What Works in Social Services," in *What Matters: Investing in Results to Build Strong, Vibrant Communities* (Federal Reserve Bank of San Francisco, 2018). Retrieved from: https://investinresults.org/chapter/performance-based-contracting-can-provide-flexibility-drive-efficiency-and-focus-resources.html

7. James Buchanan, *Calculus of Consent: The Logical Foundations of Constitutional Democracy*, (Liberty Fund, 1999).

8. Dan Rothschild, "Interview with Dan Rothschild, Executive Director, Mercatus Center," by Leah Kral, February 2021.

9. Graham, *Innovation the Cleveland Clinic Way*: 37.

10. Patton McDowell, "Challenging the Nonprofit Status Quo," podcast interview with Tina Postel, episode 42, June 2020. Retrieved from: https://www.pattonmcdowell.com/news/2020-06/challenging-nonprofit-status-quo-tina-postel/

11. Maria Popova, "David Foster Wallace on Leadership," *Marginalia* (February 17, 2014). Retrieved from: https://www.themarginalian.org/2014/02/17/dfw-leadership-debbie-millman/

12. Larry J. Prather and Dan Delich, "In Flood Resilience Debate, There Are No Solutions—Only Trade-offs." *The Hill* (February 2, 2019). Retrieved from: https://thehill.com/opinion/energy-environment/428193-in-flood-resilience-debate-there-are-no-solutions-only-trade-offs/

13. John Rosemond, "Steer Away from Trying to Micromanage Teen," *Arkansas Democrat Gazette* (January 11, 2012). Retrieved from: https://www.arkansasonline.com/news/2012/jan/11/steer-away-trying-micromanage-teen-20120111/?features-family

14. The W. Edwards Deming Institute. Retrieved from: https://deming.org/quotes/10091/

15. David Hunter, *Working Hard & Working Well: A Practical Guide to Performance Management* (Hunter Consulting LLC, 2013): 5–7.

16. Tim Brown, *Change by Design: How Design Thinking Transforms Organizations and Inspires Innovation* (Harper Business, 2019): 79–81.

17. Jay Galbraith, *Designing Dynamic Organizations: A Hands-on Guide for Leaders at All Levels* (AMACOM, 2001): 60.

18. Doreen Fagan, "Real-Life Examples of Opportunity Cost," The Federal Reserve Bank of St. Louis (January 29, 2020). Retrieved from: https://www.stlouisfed.org/open-vault/2020/january/real-life-examples-opportunity-cost

19. Gary Leff, "Roadmaps: A Guide for Intellectual Entrepreneurs" (Atlas Leadership Academy, 2020): 3.

20. Katie Grivna and Sandi Toben, "The Transformation of One Nonprofit, the Creation of Another, and the Impending Closure of Both," (Part 3 of a 5-part series, "Nonprofit Deaths, Near Deaths and Reincarnations"), *Nonprofit Quarterly* (February 17, 2015). Retrieved from: https://nonprofitquarterly.org/the-transformation-of-the-otto-schiff-housing-association-the-creation-of-the-six-point-foundation-and-the-impending-closure-of-both/

21. "Abstinence-Only Education Is a Failure," Colombia Mailman School of Public Health (August 22, 2017). Retrieved from: https://www.publichealth.columbia.edu/public-health-now/news/abstinence-only-education-failure And, Sarah McCammon, "Abstinence-Only Education Is Ineffective and Unethical, Report Argues," *National Public Radio* (August 23, 2017). Retrieved from: https://www.npr.org/sections/health-shots/2017/08/23/545289168/abstinence-education-is-ineffective-and-unethical-report-argues#:~:text=The%20analysis%20confirms%20previous%20public,intercourse%2C%22%20the%20authors%20write

22. Marie Kondo, *The Life Changing Magic of Tidying Up: The Japanese Art of Decluttering and Organizing* (Ten Speed Press, 2014): 63.

23. Paul Brest and Hal Harvey, *Money Well Spent: A Strategic Plan for Smart Philanthropy* (Stanford Business Books, 2018): 11.

24. Buzz Aldrin and Ken Abraham, *No Dream Is Too High: Life Lessons from a Man Who Walked on the Moon* (National Geographic, 2016): 103.

25. Jennifer Zambone, "Interview with Jennifer Zambone, Chief Executive Officer, Mercatus Center," by Leah Kral, February 2021.

26. Recovery: the Many Paths to Wellness," The U.S. Surgeon General's 2016 Report on Alcohol, Drugs, and Health, Chapter 5, 2016: 2. Retrieved from https://addiction.surgeongeneral.gov/sites/default/files/chapter-5-recovery.pdf

27. Ernest Kurtz, *Not God: A History of Alcoholics Anonymous* (Hazelden Publishing, 2010): 22.

28. Kurtz, *Not God*: 29.

29. Kurtz, *Not God*: 103.

30. Kurtz, *Not God*: 161.

31. The AA website includes an audio talk by Bill W., "AA and Its Critics," describing how AA encourages openness and debate. Additionally, there are website forums such as Rebellion Dogs Radio where there is a lively debate among AA members and others about its rules, processes, and claims for success. Retrieved from: https://rebelliondogspublishing.com/home/blog/sober-truths-50-years-of-aa-critics-bad-science-and-bad-attitudes There are a number of criticisms about AA's model such as: Penn and Teller's television show "Fool Us" where they aimed to "debunk the science of AA," and books such as this work by Lance and Zachary Dodes, *The Sober Truth: Debunking the Bad Science Behind 12-Step Programs and the Rehab Industry* (Beacon Press, 2014).

32. Adam Thierer, *Evasive Entrepreneurs and the Future of Governance: How Innovation Improves Economies* and Governments (Cato Institute 2020); also see e-NABLE website, retrieved from: https://enablingthefuture.org/about/

33. Nightscout Foundation website, retrieved from: https://www.nightscout-foundation.org/about

34. Nightscout Foundation website, retrieved from https://www.nightscout-foundation.org/faqs

35. Isabelle Gerretsen, "How India's Air Pollution Is Being Turned into Floor Tiles," BBC.com (September 12, 2021). Retrieved from: https://www.bbc.com/future/article/20210909-the-young-inventor-purifying-indias-dirty-air?ocid=twfut

36. Bill Murphy Jr. "Google Says It Still Uses the '20-Percent Rule,' and You Should Totally Copy It," *Inc.* (November 1, 2020). Retrieved from: https://www.inc.com/bill-murphy-jr/google-says-it-still-uses-20-percent-rule-you-should-totally-copy-it.html

37. David Hunter, *Working Hard & Working Well: A Practical Guide to Performance Management* (Hunter Consulting LLC, 2013): 22.

Chapter 10

1. Paul Brest and Hal Harvey, *Money Well Spent: A Strategic Plan for Smart Philanthropy* (Stanford Business Books, 2018): 51.

2. Jessica Poiner, "So Far, LeBron's IPromise School Is Keeping Its Promise," Thomas B. Fordham Institute (October 23, 2019). Retrieved from: https://fordhaminstitute.org/ohio/commentary/so-far-lebrons-i-promise-school-keeping-its-promise

3. Jordan Weissmann, "It's a Big Deal That LeBron James Decided to Fund a Public School," *Slate* (August 6, 2018). Retrieved from: https://slate.com/business/2018/08/lebron-james-akron-school-why-it-matters-that-i-promise-is-public.html

4. Helmut K. Anheier and David C. Hammack (eds.), *American Foundations: Roles and Contributions* (Brookings Institution Press, 2010): 212.

5. Brest and Harvey, *Money Well Spent*: 159.

6. Anheier and Hammack, *American Foundations*: 398.

7. Liliane Loya, "Small Steps in the Right Direction: Making General Operating Support the Norm," *The Center for Effective Philanthropy* (July 29, 2021). Retrieved from: https://cep.org/small-steps-in-the-right-direction/

8. "Lindbergh Given Check by Orteig," *The Gettysburg Times*, New York. Associated Press (June 17, 1927). Retrieved from: https://news.google.com/newspapers?nid=2202&dat=19270617&id=DOMlAAAAIBAJ&sjid=o_UFAAAAIBAJ&pg=920,1399980

9. Jonathan Bays, Tony Goland, and Joe Newsum, "Using Prizes to Spur Innovation," *McKinsey* (July 1, 2009). Retrieved from: https://www.mckinsey.com/business-functions/strategy-and-corporate-finance/our-insights/using-prizes-to-spur-innovation# And Robert Lee Hotz, "Need a Breakthrough? Offer Prize Money!" *Wall Street Journal* (December 13, 2016). Retrieved from: https://www.wsj.com/articles/need-a-breakthrough-offer-prize-money-1481043131

10. Aaron Holmes, "A Group of Tech Billionaires Is Funding 'Fast Grants' of up to $500,000 for COVID-19 Research, with Every Grant Decision Made in Less Than 48 Hours," *Business Insider* (April 7, 2020). Retrieved from: https://www.businessinsider.com/fast-grants-500k-covid-19-coronavirus-research-48-hours-billionaires-2020-4

11. "Task Shifting to Tackle Health Worker Shortages," World Health Organization, 2007. Retrieved from: https://www.who.int/healthsystems/task_shifting_booklet.pdf

12. "The International Response to HIV/AIDS," Population Reference Bureau (July 2, 2002). Retrieved from: https://www.prb.org/resources/the-international-response-to-hiv-aids/

13. Juliette Martin, "Africa's New Strategies to Defeat HIV/AIDS," Africa Renewal, United Nations. Retrieved from: https://www.un.org/africarenewal/magazine/december-2016-march-2017/africas-new-strategies-defeat-hivaids

14. Brest and Harvey, *Money Well Spent*: 280.

15. Anheier and Hammack, *American Foundations*: 64.

Notes

16. Marilyn Waite, "A Year in Review and What's Ahead for Our Climate Finance Strategy," William and Flora Hewlett Foundation (December 18, 2018).Retrievedfrom:https://hewlett.org/a-year-in-review-and-whats-ahead-for-our-climate-finance-strategy/ And Marilyn Waite, "Blending Philanthropic, Public and Private Capital to Finance Climate Infrastructure in Emerging Economies," William and Flora Hewlett Foundation (February 3, 2020). Retrieved from: https://hewlett.org/blending-philanthropic-public-and-private-capital-to-finance-climate-infrastructure-in-emerging-economies/

17. Yvonne Wenger, "Nonprofit Offers Low-cost Mortgages for Modest Income Baltimore Residents, Including Those on Rent Subsidies," *Baltimore Sun* (April 24, 2018). Retrieved from: https://www.baltimoresun.com/politics/bs-md-mortgage-approvals-20180424-story.html

18. "Sliding Scale Individual Therapy," Rock Recovery website. Retrieved from: https://rockrecoveryed.org/sliding-scale-individual-therapy/

19. Brest and Harvey, *Money Well Spent*: 100.

20. Jared Lindzon, "Tulsa Paid People $10k to Move There and Work Remotely. Here's How It Worked Out." *FastCompany* (December 2, 2021). Retrieved from: https://www.fastcompany.com/90700766/tulsa-paid-people-10k-to-move-there-and-work-remotely-heres-how-it-worked-out

21. "Recoverable Grant Program, The Power of a Grant Amplified," Vanguard Charitable. Retrieved from: https://www.vanguardcharitable.org/economic-relief-local

22. "The Risks of Lending," KIVA. Retrieved from: https://www.kiva.org/about/due-diligence/risk

23. Anheier and Hammack, *American Foundations*: 3–18.

24. William F. Meehan and Kim Starkey Jonker, *Engine of Impact: Essentials of Strategic Leadership in the Nonprofit Sector* (Stanford University Press, 2017): 13–16.

25. Jennifer Zambone, "Interview with Jennifer Zambone, Chief Operating Officer, Mercatus Center at George Mason University," by Leah Kral, February 2021.

26. Mario Morino, *Leap of Reason: Managing to Outcomes In an Era of Scarcity* (Venture Philanthropy Partners, 2011), Chapter 1, "We're Lost But Making Good Time," Kindle location 476.

27. Morino, *Leap of Reason:* Kindle location 484.

Notes

Part 4

1. Clayton Christensen, Jeff Dyer, and Hal Gregersen, *The Innovator's DNA: Mastering the Five Skills of Disruptive Innovators* (Harvard Business Review Press, 2011): 6.

Chapter 11

1. Tyler Cowen and Daniel Gross, *Talent: How to Identify Energizers, Creatives, and Winners Around the World* (Nicholas Brealey, 2022): 230.
2. Baltimore Sun Staff, "Full Transcript: Rep. Elijah Cummings' Closing Statements at Michael Cohen Hearing," *Baltimore Sun* (February 28, 2019). Retrieved from: https://www.baltimoresun.com/politics/bs-md-cummings-transcript-20190228-story.html
3. Cowen and Gross, *Talent*: 127.
4. Cowen and Gross, *Talent*: 247.

Chapter 12

1. The Franciscan Sisters of Allegany, https://www.alleganyfranciscans.org/
2. Matt Ridley, *How Innovation Works: And Why It Flourishes in Freedom* (Harper, 2020): 8.
3. Staff survey on workplace culture, Mercatus Center at George Mason University, 2020.
4. Ben Klutsey, "Liberalism Starts with the Individual," podcast interview with Dr. Emily Chamlee-Wright, *Discourse Magazine*, minutes 33–47 (August 7, 2020). Retrieved from: https://www.discoursemagazine.com/culture-and-society/2020/08/07/liberalism-starts-with-the-individual/
5. Kathryn Shulz, *Being Wrong: Adventures in the Margin of Error* (HarperCollins, 2010).
6. Julie Straw, Barry Davis, Mark Scullard, Susie Kukkonen, *The Work of Leaders: How Vision, Alignment, and Execution Will Change the Way You Lead* (Pfeiffer, 2013): 139.
7. Peter M. Senge, *The Fifth Discipline: The Art & Practice of the Learning Organization* (Currency, 2010): 176.
8. "Cultivated Meat" Good Food Institute website. Retrieved from: https://gfi.org/cultivated/

9. "Women & Land Ownership" Working Group for Women and Land Ownership website. Retrieved from: https://www.wgwlo.org/women-land-ownership.php

10. Edward Miguel and Michael Kremer, "Worms: Identifying Impact on Education and Health in the Presence of Treatment Externalities." *Econometrica* 72, no. 1 (January, 2004): 159–217. Retrieved from: https://cega.berkeley.edu/assets/cega_research_projects/1/Identifying-Impacts-on-Education-and-Health-in-the-Presence-of-Treatment-Externalities.pdf

11. Gary Klein, "Performing a Project Premortem," *Harvard Business Review Magazine* (September 2007). Retrieved from: https://hbr.org/2007/09/performing-a-project-premortem

12. Matt Berry, "3 Reasons Why the DARE Program Failed," American Addiction Centers (February 9, 2021). Retrieved from: https://americanaddictioncenters.org/blog/why-the-dare-program-failed

13. Jayna Fey, "Workplace Conflict Resolution Techniques For PMs," *Digital Project Manager* (August 5, 2018). Retrieved from: https://thedigitalprojectmanager.com/12-conflict-resolution-techniques-workplace/

14. Juliana Schroeder and Jane L. Risen, "Peace Through Friendship," Opinion, *New York Times* (August 22, 2014). Retrieved from: https://www.nytimes.com/2014/08/24/opinion/sunday/peace-through-friendship.html

15. Shannon White, Juliana Schroeder, and Jane L. Risen, "When 'Enemies' Become Close: Relationship Formation Among Palestinians and Jewish Israelis at a Youth Camp," *Journal of Personality and Social Psychology* (September 17, 2020). Retrieved from: http://dx.doi.org/10.1037/pspi0000331

16. Nathan Taylor, "The Ideological Turing Test. What It Is. Why It's Worth Taking Seriously," *Praxtime* (May 27, 2014). Retrieved from: https://praxtime.com/2014/05/27/ideological-turing-test/

17. Daniel C. Dennett, *Intuition Pumps and Other Tools for Thinking* (Norton, 2013): 33.

Chapter 13

1. Adapted with permission from Nan Alexander Doyal. Nan Alexander Doyal, "The Warrior: Nancy Harris," *Dig Where You Are: How One Person's Effort Can Save a Life, Empower a Community and Create Meaningful Change in the World* (Casper Press, 2017).

2. Doyal, "The Warrior: Nancy Harris," *Dig Where You Are*: 105.

3. Doyal, "The Warrior": 117.

4. The Terma Foundation, retrieved from: https://www.terma.org/

5. Katherine Spink, *Mother Teresa, An Authorized Biography* (HarperOne, 2011), Chapter Two, "The Will of God."

6. "Identifying Grantees to Deliver Results," *NGOTips* (October, 2011): 4. Retrieved from: https://www.ngoconnect.net/sites/default/files/resources/NGOTips%20-%20Identifying%20Grantees%20to%20Deliver%20Results.pdf

7. "A Bright Light for Mabouba," Mercy Ships website. Retrieved from: https://mercyships.ca/en/a-bright-light-for-mabouba/

8. DonorSee website. Retrieved from: https://www.donorsee.com/

9. "American Cancer Society Brand Platform Frequently Asked Questions," American Cancer Society. Retrieved from: https://secure.acsevents.org/site/DocServer/brand_campaign_FAQ.pdf;jsessionid=00000000.app332a?NONCE_TOKEN=412294C1417987F565D25EF6D50946F9

Epilogue

1. Paul Brest and Hal Harvey, *Money Well Spent: A Strategic Plan for Smart Philanthropy* (Stanford Business Books, 2018): 51.

References

"A Bright Light for Mabouba," Mercy Ships website. Retrieved from: https://mercyships.ca/en/a-bright-light-for-mabouba/

"A Historical Review of Efforts to Reduce Smoking in the United States," 2000 Surgeon General's Report Chapter 2. Center for Disease Control, 2000. Retrieved from: https://www.cdc.gov/tobacco/data_statistics/sgr/2000/complete_report/pdfs/chapter2.pdf

Abelson, R. "Managing Outcomes Helps a Children's Hospital Climb in Renown," *New York Times,* September 15, 2007. Retrieved from: https://www.nytimes.com/2007/09/15/business/15child.html

"Abstinence-Only Education Is a Failure," Colombia Mailman School of Public Health, August 22, 2017. Retrieved from: https://www.publichealth.columbia.edu/public-health-now/news/abstinence-only-education-failure

Aggarwal, Sunny. Book Review of "The Tipping Point by Malcolm Gladwell—Chapter 1." Review of *The Tipping Point* by Malcolm Gladwell, Medium, August 13, 2013. Retrieved from: https://medium.com/sunnya97/the-tipping-point-by-malcolm-gladwell-ch-1-b3271f1e23ed#:~:text=The%20name%20given%20to%20that,threshold%2C%20the%20boiling%20point.%E2%80%9D

Aldrin, Buzz and Ken Abraham. *No Dream Is Too High: Life Lessons From a Man Who Walked on the Moon* (National Geographic, 2016).

American Cancer Society Brand Platform Frequently Asked Questions Retrieved from: https://secure.acsevents.org/site/DocServer/brand_campaign_FAQ.pdf; jsessionid=00000000.app332a?NONCE_TOKEN=412294C1417987F565D25EF6D50946F9

"Anecdotes Aren't Enough: An Evidence-Based Approach to Accountability for Alternative Charter Schools." National Association of Charter School Authorizers, 2017. Retrieved from: https://www.qualitycharters.org/wp-content/uploads/2017/08/AnnecdotesArentEnoughNACSAReport.pdf

Anheier, Helmut K. and David C. Hammack (Editors). *American Foundations: Roles and Contributions* (Brookings Institution Press, 2010), Ch. 1, 3, 10, 18.

Association for Vision Rehabilitation and Employment, Inc. Website. Retrieved from: https://www.avreus.org/services/career-opportunities-46.html

Baldwin, James. "As Much Truth As One Can Bear." *New York Times Book Review,* January 14, 1962.

Baltimore Sun Staff. "Full transcript: Rep. Elijah Cummings' closing statements at Michael Cohen hearing" *Baltimore Sun*, February 28, 2019. Retrieved from: https://www.baltimoresun.com/politics/bs-md-cummings-transcript-20190228-story.html

Bays, Jonathan, Tony Goland, and Joe Newsum. "Using Prizes to Spur Innovation," McKinsey, July 1, 2009. Retrieved from: https://www.mckinsey.com/business-functions/strategy-and-corporate-finance/our-insights/using-prizes-to-spur-innovation#

Berry, Matt. "3 Reasons Why the DARE Program Failed," American Addiction Centers, February 9, 2021. Retrieved from: https://americanaddictioncenters.org/blog/why-the-dare-program-failed

Brest, Paul and Hal Harvey. *Money Well Spent: A Strategic Plan for Smart Philanthropy* (Stanford Business Books, 2018).

Brown, Tim. *Change by Design: How Design Thinking Transforms Organizations and Inspires Innovation* (Harper Business, 2019).

Buchanan, James. *Calculus of Consent: The Logical Foundations of Constitutional Democracy*, (Liberty Fund, 1999).

Butterfield, Fox. "From Ben Franklin, a Gift That's Worth Two Fights," *New York Times,* April 21, 1990. Retrieved from: https://www.nytimes.com/1990/04/21/us/from-ben-franklin-a-gift-that-s-worth-two-fights.html

Canales, Katie. "Austin's homeless crisis is so dire, a nonprofit built an $18 million tiny-home village to get the chronically homeless off the streets. Take a look inside Community First Village." *Business Insider,* Oct 10, 2019. Retrieved from: https://www.businessinsider.com/austin-homeless-tiny-homes-village-community-first-photos-2019-10

Cascone, Sarah. "In a Landmark Move, the Metropolitan Museum of Art Has Removed the Sackler Name From Its Walls," *Art.net News,* December 9, 2021. Retrieved from: https://news.artnet.com/art-world/met-museum-removing-sackler-name-2046380

Case, Jean. *Be Fearless: 5 Principles for a Life of Breakthroughs and Purpose* (Simon & Schuster, 2019).

Chamlee-Wright, Emily L. and Virgil Henry Storr. "Filling the Civil-Society Vacuum: Post-Disaster Policy and Community Response," *Mercatus Policy Series*, Policy Comment No. 22, February 20, 2009. Retrieved from: https://papers.ssrn.com/sol3/papers.cfm?abstract_id=1349871

Chamlee-Wright, Emily. "Local Knowledge and the Philanthropic Process: Comment on Boettke & Prychitko." *Conversations in Philanthropy* 1, no. 1 (2004).

Christensen, Clayton, Jeff Dyer, and Hal Gregersen. *The Innovator's DNA: Mastering the Five Skills of Disruptive Innovators* (Harvard Business Review Press, 2011).

Coles, Matt. "Winning Marriage: What We Need to Do," *white paper*, 2005.

Cowen, Tyler and Daniel Gross. *Talent: How to Identify Energizers, Creatives, and Winners Around the World* (Nicholas Brealey, 2022).

Coyne, Christopher. *Doing Bad by Doing Good: Why Humanitarian Action Fails* (Stanford Economics and Finance, 2013).

Crutchfield, Leslie and Heather McCleod Grant. *Forces for Good: The Six Practices of High-Impact Nonprofits* (Jossey-Bass, 2012).

Crutchfield, Leslie. *How Change Happens: Why Some Social Movements Succeed While Others Don't* (Wiley, 2018).

"Cultivated Meat," Good Food Institute website. Retrieved from: https://gfi.org/cultivated/

Dennett, Daniel C. *Intuition Pumps and Other Tools for Thinking* (Norton, 2013).

Diehl, Digby. "The Emergency Medical Services Program, 2000a," Robert Woods Johnson Foundation. Retrieved from: file:///C:/Users/lkral/Downloads/rwjf13484.pdf

Diehl, Digby. "To Improve Health and HealthCare," Chapter 10, The Emergency Medical Services Program, 2000, Robert Woods Johnson Foundation. Retrieved from: file:///C:/Users/lkral/Downloads/rwjf13484.pdf

Do Good Jamaica, Habitat For Humanity. Retrieved from: https://dogood-jamaica.org/organization-search/item/habitat_for_humanityjamaica_abode/#:~:text=Habitat%20for%20Humanity%20Jamaica%20Ltd,foot%20lot%2C%20costs%20%24250%2C000.00%20Jamaican.

Doyal, Nan Alexander. "The Warrior: Nancy Harris." *Dig Where You Are: How One Person's Effort Can Save a Life, Empower a Community and Create Meaningful Change in the World* (Casper Press, 2017).

Easterly, Bill. *The White Man's Burden: Why the West's Efforts to Aid the Rest Have Done So Much Ill and So Little Good* (Penguin Books, 2006).

"Embrace," Extreme Design for Extreme Affordability, Stanford, 2007. Retrieved from: https://extreme.stanford.edu/projects/embrace/

e-NABLE website, Retrieved from: https://enablingthefuture.org/about/

Fey, Jayna. "Workplace Conflict Resolution Techniques For PMs," Digital Project Manager. Retrieved from: https://thedigitalprojectmanager.com/12-conflict-resolution-techniques-workplace/

Flynn, Daniel and Yunhe (Evelyn) Tian. "Nonprofit Deaths, Near Deaths and Reincarnations: Part 1 of 5, Hull House," *Nonprofit Quarterly* (February 10, 2015). Retrieved from: https://nonprofitquarterly.org/nonprofit-deaths-near-deaths-and-reincarnations-part-1-of-5-hull-house/

Franciosa, Stephen. "Voices FEGS: Is the Nonprofit's Collapse a Debacle, or a Cautionary Tale?" *Accounting Today* (May 19, 2017). Retrieved from: https://www.accountingtoday.com/opinion/fegs-debacle-or-cautionary-tale

Frey, Chuck. "How Do You Define Innovation and Make It Practical and Saleable to Senior Management?" *Innovation Management* (January 7, 2008). Retrieved from https://innovationmanagement.se/imtool-articles/how-do-you-define-innovation-and-make-it-practical-and-saleable-to-senior-management/

Fuller, Millard. *A Simple,* Decent Place to Live*: The Building Realization of Habitat for Humanity* (Thomas Nelson, 1995).

Galbraith, Jay. *Designing Dynamic Organizations: A Hands-on Guide for Leaders at All Levels* (AMACOM, 2001).

Gerretsen, Isabelle. "How India's Air Pollution Is Being Turned into Floor Tiles," BBC.com, September 12, 2021. Retrieved from: https://www.bbc.com/future/article/20210909-the-young-inventor-purifying-indias-dirty-air?ocid=twfut

Gilpin, Lyndsey. "The Woman Who Turned Her High School Science Project into a Global Solar Nonprofit," *Forbes* (October 28, 2015). Retrieved from: https://www.forbes.com/sites/lyndseygilpin/2015/10/28/the-woman-who-turned-her-high-school-science-project-into-a-global-solar-nonprofit/?sh=4f15d2a64cb8

Graham, Thomas. *Innovation the Cleveland Clinic Way: Transforming Healthcare by Putting Ideas to Work* (McGraw-Hill, 2016).

Greer, Peter. *The Spiritual Danger of Doing Good* (Bethany House Publishers, 2013).

Gregersen, Hal B. *Questions Are the Answer: A Breakthrough Approach to Your Most Vexing Problems at Work and in Life* (Harper Business 2018).

Grivna, Katie and Sandi Toben. "Nonprofit Deaths, Near Deaths and Reincarnations: Part 3 of 5 The Transformation of One Nonprofit, the Creation of Another, and the Impending Closure of Both." *Nonprofit Quarterly* (February 17, 2015). Retrieved from: https://nonprofitquarterly.org/the-transformation-of-the-otto-schiff-housing-association-the-creation-of-the-six-point-foundation-and-the-impending-closure-of-both/

"Guide to Performance-Based Contracting For Human Services Contracts, An Agency User Guide" developed by the Nonprofit Resiliency Committee (NRC) August 2019, Retrieved from: https://www1.nyc.gov/assets/nonprofits/downloads/pdf/Guide%20to%20Performance_Based%20Contracting%20PDF.pdf

Haas, Michaela. "How Richard Gere and Bernie Glassman Offer Solutions for the Homeless," *Huffington Post,* September 17, 2015, Retrieved from: https://www.huffpost.com/entry/how-richard-gere-and-bern_b_8149208

Hains, Tim. "Van Jones: Criminal Justice Reform Bill 'A Christmas Miracle,'" *RealClearPolitics,* December 19, 2018. Retrieved from: https://www.realclearpolitics.com/video/2018/12/19/van_jones_prison_reform_bill_a_christmas_miracle.html

Harder, Ben. "America's Best Hospitals: the 2021-22 Honor Roll and Overview," *U.S. News & World Report,* July 27, 2021. Retrieved from: https://health.usnews.com/health-care/best-hospitals/articles/best-hospitals-honor-roll-and-overview

Haugen, Gary. *The Locust Effect: Why the End of Poverty Requires the End of Violence* (Oxford University Press, 2014).

Holmes, Aaron. "A Group of Tech Billionaires Is Funding 'Fast Grants' of up to $500,000 for COVID-19 Research, with Every Grant Decision Made in Less Than 48 Hours" *Business Insider*, April 7, 2020. Retrieved from: https://www.businessinsider.com/fast-grants-500k-covid-19-coronavirus-research-48-hours-billionaires-2020-4

Hotz, Robert Lee. "Need a Breakthrough? Offer Prize Money!" *Wall Street Journal*, December 13, 2016. Retrieved from: https://www.wsj.com/articles/need-a-breakthrough-offer-prize-money-1481043131

Hunter, David. *Working Hard & Working Well: A Practical Guide to Performance Management* (Hunter Consulting LLC, 2013).

"Identifying Grantees to Deliver Results," NGOTips (October 2011). Retrieved from: https://www.ngoconnect.net/sites/default/files/resources/NGOTips%20-%20Identifying%20Grantees%20to%20Deliver%20Results.pdf

Kania, John and Mark Kramer. "Collective Impact," *Stanford Social Innovation Review* (Winter 2011). Retrieved from: https://ssir.org/articles/entry/collective_impact

Kealty, Céire. "Our Clothing Donations May Cause More Harm Than Good," *National Catholic Reporter*, Nov 25, 2021. Retrieved from: https://www.ncronline.org/news/opinion/our-clothing-donations-may-cause-more-harm-good

Kelley, Susan. "Rethinking Revenues at Health Care Nonprofits," *Cornell Chronicle* (November 26, 2018). Retrieved from: https://news.cornell.edu/stories/2018/11/rethinking-revenues-health-care-nonprofits

Kelly, Jaclyn and Margaret Ross-Martin. "What Matters: Investing in Results to Build Strong, Vibrant Communities: Performance-Based Contracting Can Provide Flexibility, Drive Efficiency, and Focus Resources on What Works in Social Services," *Federal Reserve Bank of San Francisco* (2018). Retrieved from: https://investinresults.org/chapter/performance-based-contracting-can-provide-flexibility-drive-efficiency-and-focus-resources.html

King, Jr., Martin Luther. *The Autobiography of Martin Luther King Jr.,* ed. Clayborne Carson (Grand Central Publishing, 2001).

King, Maxwell. *The Good Neighbor: The Life and Work of Fred Rogers* (Abrams Books, 2018).

Klein, Gary. "Performing a Project Premortem," *Harvard Business Review Magazine* (September 2007). Retrieved from: https://hbr.org/2007/09/performing-a-project-premortem

Klutsey, Ben. "Liberalism Starts with the Individual," podcast interview with Dr. Emily Chamlee-Wright, *Discourse Magazine*, minutes 33-47, August 7, 2020. Retrieved from: https://www.discoursemagazine.com/culture-and-society/2020/08/07/liberalism-starts-with-the-individual/

Kondo, Marie. *Tidying Up with Marie Kondo: The Book Collection: The Life-Changing Magic of Tidying Up and Spark Joy* (Ten Speed Press, 2020).

Kral, Leah. "Property Rights as a Precondition to Development: A Case Study of Jamaica." Thesis, Duquesne University, 2006.

Kurtz, Ernest. *Not God: A History of Alcoholics Anonymous* (Hazelden Publishing, 2010).

Langfitt, Frank. "Wal-Mart Aid Outpaced Some Federal Efforts" *NPR, All Things Considered,* September 9, 2005. Retrieved from: https://www.npr.org/templates/story/story.php?storyId=4839696

Leff, Gary. "Roadmaps: A Guide for Intellectual Entrepreneurs" (*Atlas Leadership Academy,* 2020).

Liedtka, Jeanne. "Why Design Thinking Works," *Harvard Business Review* (Sept–Oct 2018). Retrieved from https://hbr.org/2018/09/why-design-thinking-works

"Lindbergh Given Check by Orteig." *The Gettysburg Times*, New York. Associated Press, June 17, 1927. Retrieved from: https://news.google.com/newspapers?nid=2202&dat=19270617&id=DOMlAAAAIBAJ&sjid=o_UFAAAAIBAJ&pg=920,1399980

Lindzon, Jared. "Tulsa paid people $10k to move there and work remotely. Here's how it worked out." *FastCompany*, December 2, 2021. Retrieved from: https://www.fastcompany.com/90700766/tulsa-paid-people-10k-to-move-there-and-work-remotely-heres-how-it-worked-out

Loya, Liliane. "Small Steps in the Right Direction: Making General Operating Support the Norm," *The Center for Effective Philanthropy* (July 29, 2021). Retrieved from: https://cep.org/small-steps-in-the-right-direction/

Marquardt, Michael J. *Building the Learning Organization: Achieving Strategic Advantage through a Commitment to Learning* (Nicholas Brealey Publications, 2001).

Marsh, Charles. *The Beloved Community: How Faith Shapes Social Justice from the Civil Rights Movement to Today* (Basic Books, 2008).

Martin, Juliette. "Africa's New Strategies to Defeat HIV/AIDS," Africa Renewal, United Nations. Retrieved from: https://www.un.org/africarenewal/magazine/december-2016-march-2017/africas-new-strategies-defeat-hivaids

"Mayo Clinic Mission and Values," Mayo Clinic. Retrieved from: https://www.mayoclinic.org/about-mayo-clinic/mission-values

McCabe, Thomas A. *Miracle on High Street: The Rise, Fall and Resurrection of St. Benedict's Prep in Newark, N.J.* (Fordham University Press, 2010).

McCammon, Sarah. "Abstinence-Only Education Is Ineffective and Unethical, Report Argues" *National Public Radio*, August 23, 2017. Retrieved from: https://www.npr.org/sections/health-shots/2017/08/23/545289168/abstinence-education-is-ineffective-and-unethical-report-argues#:~:text=The%20analysis%20confirms%20previous%20public,intercourse%2C%22%20the%20authors%20write

McDowell, Patton. "Challenging the Nonprofit Status Quo," podcast interview with Tina Postel, episode 42, June 2020, minutes 23-30. Retrieved from: https://www.pattonmcdowell.com/news/2020-06/challenging-nonprofit-status-quo-tina-postel/

McGlone, Peggy and Manuel Roig-Franzia. "The Newseum Was a Grand Tribute to the Power of Journalism. Here's How It Failed." *Washington Post,* February 1, 2019. Retrieved from: https://www.washingtonpost.com/entertainment/museums/the-newseum-was-a-grand-tribute-to-the-power-of-journalism-heres-how-it-failed/2019/02/01/aeeb2482-25a4-11e9-81fd-b7b05d5bed90_story.html

McKeever, Brice and Marcus Gaddy. "The Nonprofit Workforce: By the Numbers," *Nonprofit Quarterly* (October 24, 2016). Retrieved from: https://nonprofitquarterly.org/nonprofit-workforce-numbers/

McKeever, Brice. "The Nonprofit Sector in Brief 2015: Public Charities, Giving and Volunteering." The Urban Institute, 2015, Retrieved from: https://www.urban.org/sites/default/files/publication/72536/2000497-The-Nonprofit-Sector-in-Brief-2015-Public-Charities-Giving-and-Volunteering.pdf

Meehan, William F. and Kim Starkey Jonker. *Engine of Impact: Essentials of Strategic Leadership in the Nonprofit Sector* (Stanford University Press, 2017).

Mehta, Pavithra and Suchitra Shenoy. *Infinite Vision: How Aravind Became the World's Greatest Business Case for Compassion* (Berrett-Koehler, 2011).

Miller, Paddy and Thomas Wedell-Wedellsborg. *Innovation as Usual: How to Help Your People Bring Great Ideas to Life* (Harvard Business Review Press, 2013).

241

References

Morino, Mario. *Leap of Reason: Managing to Outcomes in an Era of Scarcity* (Venture Philanthropy Partners, 2011).

Muller, Jerry Z. *The Tyranny of Metrics* (Princeton University Press, 2019).

Murphy, Bill Jr. "Google Says It Still Uses the '20-Percent Rule,' and You Should Totally Copy It," *Inc.* November 1, 2020. Retrieved from: https://www.inc .com/bill-murphy-jr/google-says-it-still-uses-20-percent-rule-you-should-totally-copy-it.html

Murray, Peter and Steve Ma. "The Promise of Lean Experimentation," *Stanford Social Innovation Review* (Summer 2015). Retrieved from: https://ssir.org/ articles/entry/the_promise_of_lean_experimentation

Nahmias, Laura, Dan Goldberg, and Nidhi Prakash. "The Wrecking of a Blue-chip New York Nonprofit," *Politico, March 13,* 2015. Retrieved from: https:// www.politico.com/states/new-york/albany/story/2015/03/the-wrecking-of-a-blue-chip-new-york-nonprofit-087679

Nightscout Foundation website, retrieved from: https://www.nightscoutfoundation .org/about

Nonprofit Vote website, retrieved from: https://www.nonprofitvote.org/our-mission/

Paris, Joseph. "Fail fast, fail small, learn, and move on." Operational Excellence Society, November 15, 2016. Retrieved from: https://opexsociety.org/body-of-knowledge/fail-fast-fail-small-learn-move/

Pelley, Scott. "The Resurrection of St. Benedict's." June 26, 2016, 60 Minutes, CBS News. Retrieved from: https://www.cbsnews.com/news/60-minutes-newark-school-st-benedicts-scott-pelley-2/

Poiner, Jessica. "So Far, LeBron's I Promise School Is Keeping Its Promise," October 23, 2019, Thomas B. Fordham Institute. Retrieved from: https://fordhaminstitute .org/ohio/commentary/so-far-lebrons-i-promise-school-keeping-its-promise

Popova, Maria. "David Foster Wallace on Leadership." *Marginalia.* February 17, 2014. Retrieved from: https://www.themarginalian.org/2014/02/17/ dfw-leadership-debbie-millman/

Prather, Larry J. and Dan Delich. "In Flood Resilience Debate, There Are No Solutions—Only Tradeoffs." *The Hill,* February 2, 2019. Retrieved from: https://thehill.com/opinion/energy-environment/428193-in-flood-resilience-debate-there-are-no-solutions-only-tradeoffs/

"Recoverable Grant Program, the Power of a Grant Amplified," Vanguard Charitable. Retrieved from: https://www.vanguardcharitable.org/economic-relief-local

"Recovery: The Many Paths to Wellness," The U.S. Surgeon General's 2016 Report on Alcohol, Drugs, and Health, Chapter 5, 2016, 2. Retrieved from https://addiction.surgeongeneral.gov/sites/default/files/chapter-5-recovery.pdf

Rhinos Without Borders website, retrieved from: http://www.rhinoswithoutborders.com/about-the-project/

Ridley, Matt. *How Innovation Works: And Why It Flourishes in* Freedom (Harper, 2020).

Roberts, Paul. "The Agenda—Total Teamwork," *Fast Company* (March 31, 1999). Retrieved from: https://www.fastcompany.com/36969/agenda-total-teamwork

Robertson, Adi. "OLPC'S $100 Laptop Was Going to Change the World—Then It All Went Wrong," *The Verge,* April 16, 2018. Retrieved from: https://www.theverge.com/2018/4/16/17233946/olpcs-100-laptop-education-where-is-it-now

ROCA. See "How We Do It," ROCA, Inc. Retrieved from: https://rocainc.org/work/our-intervention-model/

Rothschild, Dan. "Interview with Dan Rothschild, Executive Director, Mercatus Center," Leah Kral, February, 2021.

Saving Philanthropy, A Documentary Short Produced by Failing Forward (2011). Retrieved from: https://www.nonprofitsfailingforward.org/films

Schroeder, Juliana and Jane L. Risen. "Peace Through Friendship," Opinion, New York Times, August 22, 2014. Retrieved from: https://www.nytimes.com/2014/08/24/opinion/sunday/peace-through-friendship.html

Seltman, Kent D. and Leonard Berry, *Management Lessons from Mayo Clinic: Inside One of the World's Most Admired Service Organizations* (McGraw Hill, 2008).

Senge, Peter M. *The Fifth Discipline: The Art & Practice of the Learning Organization* (Currency, 2010).

Shah, Namank. "A Blurry Vision: Reconsidering the Failure of the One Laptop Per Child Initiative," WR: Journal of the CAS Writing Program, 3 (2010-11) 88-98, Retrieved from: https://www.bu.edu/writingprogram/journal/past-issues/issue-3/shah/#:~:text=However%2C%20it%20is%20important%20to,the%20local%20cultures%20and%20societies

Shulz, Kathryn. *Being Wrong: Adventures in the Margin of Error* (HarperCollins, 2010).

Skillicorn, Nick. "What Is Innovation? 26 Experts Share Their Innovation Definition." Idea to Value—Creativity and Innovation with Nick Skillicorn. Retrieved from: https://www.ideatovalue.com/inno/nickskillicorn/2016/03/innovation-15-experts-share-innovation-definition/

"Sliding Scale Individual Therapy," Rock Recovery website. Retrieved from: https://rockrecoveryed.org/sliding-scale-individual-therapy/

Smith, Ernie. "The Curious History of the 911 Emergency System," *Popular Mechanics* (June 28, 2017). Retrieved from https://www.popularmechanics.com/technology/infrastructure/news/a27114/911-emergency-system/

Sorrell, Charlie. "Swedish Speed-Camera Pays Drivers to Slow Down," *Wired* (December 6, 2010). Retrieved from: https://www.wired.com/2010/12/swedish-speed-camera-pays-drivers-to-slow-down/

Spink, Katherine. *Mother Teresa, An Authorized Biography* (HarperOne, 2011), Chapter Two.

"Staff Survey on Workplace Culture," Mercatus Center at George Mason University, 2020.

Steward, Barbara. "In the Hood, Jobs for the Poor," *New York Times,* February 3, 2003. Retrieved from https://www.nytimes.com/2003/02/23/nyregion/in-the-hood-jobs-for-the-poor.html

Storr, Nona Martin, Emily Chamlee-Wright, and Virgil Storr. *How We Came Back: Voices from Post-Katrina* New Orleans (Arlington, VA: Mercatus Center at George Mason University, 2015).

Straw, Julie, Barry Davis, Mark Scullard, and Susie Kukkonen. *The Work of Leaders: How Vision, Alignment, and Execution Will Change the Way You Lead* (Pfeiffer 2013).

"Study Finds High Levels of Hospital Noise," ABC News January 6, 2006. Retrieved from: https://abcnews.go.com/GMA/story?id=127795&page=1

"Task Shifting to Tackle Health Worker Shortages," World Health Organization, 2007. Retrieved from: https://www.who.int/healthsystems/task_shifting_booklet.pdf

Taylor, Nathan. "The Ideological Turing Test. What It Is. Why It's Worth Taking Seriously." *Praxtime,* May 27, 2014. Retrieved from: https://praxtime.com/2014/05/27/ideological-turing-test/

"The Five Whys Technique," Asian Development Bank (February 2009). Retrieved from: https://www.adb.org/publications/five-whys-technique

"The International Response to HIV/AIDS," Population Reference Bureau, July 2, 2002. Retrieved from: https://www.prb.org/resources/the-international-response-to-hiv-aids/

The Kellogg Foundation's "Logic Model Guide" (2004), The Kellogg Foundation. Retrieved from: https://www.wkkf.org/resource-directory-old/resources/2004/01/logic-model-development-guide

"The Mayo Clinic: Faith – Hope – Science." Ken Burns, *PBS*, 2018.

"The Risks of Lending," KIVA. Retrieved from: https://www.kiva.org/about/due-diligence/risk

The Terma Foundation, retrieved from: https://www.terma.org/

The W. Edwards Deming Institute. Retrieved from: https://deming.org/quotes/10091/

"Timeline of Tobacco Industry Hollywood Involvement." Smoke Free Media. Retrieved from: https://smokefreemedia.ucsf.edu/history/timeline

Thierer, Adam. *Evasive Entrepreneurs and the Future of Governance: How Innovation Improves Economies and Governments* (Cato Institute 2020).

Timeline of Tobacco Industry Hollywood Involvement." Smoke Free Media Website. Retrieved from: https://smokefreemedia.ucsf.edu/history/timeline

Von Hayek, F. A. *The Constitution of Liberty* (University of Chicago Press. 1960).

Von Hayek, F. A. "The Dilemma of Specialization," *in The State of the Social Sciences*, edited by Leonard D. White (University of Chicago Press, 1956).

Wachter, Robert M. The Avedis Donabedian model described in, "How Measurement Fails Doctors and Teachers," *New York Times*, January 16, 2016. Retrieved from: https://www.nytimes.com/2016/01/17/opinion/sunday/how-measurement-fails-doctors-and-teachers.html

Wade, Louise C. "The Heritage from Chicago's Early Settlement Houses," *Journal of the Illinois State Historical Society* (Winter 1967) 60, no. 4: 411–441.

Wagner, Tony. *Creating Innovators: The Making of Young People Who Will Change the World* (Scribner, 2012).

Waite, Marilyn. "A Year in Review and What's Ahead for Our Climate Finance Strategy," December 18, 2018, William and Flora Hewlett Foundation. Retrieved from: https://hewlett.org/a-year-in-review-and-whats-ahead-for-our-climate-finance-strategy/

Waite, Marilyn. "Blending Philanthropic, Public and Private Capital to Finance Climate Infrastructure in Emerging Economies," February 3, 2020, William and Flora Hewlett Foundation. Retrieved from: https://hewlett.org/blending-philanthropic-public-and-private-capital-to-finance-climate-infrastructure-in-emerging-economies/

Wallace, Nicole. "Employee Feedback Helps Nonprofits Refine Programs," *The Chronicle of Philanthropy* (March 18, 2012). Retrieved from: https://www.philanthropy.com/article/employee-feedback-helps-nonprofits-refine-programs/

Ward, Alvin. "15 Fantastic Buzz Aldrin Quotes," *Mental Floss* (January 11, 2019). Retrieved from: https://www.mentalfloss.com/article/570233/buzz-aldrin-quotes

245

References

Weissmann, Jordan. "It's a Big Deal That LeBron James Decided to Fund a Public School," *Slate,* August 6, 2018. Retrieved from: https://slate.com/business/2018/08/lebron-james-akron-school-why-it-matters-that-i-promise-is-public.html

Wenger, Yvonne. "Nonprofit Offers Low-cost Mortgages for Modest Income Baltimore Residents, Including Those on Rent Subsidies," *Baltimore Sun* (April 24, 2018). Retrieved from: https://www.baltimoresun.com/politics/bs-md-mortgage-approvals-20180424-story.html

White, Shannon, Juliana Schroeder, and Jane L. Risen. "When "Enemies" Become Close: Relationship Formation Among Palestinians and Jewish Israelis at a Youth Camp," *Journal of Personality and Social Psychology* (September 17, 2020). Retrieved from: http://dx.doi.org/10.1037/pspi0000331

"Why It Matters," Second Chance Business Coalition website. Retrieved from: https://secondchancebusinesscoalition.org/why-it-matters

"Women & Land Ownership," Working Group for Women and Land Ownership website. Retrieved from: https://www.wgwlo.org/women-land-ownership.php

Wooster, Martin Morse. The Spectacular Failure of One Laptop Per Child, *Philanthropy Daily*, May 24, 2018. Retrieved from: https://www.philanthropydaily.com/the-spectacular-failure-of-one-laptop-per-child/

Zambone, Jennifer. "Interview with Jennifer Zambone, Chief Executive Officer, Mercatus Center." Leah Kral, February, 2021a.

Zambone, Jennifer. "Interview with Jennifer Zambone, Chief Operating Officer, Mercatus Center at George Mason University." Leah Kral, February 2021b.

About the Author

As senior director of strategy and innovation at the Mercatus Center at George Mason University, Leah Kral provides tailored workshops and consulting to internal teams and to a network of nonprofit partners across the country. For decades, she has been helping teams to break out of the busy daily routine and elicit their best creative thinking. She helps teams to design pilots, program strategies, and meaningful evaluation approaches, leading to better outcomes and more compelling stories for supporters. She has a passion for helping altruistic organizations achieve their missions and is an active volunteer in her community.

She holds a master of arts in public policy from Duquesne University and a bachelor of arts in English literature from the University of Central Oklahoma, and is a Returned Peace Corps Volunteer (Jamaica, 2002–2004). She lives in northern Virginia with her husband, Richard.

For more information, see http//:www.leahkral.com.

Index